# MILLENNIAL TEACHERS
# OF COLOR

SERIES | RACE AND EDUCATION

Series edited by H. Richard Milner IV

**OTHER BOOKS IN THIS SERIES**

# MILLENNIAL TEACHERS OF COLOR

MARY E. DILWORTH

Editor

Harvard Education Press
Cambridge, Massachusetts

Paperback ISBN 978-1-68253-142-6
Library Edition ISBN 978-1-68253-143-3

Library of Congress Cataloging-in-Publication Data
Names: Dilworth, Mary E. (Mary Elizabeth), editor.
Title: Millennial teachers of color / Mary E. Dilworth, editor.
Other titles: Race and education series.
Description: Cambridge, Massachusetts : Harvard Education Press, 2018. |
    Series: Race and education series | Includes bibliographical references and index.
Identifiers: LCCN 2017058058| ISBN 9781682531426 (pbk.) | ISBN 9781682531433
    (library edition)
Subjects: LCSH: Minority teachers—Training of—United States. | Minority
    teachers—Recruiting—United States. | Teachers—Training of—United States. |
    Minorities—Education—United States. | Generation Y. | Cultural pluralism—
    United States.
Classification: LCC LB1715 .M535 2018 | DDC 371.10082—dc23 LC record available
    at https://lccn.loc.gov/2017058058

Published by Harvard Education Press,
an imprint of the Harvard Education Publishing Group

Harvard Education Press
8 Story Street
Cambridge, MA 02138

Cover Design: Endpaper Studio
Cover Photo: gradyreese/E+/Getty Images
The typefaces used in this book are Minion Pro and Myriad Pro

*This is dedicated to my parents, Tom and Lina,*
*who truly valued a good education.*

# Contents

# Series Foreword

by H. Richard Milner IV
*Race and Education Series Editor*

This important contribution to the Race and Education series, *Millennial Teachers of Color*, offers a fascinating, much-needed look at the next generation of school leaders and teachers. The millennial generation is the largest in US history, and the one with the highest percentage of people of color. Yet, as Mary Dilworth notes in her introduction, "efforts to recruit, groom, and retain millennial teachers of color are out-of-date and woefully inadequate." In an effort to move beyond these past inadequate attempts, Dilworth and the contributors to her volume explore "how the current generation of teachers of color may have a distinctly different mind-set than their predecessors and white peers; what habits of mind and experiences contribute to their understanding of quality teaching and student learning; what constitutes good and useful preparation and practice; and what processes and policies accommodate cultural responsiveness and allow for all students to meet their full potential." In short, this book describes and examines a new wave of teachers and leaders in US schools—and how they are likely to bring notable changes to educational assumptions, goals, practices, and outcomes. A refreshingly optimistic view of what can be, the book provides historical and contextual framing and insights that will advance what we know about who teaches and leads and what is essential to understand in the journey to diversify the teaching force.

A central goal of the Race and Education series is to advance a critical, forward-thinking body of research on race that contributes to policy, theory, practice, and action. Although the series will advance scholarship in race and justice studies, a primary objective is to help educators—teachers, school counselors, leaders, coaches, and outside-of-school providers—center the humanity of students whose needs are far from being understood, responded to, and met in schools and in society.

Grounded in and substantiated by empirical research, the series aims to highlight effective practices designed to help solve intractable problems of race in education. To that end, books in the series address both societal challenges and educational equity. They highlight scholarship from leading researchers in the field as well as emerging scholars and investigate mechanisms, systems, structures, and practices that have a signifiant bearing on students' opportunities to learn.

Racial justice is arguably the most important educational imperative of our time. Considering the inextricable links between society and education, educators have the potential to help equip students with knowledge, tools, attitudes, dispositions, mind-sets, beliefs, and practices to create a world that is truly equitable and democratic for its citizenry. Thus, series titles attend to issues both inside and outside of schools as well as their nexus, shedding light on what matters and how we, in education, can improve practices that systemically improve students' opportunities to reach their full capacity.

Above all, the Race and Education series asks the important question, *Do we have the fortitude to center race in our work, or will we continue going about our business as usual?* I am always mindful of curriculum theorist Beverly Gordon's provocative observation that "critiquing your own assumptions about the world—especially if you believe the world works for you"—is an arduous endeavor. At the very heart of this series is an explicit challenge to those in power to work for the good of humanity, to interrupt systems, policies, and practices that work only for some while others remain underserved. It asks: How do the effects of poverty and compromised opportunities in transportation, housing, and employment manifest themselves in communities' responses to social (in)justice? What role does and should education play in understanding and responding to these manifestations? What roles do teachers and other educators play in helping students develop insights about the salience of race in society? How do education policy makers respond to these realities when making decisions about what gets covered in the curriculum? The books in this series address many of these questions about race, racism, and discrimination to advance what we know (theoretically and empirically) in education and to move us toward a more equitable education system.

Indeed, a primary premise of the series is that we must learn from a diverse range of disciplines to build and sustain efforts on behalf of students who continue to be underserved and marginalized in education. Thus, scholars and scholarship from a variety of disciplines—sociology, psychology, health sciences, political science, legal studies, and social work—can assist us in reversing educational trends that continue to have devastating effects on student experiences and outcomes. There is solid evidence that students succeed when responsive and relevant mechanisms are in place. The Race and Education series will contribute to the educational equity and racial justice agenda, centralizing those mechanisms that will help us reach our true ideal democracy. I am ready. I am hopeful that readers of the series are as well.

Welcome! #LetsDotheWork!

# Foreword

As I sit down to write the foreword to this exciting and timely collection, I realize that I have had a number of my own experiences with millennial teachers of color (MTOC), most of which had, until now, remained unlabeled and unexplored. My most recent encounter with the ways of MTOC occurred during a meeting of authors of this very book. The talented, insightful group of about twenty writers and researchers, a mix of millennials, generation Xers, and baby boomers, were gathered both physically around a conference table and virtually on a large screen placed in the front of the room. About halfway through the agenda, I turned to an MTOC friend and colleague sitting next to me and whispered a somewhat-off-topic idea that occurred to me about a comment that one of the MTOC virtual attendees made about engaging in political activism as teachers. The meeting continued, with each author presenting his or her chapter for discussion. Moments later my MTOC neighbor leaned over and quietly informed me that her colleagues had discussed my idea and wanted to meet with me at a later time to explore it further. Apparently, without any break in the larger meeting, the MTOC in the room and on the screen had convened a submeeting via their cell phones or other electronic contraptions, collaboratively discussed an idea about political activism, and come to a mutual agreement about its efficacy! And all this without anyone else in the room realizing it was happening.

I recognize now that this event was iconic of the experiences I have had with other MTOC in my work as a teacher- and principal-educator at a historically black university in Louisiana. The majority of my students are African American and range in age from twenty-five to fifty. Even though they are mostly of the same ethnicity, I have noticed some age-related differences. For one, the generation Xers tend to prefer to work on academic tasks individually, while the millennials prefer group work. I've also observed what seems to be a difference in their manner of response to the social issues that are currently bombarding communities of color.

Last summer was a particularly hard time in our community. Alton Sterling, an unarmed black man, was shot and killed by white police officers just blocks away from campus. That event was followed by peaceful mass demonstrations, although some members of the same police force that killed Mr. Sterling were on duty and were accused of harassing and injuring demonstrators for no cause. Naturally, these events became a part of our classroom conversation.

One young MTOC described her participation in the demonstration and the inappropriate actions of some police officers. Two of the older students strongly critiqued the demonstrators, saying things like, "Those demonstrators don't know what they're doing; they have no plan. They're just out there starting more trouble. They have no leader; they just go out and do anything." The younger student countered by saying they didn't need a leader; they planned on social media together and everyone agreed to what the rules of engagement would be after discussing the issues. They also kept everyone informed on what was happening at any given moment via various modes of technology.

And thus the discussion continued, with many Xers stating a belief in individual action and following a proscribed leader, and with the millennials insisting that group effort, collectively planned via social media, was most important. I finally ended the discussion, but came to more fully grasp that even though all of my students at the time were African American, there were age-based differences in how they responded to current issues.

The millennial generation is the most diverse generation ever to populate the United States. Whereas people of color currently constitute about 28 percent of the baby boomers, they make up more than 44 percent of the millennial generation. The "browning" of the millennials makes it imperative that we develop an understanding of how these complex young people navigate the world, and that we make explicit how the challenges and the gifts of millennial teachers will change the face of education as we know it.

I find that all of my students, of whatever age, struggle with the racism they encounter in the larger society and in schools, especially those schools where African Americans are in the minority in the teaching and/or administrative staffs. They grapple with the unveiled arrogance of some white teachers and leaders who leave them voiceless as they struggle to inject into the conversation what they know about the African American students they teach. The MTOC struggle, as well, with some of their same-ethnicity colleagues and administrators who don't understand the ways they connect with each other and their students, the activist orientation they often bring, and the ways they use technology to discuss their concerns and plan for action.

And so, I realize more and more the importance of this volume. The millennial teachers of color sometimes differ, not only from "mainstream" millennial teachers who don't have the issues of racism and oppression to contend with on a personal level, but also from teachers of the same ethnicity, who may see the world, its problems, and potential solutions through very different lenses. The chapters in this volume give us an opportunity to get a better understanding of this generation of exhilarating young people. They also provide us, the millennials' older colleagues, with some clues about how to best serve these new teachers' needs, helping them to overcome obstacles and develop their talents. If we don't do so, we risk losing some of the most vibrant educators our country has seen. Even more significantly, learning about how the millennial teachers of color approach the world can expand our own awareness of how to meet the challenges of our collective futures in this great, but often flawed country—in ways we might never have imagined.

*Lisa Delpit*
*Felton G. Clark Distinguished Professor of Education*
*Southern University and A&M College*

# Introduction

Mary E. Dilworth

D iversity includes everyone and excludes no one. It cannot be dismissed. It is a thread woven through the fabric of society that is virtually impossible to unravel. This nation is more racially, ethnically, and
linguistically diverse than at any point in its history. Its growth, economic
stamina, and well-being pivot on the strength and knowledge of African
American, Hispanic, Asian American, and Native American children and
children of two or more races who constitute more than half of the nation's
youth population. It is this cohort of preK–12 school-age children, also
known as centennials, iGeneration, or generation Z,[1] who by and large are
the least served by the nation's education system.[2] While academic excellence
and equity for all students are heralded in virtually every education policy
and program, the tangible outcomes are insufficient and do not offer these
students the necessary tools for a good quality of life as productive adults.
Teachers are the linchpin of a quality education, and a racially, ethnically,
and linguistically diverse teaching and learning community enhances and
leverages student achievement—particularly for the underserved and under-
achieving preK–12 student population.[3] Although the *millennial* cohort's
demographic profile mirrors that of the increasingly diverse and challenging student population, their representation in the nation's teaching force
is scarce and too often short-lived.

Informed education policy makers and administrators seem to understand the advantages of their presence, but efforts to recruit, groom, and
retain millennial teachers of color are out-of-date and woefully inadequate.
Try as we might, there is no silver bullet that will immediately change the

1

demographic profile of the nation's teaching force, but a cross-cultural understanding of motivation can do much to enhance recruitment efforts, while rewards and incentives can boost retention. Current efforts do not capture the motivations of this important segment of the population.[4]

This book is intended to disrupt the current line of inquiry that suggests that by simply increasing the number of teachers of color, equity has been established, the academic achievement gap among students from various socioeconomic backgrounds will close, and all will be well. The goal of this work is to probe beneath the surface to recognize and explain how the current generation of teachers of color may have a distinctly different mind-set than their predecessors and white peers; what habits of mind and experiences contribute to their understanding of quality teaching and student learning; what constitutes good and useful preparation and practice; and what processes and policies accommodate cultural responsiveness and allow for all students to meet their full potential.

## ON THE SURFACE

The evidence is stark. There is a lack of parity in the number of teachers of color and preK–12 students from similar backgrounds. Millennials are the most racially, ethnically, and linguistically diverse generation to date and in 2015 surpassed generation X to become the largest share of our nation's workforce.[5] While the proportion of African American, Hispanic, Asian, and Native American preK–12 educators varies by state and vicinity, the fact remains that teachers of color are in short supply and will remain so for the foreseeable future. It is conceivable that a significant number of preK–12 students will never have the opportunity to learn from a teacher of color.[6]

The reasons for this lack of representation are complex and varied, and have changed somewhat over time. Outlined below, using a generational lens, are factors that have largely deterred individuals of color from pursuing a teaching career as young adults.

> *Baby boomers:* More career options for women generally and for African Americans and other minorities specifically; teaching degrees conferred coincide with the height of a national teacher surplus and a simultaneous decline in teachers' salaries; a limited number of individuals from distressed urban areas pursuing teaching degrees and returning to their home communities

*Generation X:* Increased focus on accountability measures that included challenging teacher assessment licensure examinations; a reframing of four-year, university-based teacher education programs to a postbaccalaureate format that required a fifth or sixth year of study[7]

*Millennials:* Limited financial support to pursue teaching and the tendency not to stay very long in one career or work space,[8] as well as a discomfort with the preK–12 school environment[9]

Although these are trends impacting generational cohorts, there are racial, ethnic, and cultural differences among individuals who enter teaching.[10] Despite common stereotypes such as African American teachers as hard-nosed disciplinarians or Asian Americans as the best teachers of mathematics and science,[11] there are yet-to-be-determined reasons why significant proportions of educators in different racial/ethnic groups cluster in certain secondary level areas—African Americans in special education, Hispanics in foreign languages, and Asian Americans in mathematics.[12] While these are among the nation's high-need subject areas, the reasons why individuals of color gravitate toward these disciplines need further probing.[13]

Much of the research on teacher diversity focuses on white educators and their understandings and skills when teaching students coming from backgrounds other than their own.[14] There are clues in the scant literature about teachers of color and how their knowledge and cultural experiences are often disregarded in their preparation programs and as they work in schools. Moreover, the literature on preservice teachers of color exposes the "overwhelming culture of Whiteness that pervades teacher education programs."[15] In other words, whiteness frames how preservice teachers of color are recognized and treated in their programs. There is little insight into where and how matters of educator racial/ethnic and linguistic diversity intersect with generational difference.

## HABITS OF MIND

Millennials of color are a unique and valuable cohort of prospective and practicing preK–12 educators. It is difficult to precisely isolate their characteristics by the typical indicators of age or race/ethnicity. It's a challenge similar to learning how to wear bifocals: with a slight adjustment of the eyes, you can focus on either close-up or distant objects. Paul Taylor, in his book *The Next America: Boomers, Millennials and the Looming Generational Showdown*, posits that generalizing about generations can be messy given three overlapping properties of reality: *life cycle effects*—wherein younger people may be different from older people today, but as they age may become more like them; *period effects*—where major historical events (wars, social movements, booms, busts, religious awakenings, and medical, scientific, and technological breakthroughs) affect all age groups, but the depth of impact may differ according to where people are situated in the life cycle; and *cohort effects*—where period events leave a particularly deep impression on the young, who are still forming their core values and worldviews.[16] When coupled with habits of mind that guide a person's perceptions, attitudes, and approaches to difference (including race), these realities involve a myriad of individual and social/cultural positionalities that can lead to a professional commitment to teach.[17]

Parents and grandparents of the millennial generation are by and large baby boomers, who came of age during the civil rights era and framed the 1960s counterculture. As the largest generation of the last century, they used their numbers as ordnance to forge acceptance of difference as well as free and open expression. Their efforts were rewarded in varying degrees with programs and policies that were designed to offer equal access and opportunity, especially in the education sector.

Generation X and millennial teachers of color have likely heard first-hand accounts or opinions on how individuals such as Martin Luther King Jr., César Chávez, and Russell Means and organizations like El Movimiento and Asian American Political Alliance were able to find common ground and pushed hard to change policies that discriminated against minorities and women. As Grant and Agosto state, implicitly and explicitly, the various civil rights movements of the 1960s and 1970s raised fundamental questions about teacher capacity and spoke to the necessity of embedding social justice issues within the knowledge, skills, and dispositions of teacher education programs, as well as within the scholarship and actions of teacher educators.[18]

Consequently, it is not surprising that those in the generation X cohort grew up within a newly established comfort zone, finding little to challenge and assuming that education is a human right, and that millennials recognize education as accessible and a credible tool for change generally.[19] So within the teacher education sector it is typical that millennial teachers of color tend to pursue initial teacher preparation as well as continuing professional development from nontraditional sources or alternative routes, are more inclined than other cohorts to work in public and private charter schools with greater freedom to develop curriculum, and are passionate about moving the social justice agenda forward.[20] With few exceptions (for example the Institute for Teachers of Color—a university/school district collaborative effort), millennials work to establish nonthreatening spaces outside of the academy and schools for intellectual work that will fine-tune their teaching craft and nurture ideas.[21] In essence, they have created their own professional development communities.

It should not be unexpected that teachers of color seek asylum outside of mainstream institutions to learn and to exchange views.[22] Achinstein and Ogawa, in their book *Change(d) Agents: New Teachers of Color in Urban Schools*, use the metaphor of "double-bind" to describe the professional, cultural, and personal principles that inspire and the organizational pulls that challenge new teachers of color who attempt to engage in cultural/professional roles.[23] This notion helps to explain how millennial teachers generally, and those of color specifically, have come to work at their teaching craft and at the same time find space outside of the norm to focus on their own self and reality. The importance of learning about one's students is paralleled by the importance of learning about oneself.[24]

## GOOD AND USEFUL PREPARATION

Teacher preparation programs often bear the brunt of responsibility for criticism of the performance and quality of their teacher candidates.[25] Regardless of their format or approach to delivering instruction, most programs are required through state approval agencies and accrediting bodies to embrace diversity in their student body, curriculum, and faculty. Programs that are successful typically highlight their commitment in a mission statement and use it as a marketing tool in their promotional literature. But, as Gist points out, "[I]t is the residue of institutional racism and systemic policies and practices that creates different opportunities for different groups of teachers that often go unchecked in color-blind discourse in teacher education."[26] While many of these programs have sincere intentions and often meet political expectations on paper, newly licensed teachers too frequently disappoint school and district administrators and are also disappointed once they enter the classroom.

The notion that neophytes from any profession, much less those in teaching, will be able to hit the ground running and make major accomplishments is absurd; however, this is often the case for millennial teachers of color, who have been highly sought after and are considered exceptional by virtue of their skin color, second-language proficiency, or socioeconomic background. Yet, this sets up another type of double-bind experience for teacher candidates of color as they often then experience feelings of being marginalized or alienated, and their self-value is diminished in learning settings where the faculty unknowingly negate or ignore differences between candidates.[27] In sum, the negative assumptions in teacher education programs about diversity emanate from their fairly homogeneous student populations, the assimilationist ideology that undergirds a number of programs, the types of courses and clinical experiences that are offered, and the nature of the faculty.[28]

It is essential that faculty at all levels understand the precepts of culturally responsive pedagogy and demonstrate it in their work, but too often this is not the case.

According to Faltis and Vades, we currently have no information on what teacher educators in all roles understand about language and language diversity in schools, their level of competency for preparing students for teaching language integrated with content in linguistically diverse classrooms, or their competency for teaching preservice teachers about language uses and language demands in and across content areas.[29] Unfortunately, Faltis and Valdes' statement also has broad-based applicability in the teacher preparation sector.

## POLICIES AND PRACTICE

Despite the perception that schools have been notably weak instruments for disrupting the intergenerational transmission of advantage and disadvantage,[30] millennial teachers generally and those of color in particular are inspired to create a more just society through education. Sonia Nieto recognizes the changing landscape of teaching and offers a set of qualities, dispositions, values, and sensibilities that all teachers should have: a sense of mission; solidarity with, and empathy for, their students; the courage to challenge mainstream knowledge; improvisation; and a passion for social justice.[31] In this vein millennials, even more numerous than their baby boomer predecessors but uniquely skilled and equipped with technology, seize many opportunities to tackle policy issues that confront them on a daily basis.

The issues of underresourced schools and facilities, limited time for professional development, and students who bring a multitude of issues from home and community that have confounded or impacted teachers' work are similar for teachers of recent generations. But it appears that younger teachers have entered the profession during a time when these issues are commonly understood. Millennials tend to accept them as part and parcel of the job. On the other hand, their more seasoned colleagues perceive issues like standards-based reform as a threat to their authority, discretion, and prior identity.[32]

This millennial generation is described as apolitical and driven by "people issues" more than by political platforms. They have also been viewed as polarized by their backgrounds. A study of black and Latino/a millennial college students indicates that they are politically engaged through modern activist movements and that personal background, prior political activism, and psychosocial factors predict such involvement. Using the Black Lives Matter movement and Deferred Action for Childhood Arrivals (DACA) as context, Hope and Keels find that participation in either of these movements is not a solitary political experience, but is accompanied by participation in various types of political activism, including protests, boycotts, and campaign donations.[33] Millennial teachers of color often choose to frame their ideas and actions outside of the academy and their workplaces as a way to check systemic policies and practices that create different opportunities for different groups of teachers. Once they are firm in their convictions, they will move deliberately into meaningful action. Since millennials, as well as the generation X cohort, are more inclined than their baby boomer predecessors to venture into different professions, they are often fearless about making noise and moving on to a new career space.

## OVERVIEW

This volume begins with a first-person introduction to four millennial teachers, leading us into the focus of this work. In the chapter "Stagger Lee: Millennial Teachers' Perspectives, Politics, and Prose," the reader gets to know Sarah Ishmael, Adam T. Kuranishi, Genesis A. Chavez, and Lindsay A. Miller as I did when chatting about how they feel concerning issues of teacher diversity; about the things that their professors, school colleagues, and the authors in this book got right or wrong; and about the primary experiences that help frame their approach to teaching. Understanding where millennials are situated within the nation's population provides a necessary context for each of the following chapters. In chapter 2, "Millennials, Generation Xers, and Boomers—A Demographic Overview," Janice Hamilton Outtz and Marcus J. Coleman describe how the very diverse millennial cohort is similar to its predecessors but in many ways different in its commitment to the profession. The data explains why some call them the most threatening and exciting generation since the baby boomers.

Chapter 3, "Understanding 'Me' Within 'Generation Me': The Meaning Perspectives Held Toward and by Millennial Culturally and Linguistically Diverse Teachers," from Socorro G. Herrera and Amanda R. Morales, reveals a number of key but typically overlooked socioeconomic and cultural factors that encourage or discourage millennials of color as they prepare for and enter their teaching careers. In chapter 4, "Millennial Teachers of Color and Their Quest for Community," Hollee R. Freeman broadens our understanding of how teachers of color use this tool to enhance and advance student learning and at the same time fulfill their own social justice goals.

As Keith C. Catone and Dulari Tahbildar offer in chapter 5, "Ushering in a New Era of Teacher Activism: Beyond Hashtags, Building Hope," activism for social justice, or any cause, has many challenging facets. How millennial educators of color work to advance their agenda within schools is guided not so much from their formal preparation, but rather from their personal experiences in schools and communities. Similarly, in chapter 6, "Black Preservice Teachers on Race and Racism in the Millennial Era: Considerations for Teacher Education," Keffrelyn D. Brown and Angela M. Ward posit that African American teachers possess an authentic understanding of bigotry from family peers and experiences external to the academy.

There are scores of initiatives designed to recruit millennial teachers of color into the nation's preK–12 schools, but as Sabrina Hope King explains in chapter 7, "Advancing the Practices of Millennial Teachers of Color with the EquityEd Professional Learning Framework," the work is not complete once they enter the classroom. If we hope to retain these bright, socially conscious young educators, then professional development and other opportunities must be tailored to engage them.

States and school districts have at their disposal federal and other resources for quality teacher recruitment and professional development. In chapter 8, "Removing Barriers to the Recruitment and Retention of Millennial Teachers of Color," Zollie Stevenson Jr. advises that decision makers should consider more closely how these funds are distributed on behalf of a more racially, ethnically, and linguistically diverse corps of preK–12 teachers.

Many of the thoughts and recommendations presented in this volume are viable, but must be considered within the political landscape of the nation. In the final chapter, "The Double-Edged Sword of Education Policy Trends," Michael Hansen provides insights into a number of contemporary issues that either advance or impede progress in establishing a high-quality teaching and learning community that includes everyone—and excludes no one.

# 1

# Stagger Lee

*Millennial Teachers' Perspectives, Politics, and Prose*

Sarah Ishmael, Adam T. Kuranishi, Genesis A. Chavez, and Lindsay A. Miller

Frederick J. Brown's painting *Stagger Lee* captivates one's attention. The Chicago-raised abstract artist based this painting on the song "Stagger Lee," or "Stack-o-Lee"—a song about a real-life man turned mythic character in American blues history. Stagger Lee represents the trickster hero, the black man who breaks society's rules unapologetically, a man who is not imprisoned by society's definitions of him.[1]

This is a song that spans generations. Over four hundred artists have recorded it since its first recording in 1923. Lloyd Price, James Brown, Neil Diamond, the Clash, Pat Boone, Fats Domino, Bob Dylan, Duke Ellington, the Grateful Dead, and Ike and Tina Turner are all among the artists who have recorded some version of this song. About the song, Frederick Brown said, "My grandfather used to listen to Stagger Lee . . . he liked that tune. So when I did my series, 'The Blues,' I thought, well, let's paint Stagger Lee. And it's between abstract and figurative painting, because the story of America, the mythological story of America, is a very abstract story, and all of that story is in there."[2]

Stagger Lee, both the painting and the song, is the perfect metaphor for this chapter for a couple of reasons. First, the song spans several generations—each new artist in each generation, whether Duke Ellington or the Clash, keeps the essence of the message and yet adds their own unique sounds. Similarly, though the times have changed and each generation of teachers has brought something new to the profession, the underlying message of education for justice—for democracy—has not changed.

Second, if you try to look at the painting all at once—try to make sense of the whole thing—you get confused by the colors flowing into and out of different forms. But what the painting forces you to do is to look at the iteration of each figure. Different colors, traditions, and cultures make up each one. Brown forces you to pay attention to the minute detail in order to understand each figure and then the entire painting's message. Stagger Lee, both the painting and the song, is the story of America—the spirit of breaking free from society's expectations and the spirit of personhood despite oppression. However, it is a story that you need to get up close to, almost nose to nose, to understand.

This chapter features the narratives of four millennial teachers. And like the painting *Stagger Lee*, you have to look at each story, each brushstroke, and each color combination to grasp how we four millennial teachers understand, interpret, and remix the call to teach in today's complicated world. Each figure in the painting *Stagger Lee* has a history—*it is history*. Each has a color palette and a story all to itself. And as with each figure in *Stagger Lee*, you must stay with each narrative to understand how we teach, why we teach, and some of the experiences that we've had along our paths.

This volume comprises compelling chapters about millennial teachers— specifically millennial teachers of color. You will read research about our quest for community, our aptitude for technology, our activism, the struggles that we have regarding race, our identity as teachers, and how we fit into the workplace. Like Brown's artistic message, this volume's message is deeper than what you see at first glance; like the painting, this volume goes beyond understanding—to *illustrating* the complexity of how these differences interact *between and through* generations. It's understanding how, as Herrera and Morales describe in chapter 3, we both *think back* to the myths, stories, and lessons passed down by our families, elders, and other generations of teachers, and yet *look forward* by taking those lessons and remixing them to create something that reflects the story of America at present and, more importantly, what the needs of our students are today.

And so we invite you to read our stories. We invite you to read them as you would look at the painting of Stagger Lee—carefully, up close, with the intention of sitting a while and understanding the complexities of how experiences mix together like Frederick Brown mixes paint to depict an abstract cacophony of experiences. We invite you to see how we respond to the call to break society's rules for the students we teach, a call that spans generations—one that has been remixed and remastered to meet these unique times in which we live.

## ADAM T. KURANISHI

I am concerned with developing a teaching practice that is authentic to my identity as a millennial of color. Do my students see themselves in the curriculum? Do I see myself in the content? What ethical and political dilemmas do I encounter in the classroom? How do I respond? Does my pedagogy promote democracy and work toward a more just and equitable world? My teacher education program supported my search for answers. Following a year-long residency model, my coursework focused on curricular planning using Universal Design for Learning and culturally sustaining pedagogy to ensure accessibility for all students, in light of (dis)ability, gender, race, class, language, ethnicity, and immigration status. My professors emphasized relational, relationship-building solutions rather than punishment and reward approaches to classroom management; these included collaborative problem solving and trauma-sensitive frameworks.

Like the millennials surveyed by Sabrina Hope King in chapter 7, I am deeply committed to teaching in a learning environment that promotes equity and affirms the experiences of diverse people. I want my students to explore real-world issues and recognize their capacity as agents for change. In chapter 5, Catone and Tahbildar assert that reflection is key to being a responsive, prepared, and overall excellent educator. As someone committed to social justice in education, I constantly reflect on my role as a millennial teacher activist. How do I navigate teaching standards and school bureaucracy while fulfilling a social justice purpose?

I designed a unit for my culminating edTPA (Teacher Performance Assessment) portfolio that was aligned with my teacher training and identity. I surveyed students' learning styles and histories, and shared my background as a necessary first step to forge trust in the tenth-grade humanities classroom. The students were primarily first- and second-generation Caribbean and Latinx youth. Most lived in underresourced communities. When the students discovered that I am a Chicago native, they expressed their interest in the city's hip-hop community as well as concern for youth violence. They referred to Chicago as "Chiraq," a nickname characterizing the city as a war zone. The students and I focused on two questions: (1) How did

Chicago become Chiraq? and (2) how do communities work together to address violence?

We began our inquiry by researching victims of gun violence in Chicago. Students researched and wrote biographies of teenagers who had been murdered in recent years. They read and analyzed newspaper articles, obituaries, hip-hop lyrics, tweets, and photographs. Students also wrote diary entries from the perspective of their assigned teen with compassion and detail that revealed the experiences, fears, and challenges of urban youth. Their work raised critical questions and a call to action. We sought to answer more questions: Why was reported violence prevalent in underresourced communities of color? How did these communities become disinvested and impoverished? How do the experiences of youth in Chicago compare with those of young folks in Brooklyn? Why has society become desensitized to gun violence? How can we prevent violence?

Continuing our inquiry, we watched documentaries on Chicago's Ceasefire organization and researched community-led efforts to interrupt violence. The students developed their own community-organizing strategies and narrated how they would convince people to avoid violence. In their intervention plans, students reminded potential aggressors that violence leads to a downward spiral of trauma and death. Some urged individuals to reflect on the pain that it would cause loved ones. One student asked, "What kind of example are you setting for younger generations when you act violently?" Further, he wrote, "You have the opportunity to break the cycle. Be a role model."

Another student illustrated the consequences of incarceration. "A criminal record will follow you after you are released from jail," she argued. "You will not only encounter difficulties finding employment, but you will also be denied the right to vote."

Many described the benefits of walking away from conflict. These students referenced nonviolent civil disobedience as a vehicle for personal and political freedom. "Putting your ego aside will help you grow," a student explained. "Anger can be channeled in constructive ways such as exercising, writing poetry, and community organizing. Tomorrow is another day."

The curriculum built off students' competences and enthusiasm for learning. Our research on Chicago fostered critical thinking as well as analysis of a wide range of texts. Scaffolds were designed with consideration of students' skills and learning styles. Materials met students' reading levels, and graphic organizers were distributed to improve the clarity and organization of their writing. Critical reading skills such as surveying and annotating text were introduced. Students participated in kinesthetic and multisensory tasks that required them to move around the learning area. They were also given the opportunity to demonstrate understanding and expression through poetry and visual art.

Students and teachers were encouraged to bring their full selves to the classroom. I attempted to cultivate a learning space rooted in what King (in chapter 7) describes as an equity mind-set—where prior knowledge, interests, communities, strengths, and struggles are recognized and valued, and the ethical and academic demands are high. The significance of the unit went beyond reading and writing skill development, Common Core standards, and an edTPA portfolio. The students sought to honor Chicago's youth and humanize the murder rate statistics. A few students expressed that the unit contributed to their efforts to heal from personal trauma. Teacher education programs and school districts should provide the space for teachers to work within an equity framework. When given the planning time to develop culturally relevant lessons and collaboratively problem solve, youth and teachers have the capacity and enthusiasm to engage in democratic dialogue, be affirmed, be challenged, and grow.

## GENESIS A. CHAVEZ

Race and racism are unavoidable topics in our generation. Millennials, in general, are more willing to participate in difficult conversations. In our spaces, we are more willing to ask, challenge, and explore the unanswered questions about race and racism. As millennial teachers of color we are more open to not only talk about race, but willing to address racism in its most blatant forms in the name of our students. After all, we have endless personal experiences, tales told by our elders, and stories our students bring with them.

Brown and Ward's study in this volume (chapter 6) about preservice teachers and their knowledge of racism speaks to my experience. As Latinx teachers of color, we encounter racism and are certainly comfortable speaking about injustices, yet many of us don't have a deep knowledge base or the vernacular to be able to hold complex conversations about race/ethnicity. For example, there have been many times when people stepped into my classroom looking for the teacher and approached me as the para-educator or parent volunteer. I felt the microaggression, but was not able to name it.

I have learned a lot on my journey from a preservice teacher to an in-service teacher. I have learned how to refine the approach I take when I advocate to change racist education policies that exist locally and nationwide. I have also learned how systemic issues of social justice truly are in education. As a preservice teacher, I did not fully understand the depth and scope of these issues. I could see the trends in achievement across the country—but I did not know what it was like to live in the middle of it. Observing students fail inequitable assessments as a preservice teacher is entirely different from being held accountable for their performance as an in-service teacher.

Most preservice programs do not prepare us for dealing with race, and we see this play out in our experiences in the classroom. For example, during my first few years in the classroom, I witnessed school policy choices that I knew were unfair for the students of color that we served. Students were being tracked very early in their educational career, disenfranchising many of our students of color and English language learners. It seemed to me that benefits for a few students outweighed the needs of others, and it was infuriating. Yet I did not know how to phrase an argument in a manner that called out the racist policies. I also lacked the skill set to effectively teach the "concentrated ESOL class." It takes more than passion to teach.

My students also needed a teacher who understood her own racial and ethnic identity well enough to know *how* this impacted her craft. How does my identity impact how I teach? They needed a teacher who could analyze and constantly question her interactions to ensure equity. Why did I choose to act or react that way? Was it because of biases I am unaware of? As a cohort, millennial teachers of color need explicit and intentional training programs in order to turn our simple willingness and openness to discuss matters about race and racism into a knowledgeable force capable of creating sustainable change.

Additionally, most preservice programs do not prepare us to understand the politics around the content we teach as well as the limits on our creative freedom in the classroom. As a preservice teacher, I believed I could choose what and how I taught my students, with no repercussions. I found myself disillusioned when I stepped into the classroom as an in-service teacher and realized that my creativity was on a leash, controlled by schoolwide, districtwide, and statewide assessments, many of which are written for white, English-speaking, middle-class American children. There is a constant tug between adapting to give my students what they need and preparing them for assessments that weren't written with them in mind. Additionally, though zero-tolerance policies are being removed around the country, the existing disciplinary policies out of my control *still* echo discriminatory and racist ideals.

Despite these issues, the biggest shock was when I stepped into my school and not only felt isolated, but also recognized that no one around me shared the same sense of urgency about the racial and socioeconomic disparities that our students experience. Walking down the halls and seeing that some classes were made up entirely of white students (the "advanced" class), while other classes had only one or two white students (the "on level" or "ESOL concentrated" classes) was jarring. As if we had stepped back in time. How much had really changed? Was I the only one who found this unbearable? It is true that younger teachers of color turn to their elders when seeking support. However, this becomes nearly impossible for millennial Latinx teachers because those elders are so rare in our school settings. As a result, the feeling of isolation creeps into the small and large moments in our careers when we seek guidance and find there isn't anyone who can begin to empathize with our experiences.

Herrera and Morales's contribution (chapter 3) resonates with me because they specifically discuss the isolation that Latinx millennial teachers feel. Despite our willingness to talk openly about race and racism, and even though we can form positive relationships with colleagues, we are still marginalized in our school buildings. Whether the circumstances are formal or informal social events, team decisions, or schoolwide decisions, we are often excluded. The local watering holes, such as staff lounges, are filled with conversations we can nod along to but not contribute to with our own experiences. While our white colleagues chat away about their lives, never having to think about their race or the different realities that race creates, we challenge them while trying to smile politely—and it's lonely. The feeling of being alone in a room full of people is heavy. Our ideas and input are either forgotten or valued only when representing or speaking for our race. Sadly, this reflects many of our own educational experiences.

Furthermore, there is a misconception that because millennials are more educated in greater numbers, we have a better opportunity to move up socioeconomic brackets. While that may be true for some, for millennial teachers of color this isn't always the case. For Latinx teachers the commitment and responsibilities we have in our families complicates the journey up the socioeconomic ladder. We are a collectivist community, which isn't understood by our colleagues or the current system we still operate under.

We are emotionally tied to the sacrifices our mothers, fathers, aunts, uncles, grandmothers, and grandfathers have made for the sake of our successes. Our tongues still taste the foods of our struggling pasts, which are a daily reminder to share our economic prosperity.

Last, the structures meant to support teachers were never built with millennial teachers of color in mind. For example, the fact that I have a commitment to my younger family members, blood related or not, goes under the radar because traditionally that should be the role of a parent. Teacher support structures are built to facilitate and maintain financial support for traditional families based upon the nuclear family model. They do not support the monetary needs of those who live in extended families, assume parental roles, and monetarily support entire communities. Also, it isn't considered that many of us millennial teachers of color have had to teach ourselves about the social capital needed to pursue our careers; therefore, we have the obligation to help those who are coming after us. Our current system does not support this kind of networking, which contributes to the feelings of isolation and marginalization. It doesn't acknowledge my realities as a millennial teacher of color. Although I don't hide my realities, there certainly is no place for them.

All the facets of who I am and how I identify cannot be left at the door. I bring these things into the classroom with me in how I teach, how I relate to my students and colleagues, and how I engage with my responsibilities as an educator. A system ready to acknowledge this would support me in finding solutions for the gaps. As it stands, the educational system isn't ready for the vast numbers of millennial teachers of color needed to teach our diverse population of students.

## LINDSAY A. MILLER

Teaching in one of the largest school districts in the country has made me aware of the scarcity of millennial teachers of color and why we so desperately need them. As a preservice teacher, I sought a program with an emphasis on urban education. The embedded issues of racism, social injustice, and economic disparities were constantly topics of our discourse. The program I was in was known as a hub for the district hiring pool, and I subsequently did get hired. However, once I became an in-service teacher, the silence surrounding all these topics was deafening.

Racial variations, economic disparities, and injustices were an unspoken condition of the job. My school was 100 percent minorities (Hispanic and African America), 100 percent free and reduced-price lunch, and 75 percent staffed by white females. Yet when I asked about this in the early days of my career, not only was I met with silence, I was told in many ways, "This is just how it is, so just do your job."

As Sabrina Hope King illustrates in chapter 7, teacher preparation programs, even my socially conscious one, need to provide content on the workplace dynamics of schools and/or the bureaucracies of schools, districts, and the unions. Millennial teachers do bring a more modern approach to long-standing issues we find in our schools as well as a willingness to discuss and rectify some of them, yet having to learn the embedded politics of education has a huge impact on the quality of instruction we are able to provide for our kids—especially early in our careers.

Though millennial teachers like me look forward to having difficult discussions about what prevents us from serving our children well, many of our colleagues thrive on the motto "Don't ask, don't tell." As a result, many of my colleagues, most of them teachers of color, find it hard to both stick to their convictions and stay in the profession. Many of these teachers could have been retained at the schools in my district had our principals, district supervisors, and union offered a system, an event, or platform where teachers could genuinely come together and discuss issues beyond a new curriculum product the district bought.

Many of us have chosen to alleviate this burden by finding mentors. My few millennial colleagues of color and I searched for advocates and mentors. We found these efforts to be futile and only resulted in our being ostracized by older colleagues. When our curriculum, ideals, or views didn't align with theirs, it not only further isolated us but also gave us the reputation of being naive, ineffective, or borderline effective teachers.

Districts need to build supportive systems for teachers beyond administrators and district unions so when those don't suffice, we have reliable support structures in place. Schools might assign a mentor teacher to show you how to fill out attendance or where field trip forms are. However, our identities as educators in these districts are predetermined—and stagnant. The millennial perspective and ongoing professional growth are nonexistent. Instead, the discourse centers on phrases such as "We have been doing it like this for years" or "I don't have time to do something different."

Hope King's call for change via illuminating the perspective of millennial teachers of color and establishing an equity framework to support their ongoing development is something I feel is much needed for our educational system to be more effective. I believe these steps would retain millennial teachers of color and white teachers who are racially and socially conscious. At the end of the day, it is policy changes like these that foster schools with a diversity of teachers and students, coupled with an openness to address the realities of racism, social injustice, and economic disparities.

## SARAH ISHMAEL

Osama bin Laden was caught during my first year of teaching. The students were abuzz with conversation about what had happened. Twitter was in its heyday, and social media was becoming more and more a source of information for my kids. The topic came up during a class conversation and I decided to make a lesson out of it. I gathered stories from different newspapers about Osama bin Laden's capture and had the students compare how the story was depicted in each of the news articles. We had a conversation about author's voice, presentation, and choice of facts, and we discussed the importance of *inferring* information rather than accepting what was presented to us. One of my students raised his hand and asked, "Ms. Ishmael, that's great that we're talking about Osama bin Laden and stuff overseas and stuff, but—why don't we talk about what happens in our own neighborhood? Down the street? Can we infer about that?" I had the students push their desks into the circle and my mentor teacher and I had a class conversation about some of the things they saw every day in their neighborhoods.

Though teaching today is different, many things stay the same. Teaching content that is relevant to students' lives is not a new concept—it is an essential part of good teaching that teacher educators have imparted to their students for decades. For example, in *The Dreamkeepers*, a study of eight teachers who successfully teach African American students, Gloria Ladson-Billings asserts that education needs to be relevant to students.[3] More specifically, it needs to be relevant to their culture and to their daily experience. *The Dreamkeepers* was first published in 1995.

I did not read *Dreamkeepers* until I became a graduate student. When I did, I realized that the reason I eventually connected with my students was the same reason that the eight teachers in the study were truly masterful teachers. Their basic beliefs about who their students were and the type of teaching and intellectual rigor they needed to excel pushed them to develop a teaching practice that constantly expanded their students' thinking. For me, one of the main messages in *Dreamkeepers* is about developing a personal theory of excellent and rigorous teaching that stems from respecting your students. As I read the book and reflected on my time in the classroom, I realized that I developed such a belief because my students *demanded* that I do so. My students pushed me to respect them and to create lessons that they *knew* benefited them. They wouldn't give me the time of day otherwise.

As a teacher educator, *Dreamkeepers* is still the first text I have my preservice teachers read. Though teaching today takes on a very different tenor when students come to you with the story of Philando Castile on their iPhones and tears in their eyes asking you to explain what happened (almost the instant that he died, thanks to social media), the advice and lessons in *Dreamkeepers* and other books by teachers of color are instructive and timeless. I know that *I* was at a loss some seven years ago when my students wanted to discuss how the media focused on violence overseas, but ignored the violence present in their own neighborhoods and on their social media feeds. It is a blessing that we millennial teachers can reach back and read about how teachers of color before us taught through the LA riots, Rodney King, Emmett Till, the deaths of so many civil rights leaders, and countless other life-changing events for all students—especially students of color.

As I mentioned previously, students today *demand* excellence. They *demand* a deep understanding of the complex cultural and economic history of the world as well as a critical mind to help them learn how to navigate the layers of violence they see on social media; the incredible effects of climate change, like hurricanes that ruin cities and communities; and the fluctuation of policy and economics that often dictate their circumstances. They *demand* teachers who can help them understand how identities, societal structures, economic structures, and communities come together. They *demand* content that explains how and why these things clash in such divergent, violent, and confusing ways in their lives. This isn't new, but it *is* different—and because it is different it is *that much more difficult* today.

As Hope King indicates in her recommendations for districts, teaching requires a critical equity mind-set throughout both the school and the district. Such teaching "seeks to perpetuate, foster and sustain linguistic, literate and cultural pluralism as a part of schooling for positive social transformation."[4] Millennial teachers need monetary and administrative support from districts and administrators to develop *our own understanding* of what it means to sustain students and help them develop a critical, healthy, and investigative consciousness about the world they see around them.

In my conversations with preservice teachers, I flash back to that classroom discussion about Osama bin Laden seven years ago. I remind them that our job is to teach literacy in ways that expand and build upon the worlds their students know without devaluing them. Today, culturally sustaining pedagogy—teaching that values students' cultures while at the same time building a critical consciousness of history, and a racial/socioeconomic literacy—is *required*. My students seven years ago (and the students of my students today) refused to sit in a seat let alone *learn* unless what I taught them helped them unpack the complicated world of instant information that sometimes hurt their hearts. And that exposure means that millennial teachers of color dig deeper into who they are and what they know about life, history, and the world in order to create community with their students.

School districts and principals need to support teachers engaging in this type of exploration. To make it in a world of climate change, global economic change, demographic shifts, and political shifts, students today need teachers who have the freedom to question; to develop curriculum and pedagogical strategies that push students to master the content, then flip it and turn it into something that generations before them have never seen. They need this kind of instruction because it is what is required for them to thrive—for them to survive—in this day and age. As I talk to my preservice teachers about our work as educators today, I tell them that our job is to dig deeper into who we are and learn more about life, history, and the world so we can teach our students effectively. Don't worry, I say, because as *I* found out (as veteran teachers told me), this is something for which you *cannot* be trained. This is the art of teaching.

After having this conversation with each of my preservice teachers, I end up handing them not only the latest research on culturally sustaining pedagogy, youth culture, and critical hip-hop education, but also a copy of *Dreamkeepers*.[5] I do this because, as Herrera and Morales state in chapter 3, millennial teachers of color do think back, not only to their teacher preparation but to the wisdom of teachers of color before them. I give them this book because all of the skills that it takes to teach our kids today—namely, (1) "using historical and cultural references," (2) using social media "to impart knowledge, skills and attitudes . . . [as] aspects of the curriculum in their own right," (3) "creating knowledge in conjunction with the ability (and need) to be critical of content," and (4) making knowledge problematic, as a "vehicle for emancipation, to understand the significance of their cultures, and to recognize the power of language"[6]—are lessons passed down to us by those who have come before. I hope as my students enter their own classrooms in the following years, they take those lessons from *Dreamkeepers* and make them their own. I hope they have the support, strength, and knowledge to meet their students where they are, to push them to places they demand to learn about, and as a result to places they never thought they'd go.

## SOME CONCLUDING THOUGHTS

*So when I paint from the photograph, it's like . . . What is the moment of the photograph? What is the moment of that sound? How does the Spirit choose to be portrayed? These represent different uses of paint, different kinds of pigment, different types of brushstrokes. . . . So watercolor or heavy paint, it just depends on the individual and the moment.*[7]

—Frederick J. Brown

Millennial teachers are now seeing these patterns, which are in fact "strains of music" passed down through the generations of teachers of color and teachers who have fought for education as a path to liberation. As Frederick Brown reminds us, when you paint a portrait, or when you read a narrative, it is distinctly colored by the time and by the events that take place around it. The election of 2016, climate change, and the increasing visibility through social media of youth in danger—they all provide a very particular palette that the teachers in this chapter paint. Often it is our students, the realities they face, and the fact that those realities are often constituted through social media, that drive us to engage in teaching that analyzes broader social, economic, identity, and racial issues. As Catone and Tahbildar assert in chapter 5, they drive us to work as community activists. They drive us to build upon the work of generations to help prepare them for the future. We each do this in dynamically different, complicated, and sometimes contradictory ways. And yet, like the story of Stagger Lee, you can find some of the lyrics, hooks, and beats of the original song and sentiment somewhere in all of our stories. Each narrative in this chapter is an individual figure in the overall painting. Each one sits in a *particular* moment, affected by this particular time in history. When you pan out to view the whole painting, you see that each of these narratives is but a single brushstroke in this massive work of art. We hope that by looking closely at each story, and taking in the texture of each narrative, the colors infused in each experience, you've gained a greater understanding of the entire painting overall.

*Acknowledgments*

*Sarah Ishmael thanks Erin Matthias, Dr. Don E. Ishmael, and Sheltreese McCoy. Adam Kuranishi thanks Celia Oyler and Simone Ousset. Genesis Chavez would like to thank her mentors, Dr. Alana Murray and Heather Yuhaniak, for their encouragement and guidance; and her partner, Kevin DeLeon, for his unwavering support of her work. Lindsay Miller thanks Vicki Trinder and Melissa Gude.*

# 2

# Millennials, Generation Xers, and Boomers—A Demographic Overview

Janice Hamilton Outtz and Marcus J. Coleman

This chapter gives an overview of demographic distinctions between three generations of teachers—millennials, generation Xers, and baby boomers. The generational perspective offered here helps to provide a temporal look at some familiar trends. Namely, we focus on population growth, changes in race and ethnicity, educational attainment, labor force participation, and public school teachers by generation, gender, race, and ethnicity. We also look at the growth of public school teachers compared to the student population.

Millennials are on track to be the most highly educated generation to date, and in the first quarter of 2015 they held the largest share of the American workforce. As increasing numbers join the labor force and become teachers, what does it mean for our public schools? The following discussions will provide some context for millennials and for the teaching profession going forward.

## OVERVIEW

Generational cohorts are just one way to categorize a group of people with similarities—in this case, the era when they were born until they came of age. Other ways of categorizing a group of people include by age, which generally divides a population into five-year age groups (i.e., birth to four, five to nine, etc.), and by race and ethnicity. In contrast to the baby boom cohort, whose membership is defined by substantial changes in the US birth rates, the millennial cohort is a generation largely defined by shared experiences.[1]

## Characteristics

Generation X, those in the middle, were born between 1965 and 1980 and are often characterized as skeptical, independent, savvy, and entrepreneurial loners who were shaped by latchkeys.[2] Baby boomers, born between 1946 and 1964, are described as idealists, shaped by Woodstock, JFK, and MLK.[3] Baby boomers have been driving change in the US population since their birth. One thing to note with regard to millennials is the lack of consistency with the birth span identifying them. Most agree that millennials are those born in the last two decades of the twentieth century, but there is considerable variation in the exact range of years specified. For example, some say millennials are those born between 1982 and 2000; others have different ranges—1982–2003, 1983–2001, and 1981–1997. As much as possible, we try to focus on millennials as those who, in 2017, are ages eighteen to thirty-three. Millennials, likely the most studied generation to date, are described as multitaskers extraordinaire who are caring, community oriented, and more politically engaged than previous generations. And, according to data from the Pew Research Center, millennials are markedly less likely to be married or to have children than earlier generations were at comparable ages.[4] Seventy-five percent have never married, compared with 67 percent for generation X and 52 percent of baby boomers. In addition, the US Census Bureau reports that more millennials are living in poverty and have higher rates of unemployment, compared with their counterparts. For our purposes, we will focus on the age groups (as of 2017) of eighteen to thirty-three (millennials), thirty-five to fifty (generation X), and fifty-one to sixty-nine (baby boomers).

## Population growth

In terms of population, as of 2015, millennials have surpassed baby boomers as the nation's largest living generation, according to estimates from the US Census Bureau. In 2015, millennials numbered 75.3 million, surpassing the 74.9 million baby boomers. Generation X made up 65.7 million. By 2030, the gap between the millennials and boomers will widen—77.8 million compared to 76 million, and generation X will be very close to the millennials with 77.5 million (see figure 2.1). While baby boomers are transitioning into retirement ages, millennials are beginning to pass through the traditional benchmarks of adulthood (e.g., completing college, finding jobs, and establishing independent households).

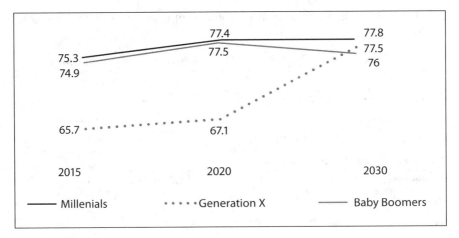

FIGURE 2.1    Millennials outnumber baby boomers in the United States (millions)

*Source:* U.S. Census Bureau, 2014 Population Projections, Table NP2014.

Large-scale immigration from Asia and Latin America, the rise in racial intermarriage, and differences in fertility patterns across racial and ethnic groups have contributed to the change. As noted by many researchers, these differences show us that millennials are more diverse than the generations that preceded them. In 2015, millennials of color in the United States (African Americans, Asians, American Indian/Alaskan Natives, Native Hawaiian and Pacific Islanders, and persons claiming two or more races) made up 26 percent of the total population compared to 23 percent for generation X and 19 percent for baby boomers. Millennial Hispanics (of any race) made up 21 percent of the total population in 2015 compared to 19 percent for generation X and just 11 percent for baby boomers.[5]

When we take a closer look, separating race and Hispanic origin, the picture is even more telling. Non-Hispanic white millennials in the United States made up 56 percent of the population in 2015 compared to 72 percent for baby boomers. The total for millennials of color compared to baby boomers was 44 percent and 28 percent, respectively (see table 2.1).

### Education and work

Millennials are on track to be the most educated generation to date. The Pew Research Center has done extensive research on the generations. Pew found

TABLE 2.1   US millennials and baby boomers compared by race and Hispanic origin, 2015

| Race/Hispanic origin | Millennials | Baby boomers |
| --- | --- | --- |
| Non-Hispanic White | 55.5% | 71.8% |
| Non-Hispanic African American | 14.0% | 11.1% |
| Non-Hispanic Asian | 5.7% | 4.7% |
| Non-Hispanic American Indian, Alaskan Native | 0.8% | 0.7% |
| Non-Hispanic Native Hawaiian, Pacific Islander | 0.2% | 0.1% |
| Non-Hispanic, Two or More Races | 2.4% | 1.0% |
| Hispanic | 21.3% | 10.7% |

*Source*: U.S. Census Bureau, 2014 National Projections.

*Note*: The racial categories from the Census Bureau generally reflect a social definition of race recognized in the United States and not an attempt to define race biologically, anthropologically, or genetically. In addition, it is recognized that the categories of the race item include racial and national origin or sociocultural groups. People may choose to report more than one race to indicate their racial mixture, such as "Non-Hispanic White" and "Non-Hispanic American Indian." People who identify their origin as Hispanic, Latino, or Spanish may be of any race.

that 27 percent of female millennials had completed at least a bachelor's degree at ages eighteen to thirty-three compared to 21 percent of millennial males. However, the percentages for millennial women and men are considerably higher than for both generation X and boomers. This is an important statistic since a bachelor's degree is necessary to pursue a teaching career.

Similarly, millennials in the first quarter of 2015 surpassed generation X to become the largest share of the American workforce, according to the Pew Research Center's analysis of US Census Bureau data; 53.5 million compared to 52.7 million are in the labor force. By comparison, in the first quarter of 2015, about 45 million baby boomers were in the labor force. Although millennials are in the labor force in high percentages, the recession of 2008 caused them to face some difficulties. According to the New York Federal Reserve Board, as reported by the US Bureau of Labor Statistics, since 2005, the educational debt of Americans under age thirty has increased from about $13,000 to $21,000.[6] While there has been a decrease in every other type of debt, student loan debt has seen a dramatic increase. This may be a reason why more than one-third of millennials (36%) depend on their parents or other family members for financial assistance and why millennials have a

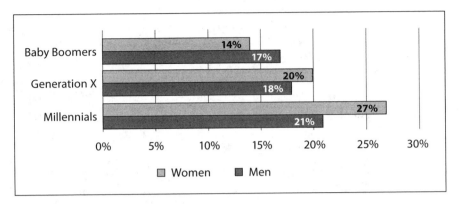

FIGURE 2.2   Educational attainment: Bachelor's degree completion at ages 18–33, by gender

*Source:* Pew Research Center, Fact Tank, "How Millennials Compare with Their Grandparents 50 Years Ago," March 2015. Tabulations from the U.S. Census Bureau, Current Population Survey.

higher poverty rate.[7] Moreover, the historical context of racial oppression in the United States continues to fuel wealth inequality in the United States.[8] For example, as it relates to educational attainment, in 2013, 42 percent of African American families carried student loan debt compared to 28 percent of white families.[9] Wealth inequality in concert with student loan debt contributes to the following financial maladies in minority communities: decreased home homeownership, lower liquid retirement, and significantly lower net worth per household.[10]

## GENERATIONAL VOICES OF THE TEACHING CORPS

Of central concern here is the continued vitality of the teaching corps for public schools, which is assessed regularly. However, the assessment of the teaching corps is usually done from a perspective that highlights racial and experiential distinctions. In this chapter we provide a generational look at teacher distribution, by race and gender, which may offer a different representation of our teaching workforce.

To ground our discussion, we begin with the voices of minority teachers who relay their respective generational perspectives on occupational perseverance, education technology innovation, and the economic pressures of being a part of the teaching corps.

## Millennial teacher

A twenty-eight-year-old minority female teacher at a high school in the Baltimore, Maryland, metropolitan area asserts:

> Economics was a motivator for me to seek graduate education so that I could eventually make the move into administration and/or policy. . . . I can't redo or beautify my classroom because I can't afford to foot the bill myself.

This teacher expresses both the desire to advance in her career as a teacher and her wish to improve her classroom. Unfortunately, the economic pressures inherent to self-improvement and to the improvement of children's learning environment, particularly inadequate teacher pay, constrain both desires. This economic conundrum may be a disincentive to many willing teachers who want to improve themselves and their communities.

## Generation X teacher

A forty-five-year-old minority male teacher at a middle school in the Jackson, Mississippi, metropolitan area states:

> Occupational perseverance came with the enjoyment of the work. It is true that it's a calling. If it's not for you, get out and move forward with a new career and do yourself and the kids a favor. . . . I started as a noncertified staffer making $500 per month. It was tough. I had another job too . . . working at a hotel.

Again, the economic hardships of being a teacher can be challenging and may prove, for some, to be too much. Even so, this generation X teacher weathered the storm due to his passion for teaching kids. In this instance, the teacher sees economic hardship as part of being engaged in community building. So, regardless of the difficulty, it is always about the kids.

## Baby boomer teacher

A sixty-one-year-old female minority teacher in Monroe, Louisiana, said:

> I started teaching at age twenty-one and have been teaching for forty years. What I think is different now—some parents' expectations are not as high as they were when I first started teaching. Educators are not as respected as they used to be. Parents baby their children. Many millennials, I think,

see this as just a job and not educating children and developing them into mature adults. They can't wait for 3:00 p.m. dismissal and days off. Today, the wrong people make decisions on what needs to be done in the school, what should be taught and how it should be taught. I loved my forty years of teaching and coaching. Yes, every now and then you have some low points but it is a profession I loved. But because of all the paper work, added pressures put on content, teachers and administrators, and salary, I can see where it is a job a lot of people do not want to take.

This teacher is critical of millennial teachers due to their lack of dedication to the job. She credits the lack of occupational perseverance to a failure of parenting. Ironically, the caretakers for millennials have primarily been baby boomers. She also acknowledges the additional administrative burden that may, again, hinder teacher retention within the teaching corps. Even so, at the core of her critique of millennial teachers is the well-being of the students.

## Baby boomer teacher

A fifty-nine-year-old female minority teacher in San Diego, California, explained:

> I started teaching at age twenty-six. So much has changed since I started. There is less support from parents; students are not grouped anymore—exceptionalities (too many children being labeled); and students are taught more by technology now. Computers can introduce, teach, and score student's work. The economic pressures of being a teacher include the fact that teaching techniques are based more on standardized testing. Teaching is political, which means too much pressure on the teacher. Curriculums are so broad that there is less time for teaching.

In this passage, the teacher provides a critique of the system within which teachers work. Support from home, the rise of technology, economic hardship, and political pressures of teaching all present challenges to occupational perseverance. A generational outlook highlights some familiar trends seen in other public school teacher data (i.e., race, ethnicity, and gender), but it also provides an uncommon perspective on new teacher recruitment and retention. In the sections that follow, we focus on generational distinctions that are exacerbated by systematic pressures that impact the teaching profession and, by extension, the students.

## PUBLIC SCHOOL TEACHERS BY GENERATION

The National Center for Education Statistics' Schools and Staffing Survey (SASS) data show that, preK–12 teachers formed the largest occupational group in the nation in 2012, and since then it has grown even larger. Right after World War II and before the postwar baby boom, there were fewer than one million elementary and secondary teachers in the United States. In 1997–98, the total number of elementary and secondary teachers in public schools was about 2.6 million. Between 1997 and 2011, there was an increase of 13 percent. According to the US Department of Education, that number is expected to increase another 13 percent by 2022.[11]

The SASS data also indicate that millennials lag considerably behind generation Xers in terms of filling the ranks of our teaching corps (see figure 2.3). It is difficult to make projections or assertions as to what this means for the teaching corps in the future, but research states: "In 2011–12, while 82 percent of public school teachers were white, 78 percent of teachers with three or fewer years of experience were white. While 7 percent of all teachers were black, 8 percent of all teachers with three or fewer years of experience were black. While 8 percent of all teachers were Hispanic, 10 percent of all teachers with three or fewer years of experience were Hispanic."[12]

That passage helps paint a picture of the lack of racial and experiential diversity that exists for teachers who are at the beginning of their careers. We also know from research that, nationally, young teachers of color are also "overwhelmingly employed in public schools . . . and are two to three times more likely than white teachers to work in such hard-to-staff schools serving high-poverty, high-minority, and urban communities."[13] We continue to see a lack of diversity among millennials, generation Xers, and baby boomers in the teaching profession.

The SASS data also show that millennials in the 2011–12 school year had far less teaching experience than either generation Xers or the baby boomers. Eighty percent of millennials teaching public school had five or fewer years of teaching experience, with an average of 3.7 years. The data show that the number of beginning teachers with less than five years' experience increased by 43 percent between 1987–88 and 2011–12—a gain of over 250,000. Probably not surprising to some, the data also show that the

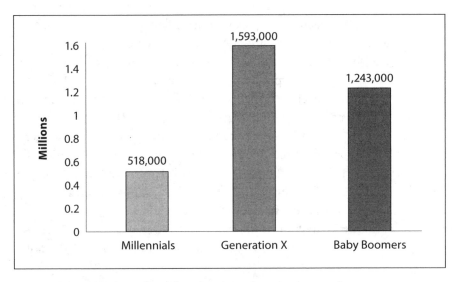

FIGURE 2.3    Number of public school teachers by generation

*Source:* U.S. Department of Education, National Center for Education Statistics, Schools and Staffing Survey, "Public School Teacher Data File," 2011–12.

number of beginning teachers in high-poverty public schools increased from 41,000 to 189,000 during that same time period—a gain of more than 350 percent. Thus, in 2011–12, there were more than four times as many beginning teachers employed in high-poverty schools as in 1987–88.[14]

Thus far, data demonstrate that millennials are entering the teaching profession in great volume, but the overarching unknown is their occupational perseverance as career teachers. The general trend is high teacher turnover in public schools in urban and/or rural communities that are characterized as being densely populated with minorities and that have high levels of poverty.[15] Considering that a significant number of millennial teachers of color are employed in public schools, this trend is disturbing and foreshadows our discussion of the need for increased gender and racial diversity in recruiting and retaining the emerging teaching corps.

## PUBLIC SCHOOL TEACHERS BY GENDER

Historically, women have outnumbered men as teachers, and that trend continues today (see figure 2.4). Female teachers increased by 56 percent and males by 22 percent between 1987–88 and 2011–12.[16] Although the number of men entering the teaching corps continues to lag that of women, regardless of generation, the overall number of teachers entering the profession is increasing. The number of teachers in public elementary and secondary schools increased by 13 percent between 1997 and 2011 (a period of fourteen years) and is projected to increase by the same percentage between 2011 and 2022 (a period of eleven years).[17]

While there is very little difference between the percentages of teachers by gender across the three generations as seen in figure 2.4, nationally the percentage of female teachers has increased. The SASS data, along with other National Center for Education Statistics data, show that since the early 1980s there has been a steady increase in the proportion of teachers who are female, from 67 percent in 1980–81 to over 76 percent in 2011–12. As the authors of *Seven Trends: The Transformation of the Teaching Force* note:

> The change in the male-to-female ratio in teaching is not due to a decline in males entering the occupation. The number of males entering teaching has also grown, by 22 percent, which is faster than the rate of increase of the

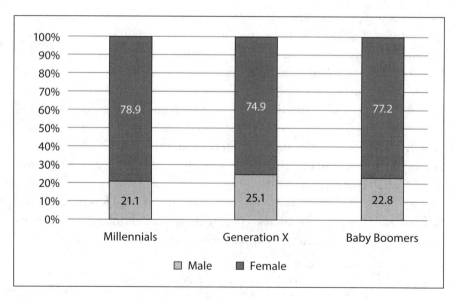

FIGURE 2.4   Percentage of US public school teachers by gender for each generation

*Source:* U.S. Department of Education, National Center for Education Statistics, Schools and Staffing Survey, "Public School Teacher Data File," 2011–12.

student population. But the number of females in teaching has increased at over twice that rate.[18]

Thus, while there is proportional growth in both males and females in the teaching force, the percentage of men entering the profession continues to lag that of women.

## PUBLIC SCHOOL TEACHERS BY RACE AND ETHNICITY

As the data show, teaching remains a primarily white workforce. From a generational data perspective, the racial disparity among those entering and staying in the teaching profession remains dire. White, non-Hispanic teachers outnumber all other teachers combined, regardless of generation (see figure 2.5.) While the increase in teachers of color between 1987 and 2012 was notable (104 percent), white, non-Hispanic teachers still made up 82 percent of all elementary and secondary public school teachers (increasing by 38 percent during that same period).[19] Shortages of minority teachers

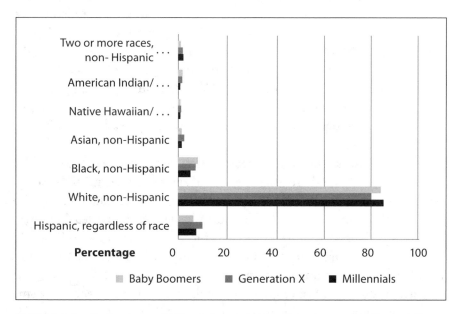

FIGURE 2.5    Percentage of US public school teachers by race and ethnicity for each generation, 2011–12

*Source:* U.S. Department of Education, National Center for Education Statistics, Schools and Staffing Survey, "Public School Teacher Data File," 2011–12.

have been an issue for the US school system for decades. The result is that students of color increasingly do not have role models and lack contact with teachers who understand their racial and cultural background. For example, in the 2011–12 school year, 37 percent of the nation's population belonged to a minority group according to the US Census Bureau (2012); 44 percent of all elementary and secondary students were of color, but only 17 percent of all elementary and secondary teachers were.[20]

At the intersection of race and gender, black males make up 2 percent of the teaching workforce nationwide, but there have been concerted efforts to increase the number of men of color in K–12 education. For example, the "Call Me Mister" program's mission is to increase the pool of available teachers from a broader, more diverse background, particularly among the lowest performing schools. *Mister* is an acronym for Mentors Instructing Students Toward Effective Role Models.[21] Programs like this are helping to increase the number of nonwhite male teachers. Some researchers have found that there are academic benefits when students and teachers share race/ethnicity because such teachers can serve as role models, mentors, advocates, or cultural translators. For example, researchers found small but significant positive performance effects when black and white students were assigned to teachers of their own race/ethnicity, but there was particular benefit found for lower-performing black students.[22] In addition, longitudinal data findings have shown there are positive effects on standardized test scores, suspensions, and attendance.[23] Also, black students who were randomly assigned to at least one black teacher between grades three and five were less likely to drop out of school and more likely to affirm their intent to attend college.[24]

Research has also shown that male teachers are necessary to the development of students, but there is debate and no agreement regarding the long-term impact on educational outcomes of matching students of color with teachers of color.[25] The dearth of minority males going into teaching may contribute to lapses in cultural awareness for both teachers and students due to a lack of exposure to male figures who can contribute alternative views to policy and procedural efforts in schools.[26]

Further, students of color are expected to make up 56 percent of the student population by 2024 due to a dramatic growth in the Latino/a population, a decrease in the white population, and a steady rise in the number of Asian Americans. African American growth has been mostly flat, according to the National Center for Education Statistics. Thus, the significant increase in minority students outpaces the increase of minority male teachers in public schools.

Ultimately, there is no silver bullet to alleviate these overwhelming disparities, whether racial or generational. As reported by many researchers, the lack of diverse teachers may mean that students of color have no contact with teachers who look like them. Further, nonminority teachers may not understand the racial and/or cultural background of students of color. Conversely, teachers of color have higher expectations for students of color, which promotes educational ambition.[27] Some researchers go so far as to suggest that this shortage in teachers of color is a key reason for the minority achievement gap and other less successful life outcomes for students of color.[28] But, as we have mentioned before, there is some debate on whether matching students and teachers of the same race influences student outcomes.

## CONCLUSION

We know that the three generations—millennials, generation Xers, and baby boomers—are similar in some regards and very different in others. No one had to tell us that. But the large *number* of millennials makes us pay attention. Some call millennials the most threatening and exciting generation since the baby boomers. Pew Research says that they are history's first "always connected" generation, steeped in digital technology and social media. In a few years, they will be the largest population group. Will their differences— their connectiveness, their large numbers, their increased levels of education—lead to improved student learning outcomes? That remains to be seen.

*Acknowledgments*

*Special thanks to Dr. Bill O'Hare, O'Hare Data and Demographic Services, LLC.*

# 3

# Understanding "Me" Within "Generation Me"

*The Meaning Perspectives Held Toward and by Millennial*
*Culturally and Linguistically Diverse Teachers*

Socorro G. Herrera and Amanda R. Morales

Numerous scholars, commentators, and analysts have persuasively argued that the most complex and compelling of all generations is the millennial generation, also occasionally referred to as generation Y.[1] The perspectives, characteristics, and actions associated with members of this generation, which came of age at the turn of the century, are highly germane to the goals and purposes of teaching and the domain of education. This is in large part because they have been the first generation to (1) grow up in the digital age, (2) utilize computers in their classrooms, (3) access a 24/7 news cycle, (4) age alongside the ups and downs of social media, (5) read paperless books, (6) learn practically any skill via web-based "how-to" videos (YouTube), and (7) enjoy fingertip access to the largest encyclopedia ever synthesized (Wikipedia).[2]

In like manner, this generation is significantly relevant to teacher educators, school leaders, and higher education and their long-term sustainability for many reasons. It is the first generation to pass along its emergent technological and social prowess with computers, programs, and apps to a subsequent one. The millennial generation is one of the largest on record, and in many ways it is the first to live more urban and suburban, rather than rural, lifestyles.[3] Furthermore, it is the most racially and culturally diverse generation, and research indicates that its members are the most open to racial/cultural tolerance of any in history.[4] And while it is the most educated of all North American generations, it is also the most financially overburdened. The children of this generation are and will be, for the foreseeable future, the emergent population of potential candidates for teaching and teacher education.

The millennial generation and its potential for current and future impacts on institutions of teacher education (ITEs) are confounding for teacher educators and educational leaders because the perspectives and actions of its members are often skewed and oversimplified. There is a large body of literature that describes millennials as the most overeducated, coddled, undermotivated, and narcissistic generation in this country's history.[5] They have been characterized as entitled, passive, and lacking respect for authority due to existing in a world of abundance.[6] However, other analysts and researchers have characterized millennials as forward thinking, confident, active, and collaborative.[7] Donnison has conducted an extensive literature review of such perspectives and the evidence from which they arise.[8] She concludes that a narcissistic/negative characterization of millennials tends to be grounded in a perspective that singularly rewards a strong work ethic and traditional values—characteristic of the baby boomer generation; whereas the forward-thinking/collaborative characterizations are typically grounded in a team-building perspective representative of a self-described millennial view.[9]

While these conflicting depictions of millennials illustrate how generational groups can be as diverse individually as they are collectively, most would agree that this cohort undeniably has distinct qualities.[10] Current social, political, and economic shifts are being experienced, documented, shared, and reinterpreted by these young adults at lightning speed.[11] The ways in which they communicate, access information, establish priorities, and engage with educational systems has changed, requiring institutions to modify practice and to rethink traditional approaches to their work.[12] The millennial generation has not only changed the ways they communicate with educational institutions but also the languages they use to do so. They are, by far, the most linguistically diverse generation since the silent generation (i.e., traditionalists)—one in four members speak a language other than English at home.[13]

Amid the prevailing and often inconsistent social narratives characterizing millennials as the entitled "Generation Me,"[14] many culturally and linguistically diverse (CLD) millennials exist in the margins of society, struggling to define themselves within the predominantly middle-class, white normative spaces of K–12 schools and institutions of higher education.

CLD millennials (especially those who are first- or second-generation immigrants) often experience dissonance between the strong societal messages they receive about their identity from their tertiary socialization (white normative culture perpetuated in US education systems) and the messages they receive from their primary socialization (home culture shared with their families and communities).[15] These conflicting messages pervade the social, familial, educational, and professional spaces they must navigate on the road to a professional career.[16]

Therefore, as argued in this book, CLD young adults who are members of this generation embody multifaceted and varied identities that merit further, and more robust, exploration. In addition, to better understand how membership within the millennial generation can be interpreted for or applied to CLD millennials, it is necessary to situate such interpretations and applications within the context of their socialization as cultural and linguistic minorities. Their socialization profoundly impacts their identity development as they traverse white normative educational landscapes.[17]

For those CLD millennials who have chosen to become teachers, the impact of such complexities in and influences of tertiary socialization in educational contexts does not end upon college graduation. Millennial CLD teachers (CLDTs) must continue to negotiate their identities in relation to their predominantly white peers and their increasingly diverse classrooms, which are part and parcel of the inherently politicized context of schools.[18]

Given the complexity of today's social landscape, the need for well-educated, culturally and linguistically competent, strongly committed, and highly engaged education professionals has never been more compelling. The next generation of innovative leaders and engaged citizens in our K–12 schools is depending on millennials' creative potential, developed skill, and critical consciousness. However, to understand the true potentialities of any particular group or subgroup, we must be thoughtful in our approach to their identifications. At the macrolevel, the social and political factors shaping millennials have been given strong consideration; yet, at the microlevel, less has been done to understand millennials as cultural beings in situ, within the historical, sociopolitical, and psychosocial contexts they navigate.

In this chapter, we considered these social and cultural factors in our search of a more nuanced perspective of millennials, in particular preservice to in-service CLD millennial teachers. To this end, we engaged in a multi-method longitudinal study of CLD graduates of an English for Speakers of Other Languages (ESOL) teacher education program at a large midwestern university.[19] This chapter is focused on data collected specifically from the qualitative surveys and phenomenological interviews we conducted with a purposive sample of thirteen CLD millennial in-service teachers.[20] Using a blended theoretical framework, this study draws primarily on the tenets of Latino/a critical race theory (LatCrit) to examine the contextual, holistic, and thematic descriptions given by millennial CLDTs of their lived experiences as preservice and in-service teachers. As phenomenological researchers, we sought a better understanding of the nuances within this generational cohort, because "understanding brings clarity, and also an awareness of the complexity of experience."[21]

The purpose of the study, therefore, was to explore the meaning perspectives millennial CLDTs held about themselves, their peers, and their students amid the prevailing narratives of predominantly white normative educational spaces in the midwestern United States. In the process, we uncovered a counternarrative. This more nuanced perspective of a subset of the millennial population provided a different vantage point from which to analyze current discourse that potentially overgeneralizes them, as well as brought to light the increasing cultural complexities that millennial CLDTs face in schools. In this chapter we discuss and explicate study findings and implications for teacher education. Further, we provide opportunities for educational institutions to consider the various ways their policy and practice impact current and future teacher diversification.

## LITERATURE REVIEW

Several bodies of literature guided us as we engaged in this work. In addition to formal K–16 educational research, we pulled from sociology, psychology, adult education, and political science literatures to inform our study. We explored theories on identity development and psychological meaning perspectives by Holland, Lachiotte, Skinner, and Cain and Mezirow, respectively, giving us the cognitive tools for a deeper understanding of millennial CLDTs' experience and for a richer interpretation of their narratives.[22] Further, we investigated critical theories on race put forward by researchers such as Mills, Kohli, Miele, Solórzano, Delgado Bernal, and Yosso, providing us the framework for contextualizing millennial CLDTs' experience within the broader historical, political, and institutional structures that frame their personal and professional realities.[23]

## Teacher diversification

Today's institutions of teacher education (ITEs) continue their efforts to effectively recruit, retain, and graduate students, while trying to understand and define the unique characteristics of this current generation. It is understood that given millennials' broad range of racial and cultural identities, the concept of race as an ideology has come into sharper focus within colleges of education. Both teacher preparation programs and the schools that employ millennial CLDTs have come to realize that they must gain a better understanding of how race, culture, language, and class impact millennial students and teacher identity if they are to fully engage them in the critical, intellectual, and practical work of schools.[24] Understandably, as incubators for attitudes and ways of thinking about social issues, educational institutions do affect teaching and learning in profound ways.[25] This is true not only for CLD children and their families but also for CLD teachers (pre- and in-service), who must navigate within the predominantly and historically white profession of education.

Yet, given teacher preparation programs' current fight against the commercialization and privatization of education, and the struggle to remain relevant in the eyes of the general public, there seems to be little time or resources left to tackle challenges presented by the mismatch between the historically white teaching force and the CLD student populations in public classrooms.[26] As a result, shortages of teachers from diverse backgrounds remain a persistent problem in both teacher education and in public schools.[27]

Increasingly, colleges of education seek to diversify their programs by recruiting CLD millennials as preservice teachers in hopes of locating the silver bullet that will address chronic racial tensions and K–12 opportunity gaps between their white, more affluent students and their students of color from lower socioeconomic status backgrounds.[28] The effectiveness of efforts toward "cultural match" between CLD students and CLD teachers has been debated in the literature for years.[29] Being understood more and more as a civil right of children of color to *see themselves* represented in schools, teacher diversification is of increasing critical importance.[30]

Historically, however, the potential impact of teachers of color has been long understood. Albert A. Goodson, a noted musician and writer during the Harlem Renaissance, described the ideological and philosophical orientation of African American teachers as advocates for black children in segregated US schools. He argued that historically, black teachers owned the responsibility of improving the conditions for African Americans in their communities and that education was seen as an emancipatory endeavor for the uplifting of their race. This ideology carried on throughout the Jim Crow era and even into desegregation as African American educators focused on nurturing students to be independent and self-reliant as well as to take action against all forms of oppression in hopes of true democracy.[31]

This ideology is not unlike that described in Chicana feminist, LatCrit, and critical care pedagogies of the current era. There is similar evidence in this more recent literature that CLD teachers have a tendency to gravitate toward urban and majority-minority schools where student diversity is higher.[32] Researchers have found that CLDTs also demonstrate a stronger sense of responsibility not only to take up issues of diversity in their teaching and professional practice but also to serve as "potential agents of social change in addressing inequities in education."[33]

With this said, a review of the literature on culturally responsive teaching suggests that, while potentially powerful, cultural congruity between teachers and their students guarantees neither teaching effectiveness nor students' target learning.[34] It is, however, one important contributing factor to the comprehensive development of a highly qualified and culturally *conscientized* teaching force.[35]

Research further suggests that even those CLD millennials who gain strong content knowledge and pedagogical skills in high-quality, research-based teacher education programs must build certain dispositions, resiliencies, and capacities for agency and advocacy.[36] Just how CLD pre- and in-service teachers develop these skills and dispositions within formal systems needs further study. This is especially the case when such teachers are placed in predominantly white educational settings where teachers may hold unchecked beliefs, assumptions, and meaning perspectives about the identities, capacities, and commitments of the CLD students and families they are serving.[37] In particular, these issues surface many questions about CLD preservice and in-service teachers' preparation in utilizing their cultural and linguistic identities in praxis. For example, what are the particular experiences that foster or limit this type of development among millennial preservice and in-service CLD teachers in such educational settings?

### Cultural and professional identity development
In the foundational book *Identity and Agency in Cultural Worlds*, Holland, Lachiotte, Skinner, and Cain establish their concept of "figured worlds." They

posit that identities are constructed relationally in figured worlds through "socially produced, culturally constituted activities."[38] As a result of these exchanges, individuals engage in multiple internal dialogues that allow them to make sense of their place in the world within the context of their collective and individual histories; essentially, humans *self-author* what Holland and Lave call our "history in person."[39]

Similarly, Mezirow's theory of transformative learning is about making sense of our history(s) in person.[40] More specifically, meaning making is a recurrent and significant aspect of our social interactions—it is "making sense of or giving coherence to our experiences."[41] His theory emphasizes the volition we have as adults to select our own paths to understanding through critical reflection. Essentially, one's meaning perspectives are a product of complex and long-lasting frames of reference that can change, but must be negotiated. Thus, the millennial CLDTs defined as the focus of this study are (especially as they come of age) shaped by their biopsychosocial history and lived experiences as nonwhites within white normative spaces, both as students and as teachers. Their ascribed memberships in various cultural, social, economic, and political groups impact how they authored themselves in relation to their college professors and peers and later their students and school coworkers.

Mills's concept of "the racial contract" articulates how people of color must come to terms with the reality of an existing racial contract in society that has been and continues to be reinforced in acts of racism, conquest, imperialism, colonialism, slavery, exploitation, national identity, and so forth.[42] Mills argues that through social reproduction, this racial contract shapes government, political institutions, and socioeconomic structures— yet rarely is discussed or addressed in theoretical or political discourse. His theory is useful in this context because it can describe the process by which preservice and in-service millennial CLDTs negotiate the predominantly white systems of society.

Abrica and Morales argue that today, millennial CLDs in particular are challenged to interpret and respond to a new postracial contract established within the purportedly welcoming environments marketed in the promotional literature and messages generated by recruiting colleges and universities.[43] In policy, educational institutions have attempted to improve access for historically marginalized populations by adopting asset-based frameworks such as funds of knowledge, community cultural wealth, or antideficit frameworks into their collective vocabulary. However, issues of racism, commonly found at the intersections of gender, religion, class, language, and ethnic differences, act as social and historical forces, often persisting regardless of efforts toward postraciality.[44] Thus, despite the adoption of asset-based frameworks, there is often a stark contrast between the espoused and the enacted equity and inclusivity of postsecondary college campuses.

Current recruitment initiatives frequently target millennial CLDs, claiming that the students' cultural and linguistic diversity is understood and supported in their predominantly and historically white spaces. Abrica and Morales state that when CLD students enroll, they enter under this assumption, being led to believe that they belong and will find acceptance in the institution.[45] Yet, when CLD students are unable to readily meet the expectations of the hidden curriculum of the university or do not conform to the traditional monolingual, white normative structures of formal education, they often are chastised and marked as deficient.[46]

The bait-and-switch that many CLD millennials experience in higher education impacts them in profound ways long after initial recruitment. Those who are able to successfully traverse the rocky terrain of higher education take these dialogically developed histories-in-person into their professional roles. In many respects, as millennial CLDTs, they often function simultaneously as insiders (as licensed educators) and outsiders (as cultural others) within and among the figured worlds of contemporary public education.[47] Therefore, in this chapter we argue that context matters in the recruitment, appropriate support, retention, and graduation of millennial CLDTs.[48] In fact, to truly understand the realities of this differential candidate population in current educational contexts, we must go deeper. We must look more closely at both the internalized and externally assigned identities of millennial CLDTs.

## Experiences of millennial CLD teachers

In recent years, there has been limited yet important research on the experiences of pre- and in-service CLD teachers from the millennial generation.[49] Studies by scholars such as Tiffany Nyachae as well as Betty Achinstein and Julia Aguirre have captured the precarious positions that millennial CLDTs find themselves in and the delicate line that many must walk in order to thrive (or merely survive) in white normative spaces.[50] Nyachae's study focuses on the internal and external conflicts of a black female teacher in her work with black female students in an urban public conversion charter school.[51] She describes the "complicated contradictions" (a term developed by Taliaferro-Baszile) and conflicting dual identities that academically successful black female teachers negotiate as race-gendered individuals, socialized within the increasingly volatile contexts of schools.[52] Achinstein and Aguirre document the double bind that many millennial CLDTs experience based on assumptions about cultural match.[53] In their study, administrators often held unrealistic expectations of the new millennial CLDTs they employed—assuming that they would by default be able to address the schools' issues in reaching CLD students. Yet, teachers in this study also felt pressure and skepticism from students of color. They reported being held to a higher standard than white teachers and being required to prove their cultural affinity before gaining the trust of students of color.[54]

Understanding how to navigate such complex institutional dynamics or how to push past students' initial skepticisms in order to gain their trust is not easy. Unfortunately, novice CLD teachers are rarely supported in developing their skills to engage in this tenuous work.[55] As mentioned, as they move through traditional teacher preparation programs, not only are they not taught how to utilize their potential cultural capital or funds of knowledge in culturally responsive ways, but also the very assets they were recruited for are often discounted and incrementally disemboweled by the time they enter K–12 schools as teachers.[56] As a result, millennial CLDTs often lack the knowledge and support needed to leverage their culture and language as critical tools in praxis.[57]

Accordingly, it is no wonder that a recent study produced by the Albert Shanker Institute affirms that "the primary obstacle to faster diversification of the American teaching force was [is] not insufficient recruitment and hiring of more new minority teachers, but their comparatively high attrition rates."[58] The data indicate that high-pressure conditions and school climate are the main reasons for leaving. It is against this backdrop of high CLDT attrition that we delved into the experiences of millennial CLDTs who have persisted in teaching positions.

## THEORETICAL FRAMEWORK

### Latino critical race theory

We drew on a broad range of critical theoretical literatures to answer our research question: *What are the experiences, meaning perspectives, and enacted identities of millennial CLD preservice and in-service teachers in predominantly white normative educational spaces?* In particular, we used the tenets of Latino/a critical race theory (LatCrit) to guide our approach to research design and implementation.[59]

The conceptual development of LatCrit and its application in empirical social science research has flourished in recent years. Having roots in critical race theory, LatCrit provides a means for understanding power and challenging institutional and discursive forms of racism.[60] In the early 2000s researchers such as Delores Delgado Bernal, Daniel Solorzano, and Tara Yosso established LatCrit as a powerful mechanism to interrogate the dominant ideologies that shape social and educational narratives regarding Latino/a linguistic minorities. LatCrit now exists as a robust theoretical construct for analyzing historical and contemporary societal and institutional structures that perpetuate the oppression and marginalization of Latino/as in the United States.[61] In this study, we used LatCrit as a lens for exploring and interpreting the experiences and complex intersecting identities of Latino/as shaped by race, language, class, gender, and citizenship. More specifically, LatCrit provided us the language for framing how these perceptions shape the psychological, social-emotional, and educational development of millennial CLDTs within white normative educational spaces. Furthermore, LatCrit provided a strong foundation for critically theorizing implications for practice. The next sections provide an outline of our processes.

## METHODOLOGY

The methodology employed for this phenomenological study was qualitative (interpretive) in nature.[62] The specifics of the study, including the context, the participants, and the tools and methods used, follow.

### Context and participants

Participants for this study were selected through the use of purposive sampling, based on specific criteria.[63] Selection was restricted to graduates of an ESOL teacher education program at the college of education at a large midwestern university. This targeted and structured program began in 1996 and ended in 2013. It served as a differential recruitment and retention (DR&R) program focused on increasing the number of first-generation, bilingual/bicultural students in teacher education. The DR&R program brought millennial CLD candidates to the university and endeavored to guide, support, enable, retain, and empower them, as future CLDTs, professionals, and leaders, through weekly seminars. These interactive seminars were designed, according to the latest theory and research, not only to counter potential and existing pressures within the predominantly white institution, but also to offer recruited candidates differentiated curricula, team building, and academic strategies as well as opportunities for leadership and skill building for advocacy.

The pool of potential research participants from this program (totaling 155 graduates) was further narrowed based on age (millennials defined in this study as those born between 1980 and 2000) and years of teaching experience in K–12 schools (two or more). Those graduates who fit these criteria were contacted via e-mail, social media, phone, or in person and invited to participate. Ten women and three men agreed to engage in the study. Their ages spanned from twenty-five to thirty-five (mean age thirty) and years of teaching from two to thirteen (mean six and a half years). Four of the participants identified as Mexican or Mexican American, five as Hispanic, two as Latino/a, and two as bicultural Hispanic/white. At the time of the study eleven of thirteen participants worked in a school with significant cultural diversity (predominantly Latino/a, black, or mixed-race student populations). Finally, the majority (eleven) of the participants were first-generation immigrants, and two were second generation. Based on our prior experience and what we know from the field, immigrant generational status can often prove significant.[64] Therefore, we were careful to attend to this characteristic at each level of the study, understanding that generational status and linguistic background may surface as salient factors among the data.

## DATA COLLECTION AND ANALYSIS

To gain deep insights and multiple points of reference on participant experience, we utilized three tools for data collection. The first primary source of data came from an online demographic survey, adapted from an existing tool used in a similar study.[65] The survey was designed and administered to gain demographic and historical information on the participants and their familial/cultural backgrounds. From this tool we gleaned information such as immigrant generational status, languages spoken, and ethnic self-identification.

The second source of data came from a two-part survey designed to uncover participants' initial thoughts, perceptions, and beliefs (meaning perspectives) about themselves, their students, and their peers within the current social and political contexts of their work and community. In the first portion of the survey, participants used a five-point Likert scale to answer questions regarding their perceptions of their level of job satisfaction and professional support, the nature of their work environment, their evaluation of coworkers and supervisors, and their place in their communities. In the second portion of the survey, using open-ended questions, we asked participants to describe, in their own words, the climate of their school/district and their relationships with peers and administrators. This survey tool also encouraged participants to articulate their current conceptions of their own enacted identities as teachers of color and to describe their felt responsibilities or roles they had taken on as CLDTs within their schools. Finally, this tool served as a mechanism for participants to discuss the challenges they faced in teaching their CLD students.

Using thematic analysis, we analyzed participant characteristics from the demographic survey and responses to the two-part, open-ended survey. Identification of the patterns that emerged was interpreted through a critical theoretical lens and within the broader landscape of the literature on millennial teachers and teachers of color in US schools. For example, from survey responses we discovered emic codes that related to the silencing of race discourse in schools where millennial CLDTs taught, feelings of cultural isolation and battle fatigue, and a personal sense of responsibility to advocate for CLD students. The themes found in this process were used to inform the design of our third and final tool for data collection—an open-ended interview. The interview was structured with the intent to reach these deeper elements of participants' perceptions, beliefs, feelings, and assumptions about themselves as millennial teachers of color, and about their peers, their students, and their administrators. Interviews were conducted in English, Spanish, or both, depending upon the preference of the participant. Once transcribed, we analyzed the interview data using a constant comparative method. Initially, as with the survey data, we categorized and analyzed the data empirically, according to the themes arising from participant voice. Then we coded all of the data etically, as driven by the substantive theoretical framework and the comprehensive literature reviewed for the study.

## FINDINGS AND DISCUSSION

Phenomenological analysis of the data in this study yielded several compelling themes in teachers' meaning perspectives across demographic differences. Despite the range of ages and immigrant generation status, relationships were extremely significant across all narratives. These elements served as cultural anchors that kept participants grounded and helped them withstand the trials they faced on the road to teaching and beyond. Findings illustrated the struggles and the strengths of millennial CLDTs as well as the tenuous realities they navigate as simultaneous insiders/outsiders within formal education systems. That said, three key themes proved most salient among teachers' meaning perspectives within this study: (1) thinking back—looking forward, (2) being a deviation from the norm, and (3) family, faith, and fortitude—finding solace in their socialization.

As previously discussed, meaning perspectives refer to the "structure of assumptions within which one's past experience assimilates and/or transforms new experience."[66] With time, these perspectives come to provide an orienting frame of reference or perceptual filter on future experiences. As such, they are pivotal in teachers' lives and practices, since they often serve as tacit belief systems for the interpretation and evaluation of current experiences.[67] One of the first meaning perspectives shared by participating millennial CLDTs and identified by researchers was indicative of both teachers' introspections and their own horizon shaping.

## Thinking back—looking forward

Millennial CLDTs who shared the meaning perspective of thinking back—looking forward already had taken time to reflect upon the pain of past experiences as cultural and linguistic minorities in college, and associated reactions to it. Participant responses suggested that they had resolved to structure a future that transcended the failures of guidance and lack of support in the past. The following excerpt from an interview with a participant is indicative of this shared meaning perspective:

Thinking back on my teacher preparation reminds me of how ready I really wasn't . . . what little help I got . . . you know, in the classes where I struggled, and the things I had to do . . . just to get through . . . my degree. I think it was really . . . one of the worst times of my life. But, whatever. One way or another, I beat it . . . I made it to teaching . . . you know—in spite of them. For a very long time, it hurt—a lot. No matter how far I got, I couldn't . . . stop second-guessing myself. . . . Was I really ready? . . . Could I . . . last, as a teacher? . . . I was just . . . I don't know . . . always unsure.

Then, the kids and the families, they began to remind me of why I started this. It was . . . one of their [the family's] first real connections with a teacher of their kids. . . . They were so excited. . . . Me? I was just, I was so surprised. I felt good too. . . . And, before long . . . I think, I began to think less about the past and consider more . . . or maybe just trust more . . . what I knew [discovered] I could do . . . then and now. You know, like I'm going to be a good teacher . . . I was meant to be here. If I can just trust in myself . . . and what I have . . . not just learned, but also been a part of myself . . . I think, maybe I can make difference . . . in their lives.

As this participant's comments illustrate, thinking back on her experiences in higher education is both painful and empowering. In fact, her discourse suggests that her current capacities as an effective teacher for Latino/a students are a product of time spent healing old wounds and reconciling prior difficulties in completing her program of study. It is not surprising, then, that she relates the process of healing and her growth to the ups and downs of her teacher preparation experience.

Similarly, other phenomenological research on the experiences of Latinas in higher education suggest that recurrent sociocultural and psychological challenges tend to significantly influence their perspectives on American education and higher education in particular. For example, Reyes and Rios's dialogic study of Latina experiences in higher education found that the Latinas had significant and recurrent struggles tied to low expectations, self-doubt, and isolation.[68]

Yet, the participant's narrative about teaching kids like herself also indicates a new perspective and an emerging professional identity that transcends her pain and self-doubt to realize what has been enabled by her sacrifices. Through these connections to her roots and the purposes of her struggles, her focus is incrementally changing from thinking back to looking forward. That is not to say that the self-doubt no longer is a challenge to her future. Clearly, her discourse indicates that it is. But her reflections on her purpose, possibilities, and potential impact suggest that the tide is turning—she is finding the meaningfulness in her struggle to become a teacher for her predominantly Latino/a students and their families.

The thematic perspective of thinking back and looking forward shared among these millennial CLDTs is just as indicative of their more recent experiences as practicing teachers in white normative K–12 schools as it is of their preservice experiences in higher education. The following excerpt from one millennial CLDT's interview is revealing. "Many times they [university faculty and staff] were like, '[You are] not in the right place.' . . . So those are days [that] ma[de] me feel like, yes, I'm not smart enough. This is not where I'm supposed to be. But then those same people ma[de] me push myself harder . . . like [to] prove to them that I was/am capable of doing [it] . . . better than what they were doing."

As evidenced by their statements, the millennial CLDTs in the study have, throughout their lifetimes (both personally and professionally), endured the uncertainty of belonging, being in the right place, or being smart enough to be able to accomplish their goals. Such uncertainty is pervasive in both their thoughts about the past and their reservations about goal setting for the future. Especially for those who think back, experiences in white normative educational spaces have left them with feelings of inadequacy.

This participating teacher, like other millennial CLDTs, indicated that the fast-paced nature and cross-cultural demands of in-service teaching often serve to exacerbate Latino/a teachers' long-standing perspectives that they are slow or inadequate or something less. Yet Latino/a millennial CLDTs often find the strength—the resiliency—to persevere in their in-service settings of professional practice. Here they gain opportunities to reconnect with children and families who are like them, who confront similar hurdles, and who share a common culture and/or language. Through these connections they are able to look forward into a different future—to what's positive, what's promising, and what's meaningful in their personal and professional realities.

Another teacher asserts: "I ask myself what keeps me from leaving the profession. My answer is—my students. . . . If I leave, who will advocate for them?" What participants were reluctant to explicate are the sociocultural and sociopolitical protocols that they must navigate in order to successfully support learning for CLD students in their schools. However, for many of the millennial CLDTs, they have discovered both solace and impetus in opportunities to serve their students, families, and communities. Participant discourse suggests the inner tension felt by many of these teachers between their cultural identities and their professional identities in schools.

This finding echoes the experiences of teachers of color in previous studies done by Irizarry and Delgado Bernal.[69] Yet it also illustrates that they were developing agency.[70] The millennial CLDT cited, like others, came to understand that her cultural and experiential background provides capital in the classroom. She realized that her knowledge of the CLD students' realities and her very existence as a successful CLD teacher could be used to challenge the deficit meaning perspectives held by teachers toward CLD students at her school.

## Being a deviation from the norm

A second theme shared across millennial CLDTs who participated in this phenomenological investigation was characterized as being a deviation from the norm. CLDTs who held this meaning perspective reported experiences in white normative educational spaces that prompted a sense of both physical and professional isolation and personal loneliness, as if they were an unexpected deviation from the norm. The following interview excerpts voice the experiences of millennial CLDTs who struggled with their own interpretations of role, language, and authority in schools. For example, one participating teacher expressed her experience this way: "While working on my bachelor's, I did not feel like I could be myself around other people because if I was, then I would not fit in with the rest of the group. I had to learn to assimilate and act like the majority of the group. There was a point in my life when I was even ashamed [of] speaking Spanish."

She, like others in the study who have been both a student and a teacher in white normative educational spaces, has sensed long-standing sociocultural pressure to forsake both cultural socialization and home language in order to avoid being a deviation from the norm.

This finding is consistent with the work of Carnock and Ege, who reported that Latino/a students, in general, increasingly face multifaceted isolation from both white students and the best teachers.[71] De facto segregation, as a result of tracking and pull-out language programs, often relegates Latino/as to the margins in schools. Their lack of socioeconomic mobility often isolates them geographically. Moreover, lack of strategies to connect academics to their home language isolates them linguistically from meaningful connections to the curriculum that could carry them to the next level.

For other millennial CLDTs, being a deviation from the norm often meant that their capacities or their performances, or even their persistence in academics, did not match the norms or expectations that their instructors or mentors held for them. The following story illustrates how one participating teacher found that his university-appointed advisor held low expectations for him when told he was struggling in math.

He said the same thing my [high school] counselor had said to me before: "Why don't you do Spanish [as an academic major]? It would be easier for you." I felt stupid once again. . . . But I didn't quit because I was going to demonstrate to him and myself that I was capable of doing math and so I have stuck with it—you know, just to show that I can . . . I just don't understand why both of them thought that math was too hard for [me] . . . maybe because my English [was] not the best . . . they thought they were giving [doing] me a favor by recommending what they thought was easier for me . . . but . . . they just didn't know me . . . and I'm not sure they really wanted to."

The college advisor's lack of belief in his abilities is evident in this passage. The advisor provided no encouragement to motivate the student to keep going, nor did he put forth effort to provide supports or specific suggestions to increase the student's likelihood of success in the course. At one level, the university advisor assumed that an academic emphasis in math would prove too difficult for the Latino student. At another level, the high school counselor (and perhaps the undergraduate advisor, as well) assumed that the Spanish-dominant student was adequately prepared only for an academic emphasis in the native language. Further, the advisor assumed that the student would be better served by switching majors completely than by tutorial assistance or other accommodative support in pursuing his chosen academic emphasis.

Mezirow has argued that such multifaceted assumptions about individuals who are perceived by dominant group members as deviations from the norm are typical.[72] These assumptions are a product of long-standing meaning perspectives developed across years of socialization in a more or less homogeneous cultural group. Such perspectives come to act as a sociocultural filter affecting perceptions of CLD students and teachers as well as their potentials for key roles and accomplishments in society.

### Family, faith, and fortitude—finding solace in their socialization

For millennial CLDTs, the challenge of staying the course is ever daunting. The struggle to find the fortitude to stay in the teaching profession was real, especially given sociopolitical, human, and cultural boundaries often established and insensibly maintained in K–12 schools. The CLDTs' skin color, language, and socioeconomic status were often used by K–12 institutions as indicators of difference and imperceptible, sociocultural signals to question their qualifications, performances, and professionalism.[73] This persistent attention to difference, as well as the subsequent physical and psychological isolation, served as a recurrent reminder to millennial CLDTs of their deviance from the norm. Yet those in this qualitative study persisted and endured. Their discourse indicates that they found solace in their socialization.

Key elements of this third theme in millennial CLDT participants' perspectives are evident in the following passage from one participant's interview.

> It wasn't until it [Spanish] was celebrated by [the college program] that I felt it was an asset. Because [when] writing papers, giving presentations, it never was appreciated. It just got in the way. . . . So, not until I got to [the college DR&R program] did my self-esteem start building [improving] . . . one block at a time. From my teachers [in the DR&R program] . . . from my classmates in it . . . everybody . . . It was like being with family. They [the program leaders and staff] were building our self-esteem as we went along: "Don't be afraid." You know, "You are who you are, and you have to be proud." And it was that building of our self-esteem, while they were building our academic skills. . . . The two went hand in hand.

In the context of the program, the participant spoke about the program's approach to accelerated academic and linguistic support, along with mentoring and leadership development. He said:

> It wasn't [just] now you have to take a class . . . It was both at the same time. It wasn't leaving one separate from the other . . . It all . . . tapped into my talent in college. . . . And so [now] I am supposed to be doing something bigger, because I've always been told that. You have to be an advocate, and you have to fight, and you have to do this, and, you know, you have to help . . . the others like you and those who aren't [here]. . . . And that was instilled in me, not just in the program, but from friends and home, too.

Consistent with the theme in millennial CLDT perspectives, this excerpt alludes to the solace and even self-esteem building that this student and other participants found in the collective socialization they experienced in the DR&R program. The seminars of the DR&R program were intentionally designed to nurture relationship building among the millennial CLDT candidates.

For a time, faculty members and mentors were concerned that this intimacy among students might inadvertently generate cliques and/or troublesome social dynamics. And, on occasion, such contingencies were briefly factors in the group's capacity for team building. Nevertheless, candidates more often than not established strong and healthy relationships where they found commonalities in their biographies (language, culture, faith, etc.). Their similarities in primary socialization highlighted or fostered shared goals, interests, collaborations, and support in dealing with the isolation and challenges of pursuing a teaching degree in a predominantly white institution. Findings indicate that, in fact, many millennial CLDTs soon became the "family" to which the previous participant refers. This remained so—even beyond their graduation and placement in K–12 public schools, despite their being many miles or even states apart. As the discourse suggests, the solace, support, and strength that participants gained from other students in the program often was pivotal in their drive to persevere as teachers in white normative K–12 schools and their capacities to engage in challenging but essential advocacy for CLD students and families.

Even prior to graduation from college, participating millennial CLDTs had already challenged themselves and each other to become active advocates for themselves, their friends/ peers, and the CLD students and families they would soon be teaching. Finding their own agency was sometimes key to their persistence in an often hostile space. The following interview excerpt is indicative of millennial CLDTs' increasing willingness to address racist and discriminatory incidents toward fellow CLD students in their teacher preparation journey.

> I decided to talk to the instructor of the class and make her aware of some of the comments [from white classmates]. I asked her if she could talk to the class and ask the students to be more tactful in their comments. Immediately, she [the instructor] realized that she needed to address this issue . . . with the class because . . . the very next week, we were to present another microteach. A year ago . . . I probably would have . . . thought of not even getting involved because I . . . was very close to graduation and . . . well, I probably would not see these people anymore. But . . . I guess I needed to do this for my friend [in the DR&R program] and all the Latino students [at midwestern university]. I needed to do it for my children who will be attending college. . . . You know . . . and . . . I needed to do it for

those students that I was going to teach one day. I knew firsthand . . . they'd need an advocate and a person who they could trust in our world. . . . It was not an easy decision, but I am happy that I addressed it . . . I know this was just the beginning of my journey but it felt good to do the right thing.

For this participant, and others like him, the need to advocate for others who couldn't or wouldn't for themselves became part of his journey in predominantly white institutions, especially during his final years in college.

As friends with similar trials and heartaches of secondary and tertiary socialization, they prompted and supported each other in nurturing the readiness and the courage to speak out for their own and others' rights. Data indicate that together, they found the strength to cope with the discrimination, marginalization, and isolation experienced in the tertiary socialization of academia. Data further indicate that through these shared trials in advocacy as well as the commonalities of their primary socialization, they also developed the professionalism to recognize inappropriate policies and practices involving CLD students in their own schools. They built courage to advocate for accommodative changes in policy, classroom practices, and treatment of CLD families.

For this group of millennial CLDTs, the commitment to think about their communities, families, and students became a recurrent agenda of their practices. They recognized that the politics, racism, prejudice, and discrimination they had faced and endured, as a cohort community, would prove no less prevalent in the K–12 schools in which they would teach— and ultimately lead. The following participant discourse illustrates one millennial CLDT's navigation of this within the new landscape of teaching in K–12 schools.

It took a while . . . but . . . I've stopped focusing on what's going on around me—politics, news, school shootings, new policies—and started focusing on my students. . . . I do that because . . . like my friends from [the DR&R program], they remind me of why I became a teacher. I think when I put my focus on them, it allows me to forget what's going on around us . . . and, you know . . . refocus on what's really important.

In addition to the strength drawn from relationships and advocacy work, participating millennial CLDTs, both during college and in professional teaching practice, discovered the power of their primary socialization. Many participants discussed the sometimes unexpected strength they are able to draw from their background during difficult times, helping them to prioritize those activities and actions that make their lives and their practices meaningful and purposeful. Ultimately, millennial CLDTs in this case, both in preparation for and in the practice of K–12 teaching and advocating for CLD students and families, found peace and strength in the memories and artifacts of their own primary socialization. The following statement from one participant is illustrative:

> My culture and language are definitely protective factors in my life personally and professionally . . . I have deep roots! My family is always a source of strength. Professionally, I'm rooted and grounded in the great responsibility that came with the blessing of becoming a teacher of students like me. I take it very personal[ly] when both my culture and language are judged. My culture and language do not make me any less or more than anyone else.

For this millennial CLDT, and others like her, the artifacts of her primary socialization—family roots, faith, and language—are the foundation of her strength to persevere in the face of negative societal messages toward culturally and linguistically diverse populations.

Although tools such as social media were described by participants as perpetuating negativity and ignorance regarding cultural and linguistic minorities in the United States today, they also served as a vital tool for participants to sustain critical connections to each other and to immediate and extended family. Therefore, technological innovations, which are cherished by so many members of the millennial generation, played an important role in this study. Cell phones, text messaging, and web applications such as Facebook, Twitter, Skype, and What's App served to reinforce and reestablish participant connections to networks of support to both professional and home communities. In particular, these technologies allowed them to access the culture and language of their primary socialization, which was central to who they were as people and as millennial CLDTs.

## CONCLUSIONS

The perspectives of millennials, and especially those of millennial CLD teachers, are frequently misunderstood by society. In white normative educational spaces, their experiences too often are part of a silent or muted struggle, despite the spotlight of attention afforded them by their racial, sociocultural, and linguistic differences from the norm. Sadly, this is equally evident in both teacher education institutions and preK–12 schools. Yet, in spite of the convoluted misperceptions, misunderstandings, and underutilizations that millennial CLDTs suffer, many of these educators have created spaces where their desire and willingness to do what's right sets them apart from the dominant narratives about millennials found in the current research literature.

Emergent evidence, such as the findings from this study, suggests that insights about both CLDTs' challenges and their ways of coping and achieving (as teacher candidates and as professionals) often are understood best in contexts that are socioculturally particular and through methods of research that give voice to their fortitude and camaraderie in teacher education institutions and public school settings. Consistent with other studies that are similarly situated or populated, this study indicates that an investigation of the experiences, meaning perspectives, and enacted identities of preservice and in-service millennial CLDs in predominantly white normative educational spaces is effectively undertaken using a critical theoretical lens.[74]

Participants in this study clearly voiced how their biopsychosocial histories had an impact on their participation in their teacher preparation program, their induction years, and, currently, as tenured in-service teachers. Their voices clearly raise questions about the relevance of the current narratives found in the literature (and further explored in this book) related to the dispositions and characteristics of millennials. More specifically, the self-absorbed dispositions and characteristics of millennials generally described include the following: (1) possessing a high sense of entitlement, (2) having a narcissistic personality, (3) feeling empowered to negotiate with those in authority, (4) lacking critical thinking about multiculturalism, and (5) preferring to gloss over the conflicts, social dominances, and difficulties inherent in cultural competence.[75]

Millennial CLDTs navigate their sociopolitical "*cargas*," or burdens, by negotiating their professional spaces. Drawing from their primary, secondary, and tertiary socialization, millennial CLDTs engage in positioning themselves within difficult spaces by drawing strength from their collective and individual communities. Their primary socialization provides them with the core foundation of understanding who they are and what their mission is within the teaching profession. Their persistence and agency for doing what is right is anchored in their need to give to others, to ensure that those like them do not experience and suffer from the same type of discrimination and marginalization that they have endured. Their commitment is grounded in the learner, the family, and the community. With the mission to work hard to dismantle the racism, prejudice, and symbolic violence they witness in schools every day, these participants stand in complete contrast to what the literature describes as the characteristics and dispositions of millennials.

As seen in participants' narratives, a great deal can and should be done at both the preservice and in-service levels to capitalize on CLDTs' funds of knowledge, which are often dismissed in white normative educational spaces. Although millennial CLDTs often experienced silencing and race evasiveness in their educational institutions, we see hope for change.[76] By utilizing academic spaces to engage in authentic and courageous conversations about race, class, religion, language, and sexual orientation within the context of current social realities, millennial preservice and in-service teachers of all cultural backgrounds are more likely to examine and reconsider their held meaning perspectives toward CLD students in order to develop more equitable and race-conscious practices.[77] Without opportunities to work through their experiences with cultural others, this generation of teachers is left to engage in such conversations as informal, disjointed, isolated, and reactionary incidents in hallways, in break rooms, or over social media—often among uninformed peers from similar backgrounds. As a result, educational institutions deny preservice and in-service educators and administrators (of all backgrounds) opportunities to develop the critical race consciousness they need in order to work effectively within the often tumultuous social and political landscape of public education.

We cannot frame millennial CLDTs' behaviors and character through a normative millennial lens. Millennial CLDTs have much to contribute within educational spaces. What currently is absent is a systematic, intentional plan of action to utilize theory and research-based strategies that bridge the experiences and knowledge of this group into the profession. Furthermore, the findings of this study illustrate the power and potential of differently situated professional development for CLDTs that supports their use of their potential cultural capital and funds of knowledge to advocate for themselves and their CLD students.

*Acknowledgments*

*Thank you to Melissa Holmes and Kevin Murry.*

# Millennial Teachers of Color and Their Quest for Community

Hollee R. Freeman

As a classroom teacher in the early 1990s, I experienced the whole-language and constructivist mathematics movements with great energy and enthusiasm. I, like many new, young teachers, veered away from wholesale phonics and rote mathematics instruction. As a group, we felt as though we were a part of something innovative—a new approach to student engagement. As I arranged my classroom for heterogeneous math groups, built nooks for the library and books on tape, and put down large rugs for community meetings, I often wondered what my older colleagues thought of us new teachers and how they perceived our ideas and pedagogical practices.

Thirty years later, the teaching profession is once again welcoming a group of younger, excited teachers, millennials this time, who, like their predecessors the baby boomers, seem to be entering the teaching profession during a time of rapidly changing social, political, economic, and educational landscapes.

## THE PENDULUM SWINGS AGAIN—BOOMERS OUT, MILLENNIALS IN

This chapter explores the ways in which a group of millennial teachers make sense of their work with students, schools, and communities. I highlight how they use technology as an instructional tool as well as a mechanism to expand community, not only for their students but for themselves as well. Additionally, delving into the stories of several millennial teachers of color illuminates their laser-sharp focus on issues of equity and social justice and how these teachers both separate and connect their personal lives—ideas, values, experiences, and issues—with their work as a teacher.

Individual differences notwithstanding, common attitudes and behaviors within generational groups are often formed through the sharing of common knowledge of large-scale events such as war, immigration, and economic and social movements. In fact, a Pew Research Center report from 2015 cites age as "one of the most common predictors in attitudes and behaviors."[1] For baby boomers—those born within a roughly eighteen-year span beginning at the end of World War II in 1946—common occurrences such as industrialization, job availability, and unionization provided citizens with opportunities to make a living as teachers. In fact, it was during this time that many women made a lifetime commitment to the teaching profession.[2]

In many industries, baby boomers are retiring in large numbers. As they retire from teaching, they are being replaced by millennials, the youngest adult generation of workers. The exiting of these older individuals from teaching often means that important historical knowledge, certain perspectives, and ways of working are lost. However, millennials, the first generation to grow up in an environment replete with information technology, are bringing new ways of working and thinking to classrooms and schools.

Generally speaking, millennials may not ascribe to frequently held notions concerning social or political hierarchies in schools. This way of thinking about themselves in relation to the school and educational community may pose challenges for their more veteran counterparts, who have spent their careers moving up the leadership ladder in schools.[3] Also, millennial teachers may think differently than their senior counterparts about educational policies and practices. As cited in the Teach Plus report, *Great Expectations: Teachers' Views of Elevating the Teaching Profession*, 71 percent of millennial teachers (in the study) agree that student growth should be a part of teacher evaluations, compared to 41 percent of veteran teachers.[4] In the same report, only 39 percent of millennial teachers agree that teacher licensure tests cover the skills needed to be a successful teacher, compared to 51 percent of veteran teachers. In 2014, millennial teachers used their collective prowess to successfully advocate for more robust standards for teachers. The White House endorsed this recommendation, paving the way for the US Department of Education to develop these very same standards for teacher education programs.[5]

## MILLENNIAL TEACHERS OF COLOR: WINDOWS AND MIRRORS

*As a teacher of color, I'd be lying if I told you I wasn't disturbed by the lack*
*of representation of Black and Latino people, especially males, as teachers.*
*(José Luis Vilson, in "The Need for More Teachers of Color")*

Of the 3.4 million public school teachers in the United States in 2011–12, 82 percent were white and 18 percent were teachers of color.[6] Millennials, which are the most racially and culturally diverse generation thus far, are predicted to be the most educated generation in history, and close to 20 percent are seeking employment in the field of teaching.[7]

For millennials of color, who may very well experience race, culture, and class differently and more acutely than their white counterparts, teaching may be one of the few places where they can juxtapose their activism around their self-agency with agency for their communities—a kind of interoception for teaching. It is important to consider that the extent to which teachers can engage with students in particular ways may be situated in their own sense of community and impacted by their level of cultural competence.

Recently, an interview with an assistant professor of early childhood education at a large university in the southern United States yielded a reflection about this phenomenon.[8] The professor remarked that in his experience, the vast majority of the mostly white female millennial teachers in his classes (who are being trained for careers in urban schools) maintain the status quo in their teaching. That is to say, their lack of experiences outside their traditionally insular environs (with little diversity of any kind) creates a hurdle that typically hinders these new teachers from making connections between their way of being and interacting in the world and that of the students they are being trained to teach.

To explore this idea further, I interviewed three people on several occasions face-to-face, by Skype, and via phone. I posed the same set of questions to each of them and also allowed the conversation to flow more naturally when participants talked about relevant ideas that were important to them. All millennial teachers interviewed had chosen to begin their teaching career through an alternative pathway to teaching program in the northeastern portion of the United States. Although they entered the teaching profession in their twenties, they'd already experienced success in other industries. Each chose the teaching profession as a way of lending their considerable interests and talents to the success of students and communities of color.

The intersection of race, class, culture, equity, and diversity with the profession of teaching was borne out by Stephan, an African American male teacher, who reflects:

> Millennials of color are coming to the classroom more prepared since they have the experience of being "other" their whole lives. They are bringing their authentic selves into the classroom so that students can be their authentic selves. Millennials of color understand the weight of the work and do not have the "savior" mentality.

Millennials of color know that cultural competence is connected to both the curriculum and the community. This complex duality of being an example by their mere presence as millennial teachers of color and their focus on the community at large can be thought of in terms of the social construct of *windows* (eyesight into the world for themselves and their students) and *mirrors* (insight through their own and their students' reflections). Although the notion of windows and mirrors has been widely used to describe how students make sense of curriculum, it is a useful way to think about how millennials of color orient themselves as agents of change through teaching.

Stephan, a former middle school math teacher, is now working as an educational technologist at an educational nonprofit. In addition, he has started his own STEM-based nonprofit. A conversation with Stephan revealed how he came to have a resolute focus on agency and community as a teacher. Stephan's intentionality in finding his voice as a teacher of color was cemented in his third year of teaching. He recollects thinking, "How can I, as a man of color, be most effective and show students how to reach their full potential?"

This exploration of agency and voice was supported in his teaching academy (a small collection of classrooms within a large urban school). Stephan's academy, which he describes as a place of high expectations, autonomy, and community for both students and staff, was composed of fourteen teachers, nine of whom were male. Of these nine male teachers, seven were black, including the academy leader. Stephan was quick to point out that this configuration of teachers was deliberate and organized by the white female principal, who seemed to deeply understand the importance of staffing the school in this way.

When reflecting about the importance of teaching in this academy, Stephan commented that this small community of teachers shaped his view of what it meant to create a classroom community in which he could bring his authentic self. Further, he explained that this particular teaching space was where he could say the things that needed to be said and be allowed to make important ideas and ways of working in his class explicit. Stephan's level of intentionality in teaching revolved around his ability to reflect back to his students his own position as a successful black male while providing them with insight into what was happening in their lives, in their communities, and in the world.

Another millennial of color, Erik, a high school social studies teacher, describes his foray into teaching as a way to "follow in the footsteps" of his grandparents. Additionally, like Stephan, Erik says that he decided to become a teacher because he saw the need for more educators of color, particularly in urban areas. For Erik, being a millennial of color gives him a discernible advantage with students since he is connected to the popular culture—the same culture in which he says his students are "drowning." As a result, Erik acknowledges that students see him as connected to their generation (mirror) but also outside of it (window). Erik used this dual role to his benefit as he designed curriculum to help students better understand social-political issues in their communities. One such curricular unit focused on a criminal justice context featuring a female character who lost her life participating in the very activities in which some of his students engage. During this unit, Erik was able to provide a window into the complexities of the criminal justice system while also providing a model for effective self-agency and decision making.

When further describing why teaching in an urban area is important to him, Erik remarks that the very nature of working in this capacity provides a counternarrative for students. His very presence as an educated, engaged black male teacher "goes against" the dominant cultural narrative of people of color in general, and black males in particular. However, Erik is quick to point out that while he's reflecting back to students what a positive black male role model is, he is careful not to overshadow students' own experiences. In many ways, Erik provides a window for students, but he doesn't want to obstruct their view. When elaborating on this idea, Erik explains that when mirroring, he must always remember to say to students, "This is my viewpoint. What is yours?" In other words, through his work as a teacher,

Erik shares his experiences and helps students to develop and make sense of their own experiences and ideas.

## COMMUNITY AND AGENCY

Millennials typically enjoy membership in a multiplicity of communities, many of them fluid. For many millennials, it is not desirable to be separate from a community since they thrive on connecting often and in many different ways. Millennial teachers of color highlight the notion of community in teaching. For instance, Stephan recollects that one of the teaching goals in his middle school mathematics class was to help students see the world in a larger context. To this end, he conducted a daily morning meeting in which students worked on biographies of people of color. As a community, students discussed what they learned and related this to current community and world events. For Stephan, this daily exercise helped students connect to ideas and information on a larger scale than what they might typically have access to, and it also helped him build a sense of community among the students.

Erik also talked about the notion of community in his classroom as well as in his own life. During a recent protest, Erik was taken into custody for "unlawfully assembling." Erik knew that the very act of protesting and talking to students about it might not be seen favorably by school and district administrators. However, he did not want to separate his personal and professional selves. After a series of conversations with administration, families, friends, and students, Erik left his teaching position but was quickly able to secure another job within the same urban school system. The weight of the situation was not lost on Erik, as he clearly saw that this act of community and self-agency might well be the ultimate act of serving as both a window and a mirror for himself and for his students.

For millennial teachers of color, the notion of community often extends beyond the classroom walls. A recent article in the *Boston Globe*, "Boston Teachers Union Poised to Elect First Person of Color as President," illustrates the agency and community-centric notion of millennials of color, along with the multiplicity of communities in which they live and work.[9] The article highlights Jessica Tang, a Chinese American teacher in Boston, who experienced the death of a student while in her third year of teaching. This event exposed gaps in the social service system, gaps with which

Tang was uncomfortable. Tang began to galvanize teachers and went on to become an advocate for increased social services for students.

Currently, Tang is the newly elected president of the Boston Teachers Union (BTU), which represents a system populated by 62 percent white teachers. This fact is not lost on political leaders or the teachers with whom she now serves. In fact, according to the *Boston Globe,* Tang's role as the BTU president represents "a general shift in power" from her predecessor, a white male baby boomer who had occupied this position for the previous fourteen years. Tang, a millennial, is also the first woman of color to serve as president of the BTU in the fifty-two-year history of the organization. Moreover, her philosophy around education represents a new way of explicitly talking about education, students, and the interconnectedness of services to schools and the community.

## The role of technology in creating community

*I want students to be creators and curators of knowledge. (Stephan)*

Millennials have had the unprecedented experience of growing up in a world in which technology has become ubiquitous in the way that people interact and share information. In fact, millennials do not remember a time before interactive digital media existed.[10]

Millennials of color, in particular, have embraced technology in the form of social media in a way that outpaces many other racial/cultural groups. They use social media platforms as extensions of who they are and to communicate with their students and colleagues about issues that matter to them.[11] According to the 2016 Nielsen report, 55 percent of African American millennials, in particular, report spending an hour or more per day on social networking sites, as compared with the total millennial population, reported to be just under 45 percent. Twenty-nine percent of African American millennials report spending three or more hours per day on social networking sites, a figure 44 percent higher than that for the total millennial population.[12]

As teachers, they encourage students to use social media in similar ways. While the pedagogy has to reflect these goals, the sheer presence of mobile devices makes this a reachable goal. Ninety-one percent of African Americans have Internet access through smartphones, outpacing all other racial/ethnic groups. However, social media is not the only way that millennials of color are engaging students in technology. As Patrisse Cullors, one of the three founders of the #BlackLivesMatter movement, describes it, "[M]illennials are ushering in a wave of social-political energy and change that does not rely on old paradigms of one leader who has 'paid their dues.'" Rather, this change is a result of networks of communities held together via technology. During a podcast for *On Being*, Cullors reflected that the use of social media in social protests, in particular, provides a new reach and a new conversation around the issues people care about.[13]

To learn more about how millennial teachers interact on social media, I scanned the posts of a number of millennials of color. Very quickly, it became clear that the thread of social consciousness and equity appears often in their posts. It is not uncommon to see a post or repost of a social justice issue. In essence, millennial teachers of color talk about social justice on social media, and they talk about it a lot.

For example, a male South Asian teacher, Rahm, shared song lyrics through a social media platform. These lyrics were written and performed in school by his seven-year-old son for a class assignment. The song lyrics focused on the issue of water rights in Flint, Michigan (a highly publicized and highly charged news story). Rahm and those responding to his post saw the intersection of this national issue and a local curricular assignment as a magnificent tool for teaching, and they praised the teacher (in absentia) for providing the space for this to happen. During the conversation thread, educators fluidly switched back and forth to discussions about the importance of integrating education, arts, and social consciousness in their own classrooms.

In another social media post, a Latina high school science teacher, Eva, shared an article by Claudio Sanchez entitled "Gifted, But Still Learning English, Many Bright Students Get Overlooked."[14] Eva explained that she used Sanchez's article in her science class to engage students in a conversation about bilingual education. Like the previous post by Rahm, this window into community issues prompted students to wrestle with individual, local, and national issues in an authentic way. In both cases, the teachers shared their personal stories and views with their students, thus evoking the mirror through which the students could better understand and make sense of these ideas and issues with regard to themselves and their communities.

While millennial teachers of color use social media as a way to engage in the community around issues that matter to them and to their students, they also use technology in other ways. When asked about the role of technology in his work, Stephan stated that his "master plan" is to share his expertise in building technological and digital media platforms to create a space for students in which they are able to employ these technologies to better understand what is happening in their lives and in their communities. In short, he says, he wants students to be "creators and curators of knowledge."

Erik echoes this sentiment of helping students develop the skills and dispositions to sort through the vast amount of information at their fingertips and to question its validity. Erik smiles warmly as he recalls the number of times that students have asked him, "Is this real? Have you seen this?" He hears these words often from students as they sort through news reports, articles, and posts from a vast number of social media sites and attempt to connect this information to their current topic of study.

Even though more than one-third of Erik's students use social media to make sense of content and world issues, he has to reinforce their awareness of information and work with them to be discerning about what they read and experience. Like law schools, medical schools, and others that train millennials, educators must adapt their pedagogy to ensure that students become astute consumers and producers of information.[15] Erik knows that he has to continually ask students to verify their sources, even those that are well known, and that he needs to be abreast of social media outlets as well.

In reflecting on his unofficial role as "tech guy" in his school—a role that he enjoys—Erik cites his ability to navigate technology easily along with the enjoyment of problem solving and learning new applications as the impetus for this designation. Stephan is also seen as the tech guy who solves technology issues, but more importantly, he supports teachers in understanding that technology can be leveraged as a tool for learning and not a distraction. For Stephan, using technology is a way to reach all students and to provide exponentially more resources for them.

When working on a unit for a research class, for example, Stephan was able to provide students with a real-time window into experiences and data around the Flint, Michigan, water crisis. This just-in-time learning provided students with infographics, videos, legal documents, newspaper reports, and more that they were able to use in the teaching and learning moment, rather than reflecting on the issues through the lens of the teacher or an article in the aftermath of the experience. Stephan's students were able to synthesize current information, develop questions, and present their ideas in a way that effectively made use of the data collected. In addition, students were able to then make connections between the content, local water issues, and public policies with a focus on their own communities.

## A WAY TO MAKE SENSE OF THE WORLD

*What does it mean to have some teachers deeply aware of particular experiences and issues and some teachers not as aware? (Jonathan Zur)[16]*

Millennials of color use their energy from and membership in multiple community groups to talk about and effect change concerning issues that matter to them. The juxtaposition of this sense of agency with teaching positions millennial teachers of color as a powerful force in the lives of students and their families, and in their communities. Having the interest and determination to speak explicitly about local, national, and global issues from their vantage point of equity and social justice, coupled with their facility in using and understanding technology, provides their students with an environment rich in information.

However, these millennials of color are not satisfied to simply bring technology into the classroom; they are also clear about wanting students to be able to consume and produce knowledge in responsible ways. For them, social media, technology, class discussions, and content are vital tools for students to use effectively, and the pedagogical underpinning and how they situate themselves in society are purposefully aligned to help students make sense of information.

Millennial teachers of color thus provide a counternarrative for students (and for their colleagues). They also provide an important way for students to view the world. This is not to say that this ability resides *only* within millennials or teachers of color. It is to say, however, that millennials of color may very well offer students, particularly those of color, a way to make sense of the world simply *by being and by doing*. This poses a great incentive for school leaders and program administrators to continue working diligently to recruit and retain teachers of color and to provide robust training in cultural competence, equity, and diversity.

*Acknowledgments*

*When I did put fingers to keyboard, it was the experiences of courageous, competent, passionate educators who gave me their words to type: among them are E. Christaan Summerhill, Adiya White-Hammond, Charles Phillips, and Bryan Wallace, the finest educators I know.*

# 5

# Ushering in a New Era of Teacher Activism

*Beyond Hashtags, Building Hope*

Keith C. Catone and Dulari Tahbildar

P ublic education has always been an experiment in democracy. Historically benefiting some groups more than others, the experiment has recently focused more and more on bolstering the academic achievement of students who have been left behind. Coming of age in an era when public education emphasized meeting standards, making adequately yearly progress, and addressing "the civil rights issue of our generation," millennials have been conditioned to understand education as an endeavor for equality, equity, and, in some cases, social justice.[1] It is common to propose (with varying degrees of criticality) that public schooling and education reform are aimed at closing achievement and opportunity gaps and preparing all students— irrespective of zip code—for viable futures as workers and democratic citizens. For millennial teachers of color, as for many teachers from previous generations, the project of public education, then, is often deeply personal as well as political. The idea that teaching is a form of social and political activism should not be terribly controversial. In fact, the notion that teaching is an important contribution to social change and social justice is part and parcel of how many frame their entry into the profession. Teachers are activists. With this backdrop, this chapter will explore how to better understand the motivations and experiences of activist-oriented millennial teachers of color as they make up the nation's teacher corps in increasing numbers. As motivated as many millennials are for activism and social justice, it is not clear that the field of education currently has the systems and infrastructure necessary to cultivate, celebrate, and commit to this new teaching talent.

Broadly, cultural reference points for what activism is in the United States stem primarily from the civil rights, peace, and other social movements of the 1960s and 1970s. Enduring stories and images of seminal events like lunch counter sit-ins, the Montgomery bus boycott, the 1963 March on Washington, student protests against the Vietnam War, the Stonewall uprising, the fight for the Equal Rights Amendment, and more have seared into our collective consciousness examples of activism that include marches, protests, mass mobilization, and organized collective action. The popular conception of what it meant to be an activist from this era was to go to protests, march in the streets, chant at rallies, take hold of a bullhorn, and not shy away from the speaker's podium. Just as the social movements of the 1970s took their lead from the civil rights movement, so is our understanding of activism in the United States shaped by our historical memories of these movements, which guide and frame our present-day thinking.

## NEW MOMENTS FOR A NEW MOVEMENT

As children of the 1980s who came into adulthood through the 1990s, we retained these examples from the civil rights and other social movements as our reference points for what activism is and looks like. For us, contemporary models of activism did not deviate from their 1960s and '70s roots, and there did not seem to be new social movements for us to be part of. It felt more like we were living off the vestiges of what had been built by the generation before. However, the tides have turned for millennials. For young people who have come of age in the new millennium, there have been new, contemporary, real-time activist and social movement reference points. In fact, millennials, it seems to us, have been rewriting our activist and movement playbooks over the course of the past decade. From Occupy Wall Street to the Movement for Black Lives, millennials have picked up the mantle of youthful activist leadership that has always been critical to social movements. DREAMers threw out the proverbial playbook to demand rights for undocumented immigrants, and have been winning. Movement is afoot for climate justice, and marriage equality, which in so many ways was a nonstarter at the turn of the century, is now a reality. As we observe the shifting sands, we are increasingly aware that there are many new ways to be involved in activism.

Millennials who are paving new avenues for activism will increasingly make up a larger and larger portion of our teaching corps. If we believe that millennials of color, in particular, are of importance to the teaching profession, then we must think critically about how those with activist sensibilities and a drive for social justice might be engaged. To support this thinking, we will look to recent work proposing a framework for the pedagogy of teacher activism that consists of three core elements: purpose, power, and possibility.[2] According to the framework, the development of activist purpose draws heavily from personal biographies that lead individuals into teacher activism. Biographical events that expose a disruption between the way the world is versus one's sense of the way the world should be plant seeds of a sense of justice that motivate work aimed at bringing change. Gloria Anzaldúa proposes that once people become aware of the incompatibility between subdominant and dominant cultures, we might "decide to disengage from the dominant culture, write it off altogether as a lost cause, and cross the border into a wholly new and separate territory"—or in other words, a new reality.[3] Because the realities that teacher activists seek to effect are predicated upon social justice values and visions, the work itself often manifests as attempts to challenge and shift power relations. Such action is sustained through a sense of possibility that frames the work, enabling it to continue even in the face of seeming impossibility.

In this chapter, we highlight the experiences of four millennials of color who have chosen to pursue a career in teaching: Fernanda, Abena, Gabriel, and James. Fernanda is a twenty-two-year-old Chinese Brazilian woman who emigrated from Brazil as a fifth grader to a large northeast city. She recently graduated from an elite university and will be beginning her preservice training in secondary English at a notably progressive school of education on the West Coast. Abena is a twenty-four-year-old African American woman who grew up in a small northeast city. She is completing her second year of teaching fifth-grade writing at an all-girls network charter school in a large city. Gabriel is a twenty-eight-year-old Mexican American man who grew up in the South. He has four years of experience teaching art, currently at an arts-based charter school in a small northeast city. James is a twenty-nine-year-old African American man who grew up in a midsize northeast city. He is completing his seventh year of teaching history at a comprehensive high school in an inner-ring suburb of a large midwestern city.

Millennial teachers of color are relatively new to the profession. Thus, our examination here will focus primarily on the cultivation of activist purpose among these teachers and how we see them showing promising signs of exercising activist agency. Then, using this pedagogy of teacher activism as a guiding framework, we will consider how we might encourage this new generation of teachers to explore and embrace teacher activism by providing the hopeful foundations of activist possibility as they embark upon their careers in education.

## DEVELOPMENT OF ACTIVIST PURPOSE: MOVING THROUGH APPREHENSIONS

The pedagogy of teacher activism articulates purpose through a multifaceted concept of *apprehension*. Working with the multiple meanings of apprehension, teacher activists arrive with purpose for their work when they have experienced anxious, critical, and angry apprehensions.[4]

### Anxious apprehension

Most commonly, apprehension is understood to manifest as anxiety or fear; a certain unease about one's surroundings or circumstance. For people of color and other people whose identities get marginalized from the mainstream, this kind of apprehension is often experienced when their own sense of being is thrown into question. Messages and actions sanctioned by society that threaten black lives, frame human beings as illegal, deny the right to expressions of love, and place prejudicial limits on human potential all work to incite unavoidable collisions between the world as it is versus the world as it should be, especially for oppressed populations. When it feels as if the world does not see you or recognize you for your human being, this produces an anxious apprehension of and about the world. Social movement scholars have framed moments of understanding the differences between one's own moral compass and the ways of the world as "moral shocks"[5] or "moral discoveries," which become motivating forces for activism.[6]

Specifically for people of color, Anzaldúa discusses how "the clash of voices" between self-conception and culture and dominant oppressive values "results in mental and emotional states of perplexity. Internal strife results in insecurity and indecisiveness. The *mestiza*'s dual or multiple personality is plagued by psychic restlessness."[7] According to Anzaldúa, this mental anxiety is a result of the combined effects of simultaneously being "cradled" and "sandwiched" between cultures, "straddling" their practices and value systems. These "cultural collisions," termed by Anzaldúa as "*choques*," can cause people to feel attacked by the dominant culture, but can also sow seeds of consciousness about the world.

When Fernanda arrived as a sixth grader from Brazil at a bilingual school in a large northeast city, she could not speak any English. Sent by her parents to live with cousins, Fernanda was essentially on her own to navigate a brand-new country through her experience at school. As she began classes, she had a difficult time connecting with her Portuguese-speaking peers as well as the Spanish-speaking students. At the time, Fernanda did not feel strongly about her Chinese identity, and always introduced herself as simply Brazilian. When she would receive confused looks and racist comments about how she didn't look Brazilian, she felt hurt and homesick for her native country. In addition, Fernanda was keenly aware of the separation of ESL students from the rest of the student population. Aside from elective classes, ESL students did not mingle with the rest of the student population, and Fernanda did not feel like teachers did anything to foster a sense of community among the different groups of students.

Even in a linguistically diverse school with Portuguese speakers, Fernanda's initial schooling experience as a non-English-speaking immigrant was alienating. Thrust into an environment where she was "othered" because of her English proficiency as well her ethnicity, Fernanda was miserable and lonely. She left the school at the end of the year to reunite with her parents in Brazil, but this formative experience never left her. These memories now shape her emerging pedagogy as an English teacher, motivating her to think intentionally about how to foster a sense of community among her students so that they may develop a love of the English language.

A generation of teachers who come from more diverse backgrounds and more multicultural settings than previous generations will have an advantage when they can access memories like Fernanda's as motivation for activist purpose. As a nation, we are grappling with the widespread tensions between anachronistic and racist notions of what it means to be "American" and the realities of a country whose racial demographic is rapidly shifting to become majority people of color. The anxiety generated by these tensions produces both vulnerability in the world for young people of color and clarity about the world they want to bring into being.

## Critical apprehension

For teacher activists, the seeds of consciousness planted by experiences of anxious apprehension then grow into a more critical understanding of the world.[8] Paulo Freire's *Pedagogy of the Oppressed* calls for an apprehension of the world as a prerequisite for transformative action: "A deepened consciousness of their situation leads people to apprehend that situation as an historical reality susceptible of transformation."[9] This second meaning of apprehension—understanding or grasp—is what teacher activists develop out of their anxiety about the state of the world. Anzaldúa is instructive here as well. She posits that "those who do not feel psychologically or physically safe in the world are more apt to develop [la facultad]," which Anzaldúa defines as "the capacity to see in surface phenomena the meaning of deeper realities, to see the deep structure below the surface."[10] Very specifically, those of us who experience oppression in society are forced to develop la facultad as a survival tactic, consciously or subconsciously, to defend against "when the next person is going to slap us or lock us away."[11] The pedagogy of teacher activism employs deeper consciousness about the world as critical apprehension in the formation of activist purpose. This understanding and grasp of the world stems from the vulnerability created by more anxious apprehension, driving a righteous indignation about the way things are that motivates activism.[12]

Abena attended a parochial K–8 school where she was the only girl of color in her class until seventh grade and where all of her teachers were white and female. Throughout elementary school, teachers and students would make comments to her such as, "You're really smart for who you are," consistently alluding to her difference. The absence of peers and teachers of color, as well as frequent microaggressive comments directed to her, was normal for Abena until she was in high school and met her first teachers of color. Once she realized that teachers of color "were actually a thing," and she started having conversations with these teachers about the liberatory aspect of teaching, she saw her early schooling experiences through new eyes. She started to understand how her teachers' and peers' interactions with her held underlying tones of racism and classism. This newfound awareness prompted a shift in her own understanding of the possibility of her becoming a teacher as a woman of color, as well as a sense of the type of teacher she wanted to be.

The critical apprehension Abena gained about her past schooling experiences and ways in which things could and should be different led to her decision to teach. There was a sense of having been cheated out of an educational experience (at least in school) that might have been liberatory for her as a young African American girl. The critical sense of wrong that stems from the newly formed grasp of otherwise anxiety-inducing experiences feeds the next level of apprehension, which motivates and informs action.

## Angry apprehension

A dissatisfaction with the world's inability to see everyone in it as full human beings, as well as a deeper understanding of why and how that world operates, moves people toward activism. However, Warren[13] and Andrews[14] emphasize that one's entry into activism is not born overnight. Though specific events or circumstances may quickly lead to anxious and critical apprehension, the development of activist purpose and commitment is a process that develops over time. The pedagogy of teacher activism borrows from the concept of "cold anger" to help make sense of the final factor informing teacher activist purpose: angry apprehension.[15] Cold anger is borne from community organizing that "seethes at the injustices of life . . . rooted in direct experience."[16] The seething hot anger and impulse that people feel at the discovery or experience of injustice—the result of both anxious and critical apprehension—is cooled down "so it can become a useful tool to improve individual lives and quality of the common community."[17] Thus, angry apprehension is a motivating passion for action, one that results from experiences of both anxious and critical apprehension.[18]

Gabriel switched schools every year of elementary school because his parents were adamant about ensuring that his needs were being met. While these annual transitions were difficult for Gabriel socially, when he got into a performing arts magnet school in the fifth grade, he and his parents were satisfied they had found the right fit. Gabriel continued through middle school and high school via the feeder system of performing arts schools, but when he became unhappy at his performing arts high school, he decided to transfer to his neighborhood high school. The school had a majority Latino/a student population, yet Gabriel noticed that the number of Latino/a students in the honors classes he was in slowly dwindled over time. By the time Gabriel was a senior there were only a few Latino/a students in honors classes. Gabriel remembers the division between white and Latino/a students as being so stark that if you took a picture of the class, you would literally see Latino/a students on one side of the room and white students on the other.

Gabriel recognized a pattern in how his peers viewed him: "There were so many times when I was working to earn something and there would be this feeling that I was cheating or not playing fairly by my white peers. I developed attitudes and fears about white people that took me a long time to work through." While no one had ever sat him down and explained the fallacy of meritocracy, Gabriel knew he "had to play a game, to be power hungry in this competition against white people." It was a deeply motivating impulse, fueled by his discomfort, his nuanced understanding of, and his anger about the tracking and segregation of Latino/a students.

Combined, the stories shared by Fernanda, Abena, and Gabriel illustrate the importance of excavating our biographies in search of what shapes our understanding about justice in the world. Moments of anxious vulnerability can also be translated into a more enduring criticality about what is wrong and what is right. Together, these memories and experiences sow within us the seeds of activism, germinating the cold anger necessary to fuel action. For the millennials of color we've profiled here, these memories are stark and they are all related to their schooling. The same school structures and practices that produced these moments in their lives are by and large still in place. However, as they and their peers continue to make up larger proportions of the teaching corps, it will be their individual and collective actions that help shape new educational settings aimed more at supporting the world they would like to see—and one that will more clearly see them and their students.

## SHIFTING THE BALANCE OF POWER: EXERCISING AGENCY

To achieve their activist purpose, teacher activists engage with power. That is, they work in ways both inside and outside classrooms that seek to shift the balance of power so that people and communities most often on the short end of the stick are afforded more. The pedagogy of teacher activism outlines three forms of agency that teacher activists employ: relational, creative, and resistive.[19] These are tightly linked to teacher activists' apprehensions in and of the world.

### Relational agency

The pedagogy of teacher activism defines relational agency as "the proactive cultivation of relationships to build power with others in order to fulfill teacher activist purpose."[20] This form of agency is predicated upon the notion that people can build power *with* others as opposed to *over* others.[21]

James feels fortunate to have learned at an early age the value of teachers who unconditionally love their students. His kindergarten teacher made a special request to keep the thirty students who started with her in kindergarten for three consecutive years. James remembers how special and loved he and his peers felt because this teacher knew everything about their personalities and needs, and was a healthy part of their home lives. It wasn't until later in college, when he learned about identity and systems of oppression, that he realized that not all children, especially black children like him, received the same love and care that he had in school. He decided that teaching history was a vehicle through which students would be able to see themselves and be validated.

James's strong grounding in the power of relationships through his early schooling experiences seems to have influenced his commitment to build strong relationships with his colleagues as a way to change unjust systems in schools. James has been a part of his school community for eight years—one year as a student teacher and seven years as a full-time faculty member. Prior to James's joining the school community, the district superintendent embarked on an initiative to explore equity and excellence in the district through the lens of race. The cornerstone of this initiative involved a partnership with a nonprofit organization that provided professional development to every faculty member and administrator on understanding and decentering whiteness through the exploration of critical race theory and the cultivation of reflective practice. James became a teacher leader, participating in and promoting this learning. He models a commitment to analyzing the role of whiteness and power in individual mind-sets as well as school structures so that the faculty and staff can collectively make decisions to disrupt those dynamics. James points to his school's decision to de-track all of their classes as a result of this ongoing professional development. While there is still a quantifiable achievement gap between white students and students of color, James believes that the school now feels much more inclusive, with fewer stigmas associated with certain classes, which strengthens the potential for more positive relationships between teachers and students.

James's story traces how educational biographies can influence the ways in which teachers seek to build power and challenge dominant power dynamics. In his case, it was a positive personal experience that he later realized actually challenged the oppressive norms experienced by too many black students, and which now shapes his approach to teaching. The relational agency that he displays reflects the care shown by his teacher in kindergarten through second grade. His critical understanding of the formative influence of his experience, where he was fully seen as a young African American boy, motivates him to effect positive relationships that challenge normative whiteness in the experiences of his current students and to assert a new form of power that relies upon practices that value multiple identities.

### Creative agency

Creative agency is marked by efforts to "structure and create spaces within which students [and/or teachers] can understand and renegotiate their own relationship to power."[22] This form of teacher activist agency is most often seen in response to structural oppression, including traditional classroom and school structures and policies that often inhibit the recognition of students (and families and teachers and community members) as full human beings. Thus, creative agency often seeks to build alternative spaces within which everyone is fully seen.

Gabriel loves and appreciates teaching in an arts-centered school because the school leaders have established an ethos around creative thinking that has informed the development of systems and structures for learning that cultivate creative thinking among students. However, Gabriel also recognizes that the same leaders who are committed to creative thinking are not entirely free of the white supremacist ideas that undergird their views of which structures and systems are best for students. Gabriel's priorities as a teacher committed to social justice, which he describes in three levels, reflect this understanding and his desire to cultivate a classroom experience where his students can understand and renegotiate their own relationship to power.

Gabriel's first priority is to sustain his own teaching by practicing self-care. He sees that some of his colleagues are burning out after only a few years and he does not want that for himself. His second priority is to ensure that his students' basic needs are being met so that they can learn. Finally, helping students to make connections and take action around global issues affecting their school community is his third priority. He actively facilitates learning in his classroom, where his students "are making art about intersectionality and about bigger global social justice issues, but they're exploring these global issues and then *they* are deciding to make art on the way these issues have come to surface in our school community." In Gabriel's classroom this past year, students worked on a final performance that expressed their critique of the school's uniform policy, questioning the notion that khaki pants and a white shirt are the ideal outward expression of professionalism that students and their families should be aspiring toward.

Not surprisingly, given Gabriel's childhood experience of being challenged by white peers for his legitimacy as an academically high-achieving Latino, he is sensitive to school structures that reify normative whiteness. Therefore, he has used his teacher activist agency to create spaces within which students are encouraged to question these norms. The space he has created in his classroom then allowed students to problematize the school-wide dress code policy, while Gabriel was effectively speaking back to his experience as a student in an arts school where there was no space to explore and take pride in his Latino identity.

## Resistive agency

Resistive agency "subverts current structures in the interest of those who are typically excluded."[23] Through resistive agency, which is more undercover than creative agency, teacher activists can name oppressive power structures, but refuse to succumb to them by subtly working to disrupt or bend the rules to provide more equitable and just teaching and learning environments.

Abena's school has restrictive policies, including silent hallways and meals, which teachers are expected to implement and enforce. Abena has been starting to realize the impact on her students of her being "the face of those systems," of being the one who tells her students to keep silent and keep still for over eight hours a day. She reflects, "It's not the best feeling to know that you're stopping them from being their best because of what others have said is the best way for them to learn."

In addition to policing students' bodies, Abena is limited in what she can teach and how she can teach it because her curriculum is given to her by the charter network. While she feels that the scripted curriculum limits the connections she would ordinarily make between the content and students' own experiences, she "looks for other spaces" where students can think critically and be heard. Whether this means meeting up with students during recess or making time during Advisory, Abena is proud of the ways she has cultivated student-centered spaces within the larger limiting context by which she is bound.

Abena is not alone in manifesting her resistive agency. The other women of color on the faculty are aligned in their critique of the school's using control over students' bodies to mold their minds. When these women talk, they "try to find ways to undermine the systems." For example, teachers are not allowed to play music without words in class. But Abena and her like-minded colleagues will simply close their doors and make space in their individual classrooms for students to enjoy music they like to listen and dance to, an act they specifically see as a culturally responsible and developmentally appropriate thing to do for their students. While small subversive acts such as these are not coordinated to occur at certain times, Abena and her colleagues are fueled by their collective resistive agency to cultivate opportunities to humanize their students, if only for a moment.

Abena's own experience as a student of color who felt unseen by her teachers, as well as her later realization that teachers of color could serve as antidotes to the negative messages sent by dominant schooling practices, deeply influences her self-reflections as a teacher of color today. Not wanting to replicate the negative patterns she has identified in her educational experience, her resistive agency serves as an opportunity to reclaim and rewrite the restrictive policies in her school that she fears might otherwise inscribe the racist and classist messages she also received as a young student.

While all of the teachers whose stories are told here have varied reactions to identifying explicitly with the "teacher activist" label, as millennial teachers of color they are honing in on what they can do in their classrooms in ways that clearly reflect the pedagogy of teacher activism. However, if we have an interest in cultivating teachers like them, the pedagogy of teacher activism calls for one final element that is necessary to sustain this kind of work: a sense of hope and possibility.

## SUPPORTING ACTIVIST POSSIBILITY: BUILDING HOPE TO #STAYWOKE

Forever inventive, millennials of color have widely adopted the African American Vernacular English (AAVE) term of being *woke*. It is used to convey deeper levels of social consciousness, as in being awake to social realities of inequity and structural oppression, much like Anzaldúa and Freire have articulated. New activist paradigms led by millennials of color demand that we be *woke* and *stay woke*.[24] Largely credited as one of the first popular uses of *woke*, Erykah Badu's 2008 song "Master Teacher" brings clarity to the term in relation to the pedagogy of teacher activism. The song beautifully captures the apprehensions of teacher activist purpose. Naming the anxieties of the world, Badu sings of "struggle and strife" alongside her assertion of critical understanding by staying "woke" while dreaming and searching for a beautiful world. It's no mistake that Badu's song calls for "master teachers" in pursuit of these dreams. The pedagogy of teacher activism recognizes that it is teachers who can instill a sense of hope and possibility within students and for society, but also stresses the importance of being able to support the sense of hope and possibility for teacher activists themselves as a sustaining force for their work.[25]

If millennial teachers of color are poised and ready to be the master teachers we need to wake up and stay woke, then we must think critically about the systems of supports that are necessary to successfully cultivate and sustain this new generation of teachers. The pedagogy of teacher activism uses Duncan-Andrade's three elements of "critical hope" to consider how we might sustain teacher activism.[26] We conclude this chapter with some reflections on how to achieve this goal.

## Material hope

Material hope provides the resources and support necessary to feel a sense of control over the forces that affect our lives by connecting to real, material conditions.[27] We would argue that, for the most part, millennial teachers of color are woke. As a generation, they more widely believe that black lives matter, no human is illegal, gender is not binary, and people should love (and marry) whomever they please. They are confident, then, in their ability to develop relationships with their increasingly diverse array of students and to stand by them in the face of injustice. However, almost by definition, we are asking that they become teachers inside institutions that have not caught up to these beliefs in their systemic organization, policies, and practices. This gap between "wokeness" and institutional practice makes it more difficult to help millennial teachers of color connect their understanding of power and their roles as change agents to their teaching practice.

Material hope will manifest when we can reshape our school institutions to connect educational theory that aligns with being woke to the material realities of schooling and classrooms. When we support and seek the leadership of millennial teachers of color to develop school-based practices that, for example, value black lives, treat no human as illegal, and support gender inclusivity, then we can build material hope that will sustain the sense of possibility that recent millennial-led activism has helped us achieve. In conversations, Abena, Gabriel, Fernanda, and James all name the need to have more people of color in school leadership and to incorporate student and teacher voice into decision making. These actions not only provide the supports they need to sustain their work, but they also would begin to engender material hope in schools. Essentially, more woke leadership and decision-making structures responsive to student and teacher voice will tangibly help establish institutional practices and structures more aligned to concrete material realities.

## Socratic hope

Socratic hope is developed from the reflective examination of the difficulty and pain of everyday life and the recognition that shared struggle is our only path to justice.[28] Our schools and teacher preparation and professional development programs must acknowledge the intersections of the personal, professional, and political. Millennials of color know very well the lack of representation of people of color in teaching roles because very few of them had teachers of color themselves. Like Abena and James, who explicitly talk about their identities as black teachers in relationship to their black students ("these students look like me"), and Gabriel, who feels isolated and unsupported as the only Latino teacher in the school, we must support spaces that help all teachers uncover how their own biographies are reflected in their teaching.

In these examinations of biography, we must recognize that there is not only much to learn, but also much to unlearn. The unlearning is about undoing racism and other forms of systemic oppression that plague our systems and our mind-sets (becoming "woke"). We need to make space for teachers to experience the moral shock of reconciling their idea of what it is to be an effective teacher with what they have been told, or what they have absorbed from their own experiences as students. In these spaces we might instill Socratic hope by redefining how we might work together as teachers and educators toward justice. James's experience through his districtwide professional development underscores the importance of enabling teachers to unlearn together and then immediately talk about how they can collectively change structures in their school to address inequities.

## Audacious hope

Finally, audacious hope is about not just dreaming big, but also continuing to dream. Despite the overwhelming odds that seem stacked against the ideals of social justice, activists find the motivation and strength to persevere on the difficult path toward justice, time and time again.[29] For instance, how do we capture the audacious hope embedded in James's assessment of what we ultimately must transform if we are going to overcome inequity:

I think capitalism has to go, low-key. Not even low-key—high-key. That's where a lot of our problems are rooted. Unless we stop looking at our kids as products then nothing is going to change. [Our school] is still run on an industrial model. We have nine periods a day . . . we hear forty bells a day. If we're still run on an industrial model, then we're going to continue to perpetuate [inequity].

Whether the ultimate answer to our problems is dismantling capitalism or something else, the only way to cultivate a new generation of teacher activists is to do the hard work of entertaining these audacious possibilities. Anything short of that will amount to maintaining a systemwide sleep mode for our schools, while we watch the world waking up all around us. Thus, we must answer the paradoxical call that activist millennials of color are making to all of us: Dream big and stay woke.

*Acknowledgments*
*We thank Fernanda, Abena, Gabriel, and James for their commitment to acting for a better world and their willingness to share such important insights into their lives and their teaching.*

# 6

# Black Preservice Teachers on Race and Racism in the Millennial Era

*Considerations for Teacher Education*

Keffrelyn D. Brown and Angela M. Ward

The rapidly changing landscape of twenty-first-century education has sparked intense conversations around the need for a more racially and ethnically diverse preK–12 teacher population. These calls echo from myriad corners, from university teacher education programs to targeted initiatives undertaken in national organizations like the National Education Association (NEA) as well as the White House. The goal of these efforts is to address the schism between the existing and projected preK–12 teaching force that is overwhelmingly white and the concomitant growing student population that is of color. This includes black teachers, a group with a prominent, historic place in the teaching profession, but one that has witnessed a sorely diminished presence since the racial integration of US public schooling.

While not dismissing the ability of white teachers to teach students of color well, such efforts acknowledge that because of their cultural backgrounds, preservice teachers of color often (but certainly not always) possess the knowledge, experiences, and dispositions needed to work most effectively with students of color.[1] Scholars have also noted that preservice teachers of color, specifically those who are black (as well as Latinx), regularly express wanting to become a teacher in order to improve the educational experiences and outcomes of students of color.[2] Yet what does this tell us about how these teachers understand race and if and how they imagine engaging it in their classrooms?

At a time when race has taken on heightened attention, what are the implications of preparing teachers of color to acquire critical sociocultural knowledge of race and a commitment to social justice teaching in the changing terrain of race found in the twenty-first century? How can teacher education programs help millennial teacher candidates more effectively address race in the twenty-first-century racial world?

To address this question, in this chapter we explore how a group of black millennial preservice teachers talk about and understand race and racism. As members of generation X, we recognize the different and unique racial context in which millennial preservice teachers find themselves learning how to teach. Unlike our own experiences as young people preparing to teach, millennial teachers of color have witnessed the election of the first black president, Barack Obama, as well as the racial backlash that accompanied the election of Donald Trump in 2016. The complex racial terrain that black millennial teachers navigate provides a fertile space to interrogate contemporary perspectives on race and their implications for teacher education.

Drawing from critical race theory (CRT)[3] and racial formation theory,[4] we explore how millennial preservice teachers of color understand race and its role in teaching in the twenty-first-century racial context. We begin with a brief discussion on the need for more teachers of color. We situate this in the existing scholarship on the challenges, experiences, and perspectives of preservice teachers of color in teacher education programs. We then consider the generational social context surrounding millennial teachers of color, specifically around race and diversity. We relate this discussion to critical theories of race and racial formation that recognize how the larger sociopolitical landscape shapes the racial knowledge people hold. We then share the findings from interviews with a group of black preservice teachers regarding their understandings of race, racism, and teaching. The chapter concludes by offering suggestions on how teacher education might more effectively meet the needs of millennial teachers of color.

## MILLENNIALS OF COLOR, RACE, AND TEACHER EDUCATION

Millennials—born after 1980—are depicted in the literature as natives and products of the digital culture.[5] The millennial generation is also marked by the sociocultural-political climate of the new century.[6] For example, this group of college-educated and college-age students was in large part responsible for the 2008 and 2012 elections of President Barack Obama, the first black US president.[7]

It is not surprising, then, that the millennial generation is characterized as (1) more racially open, tolerant, and savvy,[8] (2) tasked with a social landscape dominated by colorblind racism,[9] and (3) tending to assume a greater social distance between self and "racists." Yet, regarding race, millennials are not monolithic, as differences exist in how young people of different races and ethnicities view the significance and extent of racism in US society.[10]

In a study on how millennials understand race and racism, Dominique Apollon found similarities and differences in how white millennials and those of color viewed race and racism.[11] While both groups agreed that race holds continuing significance in society, a majority of participants across both groups had difficulty defining "present-day racism" and often drew from "generic terms of *interpersonal* racism." Yet at the same time participants of color more easily acknowledged contemporary societal systems as "racist." Not surprisingly, Apollon also found that both white millennials and those of color who expressed an understanding of structural and institutional racism had a background in race and/or social justice or had taken courses on race and ethnicity in college. Additionally, he highlighted the limited understandings that white millennials hold regarding the impact of race on education. This stands in contrast to millennials of color, who recognize how racism operates in education, often drawing from their personal experiences with racism in K–12 schools.[12] While some students of color acquire understanding about race and racism from their direct experiences, the literature suggests that, collectively, students of color, like their white peers, can benefit from knowledge they acquire about race and racism, both through their personal experiences and from knowledge they receive in their official school curriculum.

There is an irony to the greater openness millennials are assumed to have regarding issues of race: students of color often experience racially hostile spaces in predominantly white universities.[13] These actions, sometimes called racial microaggressions, can occur in overt or covert ways.[14] They might take the form of hostile or joking discourses between strangers or occur between those who have friendly, social relations.[15]

Black preservice teachers have experience with the duality of living in a racially stratified society and navigating these social spaces in a way that recognizes, values, and affirms their sociocultural knowledge. A fundamental assumption in the work linking race and teaching is that teachers need to possess racial knowledge in order to teach in effective and equitable ways.[16] Existing literature on black preservice teachers has noted the hostile racial experiences these students often encounter in predominantly white university and teacher education programs.[17] These encounters align with those recounted in the scholarship on preservice teachers of color.

Scholars have documented the racism teachers of color often encounter in the schools and in the teaching programs they attend.[18] Additionally, while teacher candidates of color often attend teacher education programs that celebrate the "diversity" these students bring to their larger programs, paradoxically, their knowledge, experiences, and perspectives often go unacknowledged.[19] This invisibility[20] linked with the lack of knowledge these students report acquiring in their K–12[21] and teacher education programs undermine opportunities to learn about race and how to teach in culturally relevant/responsive ways.[22] Researchers present cautionary tales of missed opportunities to learn about culturally relevant/responsive teaching when it is assumed that teachers of color already possess innate knowledge of such teaching. This matters, because teachers of color often express wanting to make a difference in the lives of students of color.[23]

Black teachers, like all teachers, bring complex, intersectional identities around race, gender, class, language, and sexuality to teacher education.[24] In traditional teacher education programs, black preservice teachers must negotiate their identities as they seek to bridge the divide between their sense of self and the dominant notions of what it means to be a teacher. Yet when operating in intentionally race-conscious ways, these same teacher education spaces can hold transformative possibilities.[25]

## THEORETICAL FRAMEWORK

To guide this study, we draw from critical race theory and racial formation theory. Collectively, these frameworks speak to the nature of race as a complex, foundational, and shifting idea.

### Critical race theory

As an outgrowth and critique of critical legal studies, critical race theory offers an analytical framework to examine how race operates in US law and social relations. CRT pushed against critical approaches in legal studies that considered inequities in law, but neglected to address how race played out in these processes. The result of this work was to offer a critical framework that centers on and accounts for race.

Scholars have applied CRT in various disciplines, including education, to explore the nature of race and racism.[26] CRT in education seeks to excavate how race operates in society and in education, at both the structural and local, everyday levels. By making race the center of analysis, CRT presents a challenge to color-blind perspectives that fail to recognize the role of race in social interactions.[27] As a result, race "is precluded as a source of identification or analysis."[28] This makes it possible to disavow its importance and role in localized, microlevel activities, as well as the deeply entrenched institutional practices that support, sustain, and maintain everyday interactions.[29] The nonrecognition of race shuts off the possibility that race is an important or viable factor to consider when interpreting interactions in the social world. Concomitantly, this nonacknowledgment makes it possible to position those who do recognize the insidious role of race as hypersensitive race-baiters who see racial issues where none really exist.[30]

## Racial formation theory

Deeply aligned with CRT, racial formation theory recognizes the socially constructed nature of race.[31] Race is created through social practices with material consequences that impact our experiences, perspectives, and outcomes in everyday life. To make sense of race one must consider the larger sociopolitical contexts—current and historical—that frame and bring meaning to how race is understood. Race is fluid, political, and reproduced and redefined over time and different spaces.[32] Similarly, racism refers to discriminatory practices grounded in race-based ascriptions that also morph temporally and spatially. Race and racism are dynamic forces. They do not operate in flat or static ways. If one is to hold a complex understanding of these ideas, including how they function in everyday societal relations, one must recognize their remarkable ability to shift and adapt to specific times and circumstances.[33]

Together, CRT and racial formation theory account for race as a complex idea that has impacted social relations in the US and continues to do so, including the area of education and teacher education.

## METHODOLOGY AND METHODS

The data presented in this chapter derive from a qualitative case study that examined how millennial preservice and in-service teachers of color understand race and imagine addressing it in their teaching.[34] The following question guided this study: How do preservice and beginning millennial teachers of color understand and talk about race and teaching?

## Participants and settings

This chapter reports on data collected from six black preservice teachers aged twenty-one to twenty-two. All were considered part of the millennial generation, with birth years from 1993 to 1995. Participants were recruited using a snowball sampling technique.[35]

All of the participants were in a teacher education program housed at a predominantly white US university. Three participants (Jackie, Ashley, and Portia) attended a large research university in the South and were enrolled in a secondary social studies undergraduate teacher certification program. The program focused on teaching in an urban school context. One participant (Victoria) attended the same large research university but was enrolled in a master's secondary social studies teacher certification program. These four participants were in the second semester of their three-semester-long program, which focused on social justice teaching in an urban school context. Two participants (Lance and Marie) attended a regional university also in the South, but in a different state from the large research university. This program did not focus on any specific area. Both participants were pursuing a middle grades teacher certification (fourth through eighth grade).

## Data collection

One extended, semistructured interview was conducted with each participant.[36] The interview lasted from one to one and a half hours. Four participant interviews were conducted in person and two by phone. All interviews were audio recorded and transcribed. The interview focused on three areas. The first centered on the background of the participants regarding their identities, reasons for becoming a teacher, and the kind of schools where they wanted to teach. The second area of questions focused on the participants' experiences with race and racism, including what they learned about these issues in their K–12 schooling and teacher education programs. The third area of questions centered on the participants' perspectives on teaching, their professional goals, and if and how they imagined addressing race and racism in their own teaching. The semistructured protocol included thirty-one questions to which all participants responded. In some cases follow-up, clarifying questions were asked; most of these instances occurred during the participants' discussions of race and racism.

## Data analysis

Data analysis occurred in two phases and drew from inductive (provisional, theoretical-based) and deductive (emergent) coding methods.[37] The first phase focused on coding interview data using CRT and racial formation theory. This included theoretically coding instances of how race and racism were addressed by the participants, with particular attention to whether these ideas were generationally situated. The second phase focused on coding for emergent data not captured by the first-phase coding. Trustworthiness was established by triangulating the data, or looking for three or more instances of consistent patterns across theoretical and emergent themes. In presenting the data, we offer text-rich examples that show the salience of specific key themes across all or a majority of the participants.

## FINDINGS

Four findings emerged on the perspectives of black millennial preservice teachers around race, racism, and their future teaching. These findings speak to the continued relevance the participants felt race had in their own lives, even as they recognized differences in how race operated for them and for previous generations. The participants also identified both the university and social media as key spaces where they acquired knowledge about race. While all of the participants envisioned addressing race and racism in their future teaching, they expressed varying understandings of racism that focused primarily on micro, interpersonal perspectives, and they experienced different levels of commitment in their teacher education programs on addressing these topics.

## Relevance of and generational differences around race and racism

All of the participants felt that race and racism hold continued significance in contemporary US society. This significance was evident in what they learned from their parents' experiences with racism as well as from their own. While all of the participants said that they learned very little about race in their K–12 schooling, several highlighted how their parents talked to them about race and racism, often as a way to buffer against the everyday racial microaggressions that black people experience. Lance shared that both his great grandmother and his grandmother talked to him about the racism they encountered in their work as housekeepers for white families. Portia discussed how she remembered her father telling her stories about the racism he faced at work. At the time, she was unable to fully appreciate these "warning speeches."

> [H]e would come home almost daily and talk about the racism that he experienced in the workforce. He'd been fired and he had evidence through I guess talking and writing things down that people were treating him much differently than other people because of his race. There were slurs, microaggressions, and the like, and still at that point I didn't grasp it until I had a chance to really experience it on my own.

As a result of these stories, Portia felt more confident to recognize and name racism when it occurred later in her own life.

Some participants acknowledged talking to their parents and grandparents about race and racism. These conversations sometimes were related to the participants' experiences or were attempts to seek out knowledge about these topics. For example, Victoria shared a story of what happened to her when she encountered race for the first time while doing a project in kindergarten: "I just remember going home and telling my mom, 'Mom, I'm brown,' and she stopped everything she was doing and she was like, 'Who told you that? Why would you say that?' I remember her being upset. . . . I was excited about it and she was really upset."

Victoria acknowledged that her mother "didn't want to raise us in the way where we saw difference in other people . . . she wanted us to grow up seeing equality, everybody's equal." Here we find an example of a parent acknowledging the power of race and racism through a seemingly color-blind perspective.[38] Victoria's mother worried that if her daughter's non–African American teacher acknowledged racial differences, this might lead her students to adopt a racist lens that would compromise an equal educational experience for all. This is a complicated reading of race that acknowledges the salience of race and racism, while adopting a color-blind stance in order to protect students of color who are particularly vulnerable to racist beliefs.

The participants also acknowledged their own personal experiences with race and racism. For instance, Ashley learned about the power of race and racism during her younger years as an aspiring model and when looking at popular media. As a child, she noted, "I went to modeling school because my mom wanted me to be a model, and it was really weird to me because there weren't a lot of black girls. . . . I just felt like the odd one out just being there because I wasn't the stereotypical blonde hair[ed], blue-eyed girl, and I felt that I wouldn't be as pretty as them or they would get more contracts than me."

What she experienced was exacerbated by what she saw on television. She continued, "I used to watch *America's Next Top Model* and usually the really pretty ones with a lot of praise from Tyra were the white ones and usually they would win."

### University and social media as locations to acquire knowledge about race

When asked where they received knowledge about race, participants overwhelmingly highlighted both the university and social media as key locations. Along with the knowledge they gained from their parents and grandparents, they cited learning about race in their university coursework and in the context of university organizations in which they participated. For example, Lance expressed that his knowledge of race grew from "interactions I had with dealing with different professors, organizations on campus, community service and . . . reading." As a result, he believed that he "just grew a consciousness for race and how it affects our interactions." Lance went on to note that he participated at several conferences devoted to race as a result of his campus organization affiliations, including the National Conference on Race and Ethnicity (NCORE) and the Southwestern Black Leadership Conference.

When asked about what informed her current understanding about race and racism, Victoria asserted,

> Right now I've been doing a lot of meetings based on racism in my courses. I have read articles and excerpts out of books but [am] also reading different articles from news outlets like the *New York Times* and *USA Today*, CNN. I watch the news and I like to read it. I do look at social media because sometimes it leads me to an article that I haven't seen or I haven't heard that people are talking about.

Here, Victoria highlighted her acquisition of racial knowledge through both coursework and social media outlets. Victoria was not the only participant who gained knowledge about race and racism through social media. Ashley also noted getting most of her information about race and racism from "the Internet." She separated her use of the Internet between what she called "use" and "not for comments," where she "used" the Internet to access information but did not make remarks in the comment section of the pieces she read. She said, "I try to get facts and use [them] to sort my opinions so when we talk about Black Lives Matter, I sort through all the crap and focus on what is happening."

## Differing understandings of race and racism

Across the participants there were varying degrees of understanding about race and racism. In considering this finding, however, it is important to note that four of the participants were in the beginning stage of their teacher education program.

These participants' perspectives on racism ranged from viewing race as a biological construct to seeing it as socially constituted. A few participants recognized racism as a process that operates at the interpersonal and structural/institutional levels, while a good number of the participants discussed racism as something that plays out at the individual microlevel. They also often struggled when trying to talk about racism in complex ways that moved across micro- and macrolevel understandings.

Two of the participants offered definitions of racism that focused on its structural and systemic nature. For example, Portia stated that "racism would be someone in a position of power, at least racially, exploiting the constructed racial differences of somebody who is positioned underneath them so to speak." Lance viewed racism as "strong prejudice" that operates systemically to oppress certain people.

Jackie also acknowledged a relationship between prejudice and racism, yet she remained unclear whether they were connected to individual or structural/institutional practices. Victoria similarly linked prejudice and racism, as she noted the latter was "showing a prejudice against a different race or showing a dislike or hate of a different race other than your own."

In addition, several participants defined racism as an interpersonal, microlevel phenomenon. Marie identified racism as "one race mistreating another," and Ashley viewed it as "believing that one race is superior to another." When looking across these definitions, one notes that none of them were incorrect but most were incomplete renderings of racism, limited mainly to actions that occur between people.

## Learning about race in teacher education

The four participants who attended a teacher education program that focused on social justice teaching in urban school spaces all said they engaged directly with issues of race and racism. They recounted experiences that occurred early in their programs in at least two pedagogic contexts. These included a summer field immersion experience they participated in during their first semester in the teacher education program, in their social studies methods course. For example, Ashley stated

> I've had a lot of experience learning about racism especially during my [first semester]. We were teaching students from [a particular summer program,] and they're mostly Hispanic and there's some African Americans and they were telling me about how in their schools, people get made fun of because of their skin color and how dark they were and their accents . . . and just a lot of stereotypes that are being pushed around. You're black, you're poor, and you live in the hood and you shoot people and do drive-bys. You're Hispanic, you don't know English. Stuff like that.

In her new position as a teacher, Ashley recognized how race and racism operated as microaggressions in her students' everyday lives. Victoria felt that her course readings and the ideas she learned about race in her foundations and methods courses were helpful in preparing her to teach about race in the classroom. Yet, even as she appreciated learning about race in college, she regretted having to wait so long to do so. This was the catalyst for her wanting to teach about race and racism in her future high school classroom. She stated:

> I feel that it is important to teach about [race]. I feel like college is too late to be the first time students hear about racism. I think it's too late in the game for people to try and start understanding what racism is, because we only have four years in college to figure it out and we only have one semester in this class for us to really try and understand what racism is. That's why some of my understanding about stuff is so limited. . . . To start at a young age in high school is where I would like to start teaching kids about race and racism.

Jackie similarly noted that she appreciated learning about race and racism in her current teacher education coursework, which included foundations and social studies methods courses. She shared how she was coming to understand "different narratives to racism" that were silenced in her K–12 history courses:

> Mostly it's not always the slaves' perspective that gets told because they didn't really have a voice back then. It's like after slavery happened then they were allowed to talk more and speak more about it once they were freed. I learned a lot about it even if it's not about slavery but if it's just like about the Holocaust or something. It's more of the dominant narrative being told rather than the minorities.

Jackie's statements are an example of how race matters in the narratives found in official school curriculum. Dominant historical narratives quite often line up with the perspective of the racially privileged group. These enacted curriculum practices perpetuate racism because they render dominant narratives as neutral and correct, while systematically silencing alternative viewpoints.

Though two participants were enrolled in programs that did not have an explicit focus on teaching social justice, they both indicated a desire to address race and racism in their future teaching. They acknowledged, however, that they had not learned much in their program about race. When race was addressed, they felt it was done in a way that suggested students' racial, cultural, and linguistic identities operated as barriers to learning. For example, Lance mentioned learning only about "differentiating [instructionally] for diverse and linguistic students." He stated,

> I learned the different, I guess instructional approaches to students . . . but I know how with standardized texts it can be misleading to certain cultural backgrounds. What else did I learn? With English language learners, you have to speak slower for them and have different supports, like where I was they didn't really talk a lot about Asian Americans. They don't really talk about Native Americans. Pretty much how to support black and Latino students.

Marie also felt that she had not learned much at all about race. Though she anticipated teaching about race, when asked if she felt equipped to address these issues right now, she replied, "If I were to teach right now, I would say no." In spite of this, she said that "[when] the time comes, I feel like I will be prepared," even though she did not express why she felt this way.

## DISCUSSION AND IMPLICATIONS

The findings previously discussed support and extend the existing literature on millennial students and preservice teachers of color regarding race. First, participants acknowledged the continued relevance of race and racism in their lives.[39] While these issues still mattered to the participants, they also pointed to generational differences in their importance and operation. What the participants knew about race and racism linked to their knowledge of how past generations encountered racism. Racism had a long history and it continued to impact their lives, but these impacts were felt in more subtle ways than in the past.

Second, the participants acknowledged the power of both social media and university spaces in cultivating and curating their knowledge around race and racism. While Apollon has noted the connection between university coursework and the complexity of racial knowledge held by millennials, little if any research on preservice teachers of color, specifically black teachers, has addressed the power of social media in the acquisition and dissemination of racial knowledge.[40] Participants highlight both the affordances and challenges related to navigating race in social media.

Third, the participants talked about race and racism in different ways, with several struggling to move beyond microlevel, interpersonal understandings.[41] Fourth, while all of the participants expressed wanting to address race and racism in their future teaching—often because these topics were not part of their own K–12 official school curriculum—they were exposed to different levels of racial knowledge in their teacher education programs. These findings corroborate the existing literature on preservice teachers of color. Similar to the participants in a previous study, these millennial preservice teachers held a commitment to teaching about race and racism, often because of its near invisibility in their K–12 schooling.[42] In addition, the participants who were enrolled in a teacher education program focused on social justice teaching in urban school contexts felt their program did a good job of discussing race and racism.

The millennial teachers in this study continue to see the value of race in contemporary society. Yet, they ask us to consider the following questions:

What does it mean to acknowledge that race and racism are generationally situated? What are the implications of addressing race and racism as generationally situated in the context of teacher education? If social media and universities serve as key locations where race knowledge is found and discussed, how might teacher education programs better leverage opportunities for students to acquire such knowledge?

A clear implication from this study is that teacher education programs must approach teaching about race and racism in targeted ways. Fundamentally, these programs should help teacher candidates understand race and racism as complex factors that operate at multiple levels—micro and macro—and change in appearance, yet not in significance, over time and across generations. Racism does not cease to matter across time and space. Finding ways to incorporate social media in teacher education, while also equipping preservice teachers how to navigate it and teach their future students how to read and engage with race in social media, seems particularly important.[43]

Teacher education programs may bolster their recruitment of students of color by developing stronger relationships with programs and departments that focus on race, such as ethnic studies.[44] Students might consider double majoring in both an ethnic studies area and teacher education. Also, teacher educators might learn how to help students develop more critical race knowledge and sociopolitical consciousness by examining how ethnic studies courses are taught. Similarly, teacher education programs might work more closely with campus organizations that service students of color as an additional way to recruit candidates and provide current preservice teachers opportunities for critical community engagement with issues of race.

While it is true that preservice teachers of color generally, and black preservice teachers specifically, reflect a small percentage of the total US teaching population, looking closely at these groups serves two important purposes. First, in teacher education there is a tendency to approach knowledge related to teaching as racially and culturally neutral, including disregarding the cultural knowledge of groups of color.[45] This renders people of color as invisible and their knowledge as irrelevant to the overall work of teaching and teacher education. And, in the case of preservice teachers of color in predominantly white university teacher education programs, the existing literature is replete with reports of their experiences of isolation, alienation, and invisibility.[46] At a time when there is growing emphasis on the need to recruit more preservice teachers of color, we cannot afford to ignore their perspectives and experiences and what they offer to teacher education.

Second, there is something important to learn about race and racism when looking closely at a group recognized as both racially knowledgeable[47] and particularly vulnerable to negative enactments of race and racism.[48] The black millennials in this study discussed having to navigate racism on their campuses, in their classes, and on social media. Listening to what they have to say about race and racism provides insight into the challenging encounters they navigate around race. Here, black preservice teachers operate as canaries in the mine, highlighting the deepest resonances of race that preservice teacher education needs to consider when seeking to help candidates acquire the racial knowledge needed for teaching.[49]

Given the findings in this study, teacher education that seeks to address race must adopt practices that help millennials understand the connection between micro- and macrolevel issues that sustain racial inequality at the systemic level.[50] This is highlighted by the important role coursework plays in educating students about the complexities of race and racism.[51]

As a result, and in line with the findings from this study, teacher educators cannot assume that any particular students, including preservice teachers of color, come into their programs already possessing the experiential or content knowledge needed to teach in a socially just, relevant, and equitable way. However, this does not diminish the important knowledge and commitments to teaching that these students often bring to their programs.[52] Nor should it undermine efforts to recruit more teachers of color in K–12 schooling.[53] It does ask that teacher education programs work to affirm, draw from, and build on the knowledge historically marginalized students of color bring to teacher education programs. This work must be intentional and critically transformative. It must also actively aim to transgress the practices of whiteness that render millennial teachers of color, along with their knowledge, experiences, and perspectives, as invisible. Doing this better equips teacher education to cultivate an effective, equitable, and race-savvy teaching force for the twenty-first century.

# Advancing the Practices of Millennial Teachers of Color with the EquityEd Professional Learning Framework

Sabrina Hope King

The value of teachers of color for all of our nation's students is well documented.[1] Research demonstrates their unique contributions and impact on student success. Although there are programs to support the recruitment of teacher candidates and teachers of color, less emphasis has been placed on the ongoing professional learning needed to retain teachers and promote teacher efficacy, equity, rigorous and engaging student learning, and student success. While some preservice programs prioritize teaching for equity and social justice, district professional development typically does not.[2] Although some districts have been intentional and successful in recruiting teachers of color, most districts have not considered the need to provide specialized support to teachers of color. Some districts express a wish for more for teachers of color, others choose to be silent on the issue, and some districts still have discriminatory hiring practices against teachers of color.[3] School and district professional learning in schools that serve black and Latino/a students and students living in poverty needs to be positioned within the context of equity, empowering and supportive adult learning, and transparent understandings of the roles millennial teachers of color can play to dramatically improve student achievement. Schools and school districts can learn from the experiences and perspectives of millennial teachers of color to ensure impactful professional learning and student outcomes.

The need to improve the educational experiences and outcomes for students of color and students whose lives are affected by poverty is equally understood. Given our nation's widening achievement gap and equity challenges, many school systems recognize the importance of having teachers of color who reflect the demographics, spoken languages, and life experiences of their student population.[4] With all that is currently happening in the United States of America—including political upheaval, related civil disobedience, violence against people of color and the LBGTQ community, the systematic removal of long-fought-for civil rights, the increasing segregation of our schools—the jury is still out in terms of how the work, goals, and perspectives of millennial teachers of color will differ from those of other generations of teachers of color. However, we need to ensure that the potential of millennial teachers of color is realized so that they can use education to address student and societal improvement. We must prioritize the hiring of millennial teachers of color and support their ongoing professional learning and pedagogical practices as they relate to their work with students of color and students living in poverty, who need the best academic and social-emotional development experiences to be successful in school and in life.

For this discussion, millennial teachers of color are defined as teachers who were born in the 1980s and 1990s and who self-identify as a person of color. As districts become able to advance the perspectives and practices of teachers of color, we will further understand how millennial teachers of colors draw upon characteristics of the millennial generation and their cultural identity in their pedagogical practices to support this generation of students. We know many teachers of color choose to work in communities of color and neighborhoods of concentrated poverty.[5]

This chapter focuses on the work to advance the perspectives and practices of millennial teachers of color once they are employed by a school or district. I present the need for an equity framework to support district professional learning and offer recommendations for using the equity framework to advance the practices of millennial teachers of color.

## ILLUMINATING THE PERSPECTIVES OF MILLENNIAL TEACHERS OF COLOR

Millennial teachers of color have multiple reasons for entering the education profession, different understandings of their role as teachers of color, different understandings about teaching within the context of diversity, and useful perspectives about the best ways to spend their time as teachers and the kind of professional support they deem most valuable.[6] For the purposes of this chapter I developed a survey, which was completed by eleven teachers;

I also had informal conversations with a few other millennial teachers of color to illuminate their perspectives on professional learning. The respondents were predominantly African American and Latina, female, in their first through fifth year of teaching, and currently working in urban schools: schools with low socioeconomic status and low-achieving students of color. They describe themselves, the millennial generation, as social media driven, tech savvy, culturally diverse, and entrepreneurial. Other characteristics offered include entitled, confident, questioners, culturally diverse, possessing a voice of freedom to express differences in identity, and globally conscious.

Through the survey responses and the sharing of perspectives, I learned about some of the reasons this generation of teachers of color entered the profession and their initial perspectives about their professional learning experiences and hopes.

## Why did they enter teaching?

More than half entered teaching because of the opportunity to be creative, to work with young people, to contribute to the betterment of society, to work with students of color, and to be a role model. Only two of the respondents cited entering teaching because of an interest in promoting equality and social justice, and only three cited intellectual challenge.

## What are their goals as teachers?

As millennial teachers of color, the survey participants expressed the following goals: to ensure ample learning and to make a positive impact with their students, to be a role model for all of the kids in the school, to help students understand the importance of being bilingual in today's society, to practice liberation education, to help students understand their current life situation and how to make it better, to work to close the achievement gap, and to connect culture and ethnicity to learning. As teachers of color, over half of them noted they would benefit from professional development that included opportunities to talk about diversity, race, and equity issues with their colleagues and develop strategies to reach all students. A few expressed an interest in opportunities to develop strategies for students of color informed by their own experiences. Two participants said that these topics and opportunities to learn more about their own race and ethnicity and affinity groups would be helpful because of the ways these topics connect to each other. One participant noted that support on how to work with administrators as a teacher of color would be useful.

## What did they learn in their teacher preparation programs?

The respondents rated actual teaching in the classroom and assistance from colleagues as the factors that most helped them in learning to teach. Next, they cited their teacher preparation program and assistance from administrators and coaches. Almost half rated support or professional development by external coaches as being helpful, but only two participants said this was true of school or district professional development workshops.

The majority of respondents said that their preparation included understanding how students learn, planning for instruction, diagnosing student learning needs, and implementing classroom management. Yet only four participants noted preparation in the areas of planning for diverse achievement levels, and only four stated that they had training in culturally relevant pedagogy. Only one participant received preparation in planning within the context of cultural and linguistic diversity, understanding and addressing issues of equity and inequality, and understanding and addressing issues of race. In response to the question, "If you were given a gift of ten or more hours a week as a teacher, how would you use it?," participants said they would use the time for planning, including preparing lessons, planning more culturally relevant lessons, creating tools and activities, collaborating with colleagues, and learning how to better engage and motivate students.

## What kind of professional learning do they want?

Participants were asked to describe their vision for empowering professional learning. Responses included "honest and inclusive," "hands on," "learning new content within the context of student needs," "it looks like my ideas matter and it feels like I am more than just a teacher," and "an opportunity to address diversity, race, equity, and inequities in our society." Finally, participants were asked for suggestions for what schools and districts could do to recruit and retain millennial teachers of color. Suggestions included professional development workshops led by teachers of color, providing opportunities for teachers of color to get to know the communities they are serving, treating teachers of color with respect, and providing support when it is requested. The comments offered by this cohort support the rationale for significant district-facilitated professional learning to enable millennial teachers of color to explore their identity and perspectives as millennial teachers of color and to have input into the kind of professional learning that will be impactful. The following snapshots from the survey offer insight into the type of support that could propel millennial teachers of color to success and longevity as teachers and educators.

*Snapshot 1*

I am a second-year black male early childhood teacher. I am excited about my work, I love the community I work in and I am appreciative of the preparation I received. I received a "developing" [rating] my first year of teaching and if I receive a developing my second year, it may be impossible for me to continue to teach in this district. I don't have the support to develop my practice, I am not working in a school where collaboration is valued and I don't want to leave this school because I am committed to teaching this student population.

*Snapshot 2*

I am a third-year African American and Dominican teacher working for the New York City Department of Education. I teach in a suspension center with mostly boys of color. I am finishing my master's degree in bilingual education and special education. I am learning a lot but I basically am winging it on a day-to-day basis. My students have a lot of needs and are one step away from prison because they have been suspended from school. I try to support the other teachers at the center but we are making it up as we go. We could be doing a lot more.

*Snapshot 3*

I appreciated learning about rigor and the use of culturally relevant text to promote engaging literacy learning. I wish I had been exposed to culturally relevant text in my own learning. Students were more engaged with these texts; accountable talk came easily; it was not a chore.

The perspectives and ideas offered by these millennial teachers of color buttress those I formed as an urban educator, through evaluating and supporting schools and districts in need of improvement, leading low-performing districts, and creating a consultant practice focused on improving achievement in communities of color. Their perspectives and ideas need to be understood within the context of the tremendous difficulties districts face to effectively serve students of color as well as students affected by poverty.

## THE NEED FOR AN EQUITYED FRAMEWORK FOR PROFESSIONAL LEARNING

To improve student learning in schools that serve large numbers of under-performing students and/or sizable student populations of color, professional learning needs to be framed by principles of equity and meaningful adult learning. Some teachers made a conscious choice to work in these settings; others did not. Many have never worked with or interacted with students who live in neighborhoods of concentrated poverty; and many are unfamiliar with and have limited experience interacting with cultures other than their own. Others, like many Americans, have biased perspectives about people of color and those whose lives are affected by poverty. Some may even subscribe to the notion that genetics and socioeconomic status influence student potential to achieve. Improving educational experiences and outcomes of students in these settings is viewed as a challenge; preparing all students for college and career readiness is sometimes viewed as impossible. The concurrent work of building student confidence, self-worth, and the ability to foster academic, social-emotional, and life-skill development adds challenge, but is necessary.

Additional realities teachers encounter include a culture of low expectations; a myriad of curriculum implementation and data analysis initiatives; students who have not experienced consistent school success; students whose lived experiences, community, and family life are unfamiliar to the teachers; and students who need but have not experienced engaging, rigorous learning experiences. Even where members of the community believe in students' unlimited success, accountability systems are experienced as onerous, all-encompassing, or the main priority of school or district leaders. Staff often experience a consistent pressure to perform and produce amid an absence of rigorous and culturally relevant practices from which to learn. For a teacher of color, this is often exacerbated due to the pressure put on oneself or placed by others. It is important to note that just because a teacher is of color does not mean that he or she can relate to the experience of every student of color. Also, given that some members of the millennial generation view race as a flexible concept, work is needed to help millennial teachers of color to examine their own practice as people of color.

The challenge, the working conditions, the previously held notions about students, communities, and current student achievement levels—all converge to create schools and districts that hold low expectations for student achievement as well as for teacher learning and development, and that ultimately underserve students.

For example, the research suggests that black teachers hold higher expectations for black students than their white counterparts. In fact, students of color who have just one black teacher are more likely to succeed. Hence, advancing the practices and cultivating the sense of efficacy and well-being of teachers of color are critical to student success.[7] They are also crucial to the success of this country since in many school districts, students of color are already the majority. Based on these needs to move from obstacles to opportunities for student success, this EquityEd framework was developed to support affirming and equity-focused school and district professional learning to lead to improved outcomes in communities of color. Framing professional learning within the context of equity is best practice—period— and essential to the cultivation of working conditions and staff relationships that will motivate teachers of color to stay.

## THE EQUITYED FRAMEWORK

The framework was initially developed to support the United Way of New York City's ReadNYC initiative.[8] My colleague Tanya Friedman, an equity literacy expert, and I have used this framework in our work with teachers. This framework can serve as a tool for school and district capacity building to enable teachers to effectively and powerfully educate black and Latino/a students and students whose lives are affected by poverty. The framework includes four components: (1) the cultivation of an equity mind-set, (2) the development of an empowering culture of adult learning, (3) culturally relevant and rigorous student learning experiences, and (4) the effective mobilization and alignment of talent, resources, and strategy. Collectively, these four components frame professional learning and leadership efforts for all teachers as well as district work to advance the practices of millennial teachers of color.

### Equity mind-set

An equity mind-set is defined as possessing an up-to-date understanding of the reality of and reasons behind educational inequity in the United States, coupled with a commitment to hold high expectations for the educational success of all students—particularly those of color and/or students who live in conditions of poverty. Many teachers (as well as school leaders) have not had sufficient opportunity to contemplate the roles that race, culture, sexual orientation, socioeconomic status, immigration status, native language, and implicit bias play on beliefs, values, and actions and on the importance of affirming diversity. The intended results of an equity mind-set are actions to provide the right educational opportunities for all students to ensure that each student gets the support needed to be successful in school, college, and life. An equity mind-set is necessary to affirm diversity and to see it as strength. Educators who possess an equity mind-set are more likely to engage in multiple strategies to close the achievement gap. They are also more open to turning problems and challenges into opportunities with solutions and are less likely to engage in deficit thinking. An equity mind-set supports the development and delivery of additional teaching, learning, and programmatic resources to ensure that learning gaps are addressed and rigorous grade-level learning and above becomes the norm.

### Empowering culture of learning

An empowering culture of learning is defined as classroom, school, and professional learning environments replete with learner-centered activities that affirm the expression of diverse perspectives, involve collaborative problem solving, and foster development of student and teacher plans and products aligned to clear learning goals and outcomes. Within empowering cultures of learning, learners appreciate effective effort, collaboration, challenge, success, and failure as useful feedback. The facilitators of empowering cultures of learning can include students, teachers, instructional coaches, consultants, and/or school leaders who view their role as providing support and guidance. Empowering cultures of learning for students are impossible without empowering cultures of learning for educators. Schools and districts can create the space for this work within every classroom and content area and for all professional learning activities. Educators should not have to leave their school or district to attend an engaging professional development workshop or a phenomenal conference to feel energized or excited about new learning.

### Culturally relevant rigorous teaching and learning

Culturally relevant and rigorous teaching and learning is defined as a teaching and learning practice that assumes student success based on high expectations informed by student culture, racial identity, community, and/ or social justice needs and resulting in student work products that involve high levels of thinking, doing, and creating. A culturally relevant teaching and learning practice assumes that students' lived experiences should be part of the school curriculum and posits that students should not be expected to leave their community, their culture, their interests, their values, their needs and/or their identity at the school door.[9] Such a practice allows students to develop a strong sense of their own identities so that they can develop the confidence that will enable them to thrive in school. This is of paramount importance for students of color and students who live in neighborhoods of concentrated poverty because of pervasive views of inferiority, corresponding inequities, and internalized oppression. Through the engagement with real-world and culturally informed learning activities and projects, students can cultivate their own equity mind-set as well as the inclination and ability to work for change in their school, community, and world. Culturally relevant pedagogy involves the community, uses culture to promote racial identity, treats culture and racial identity as assets, educates all about racism and racial uplift, develops caring relationships informed by culture, and assumes success.[10]

### Effective mobilization and alignment of resources, talent, and strategy

The final component of the EquityEd framework is the effective mobilization and alignment of resources, talent, and strategy. Providing the best for students of color and students of poverty and the educators of all backgrounds who serve them requires a very deliberate strategy. Often, due to the low-performing status of a school or district, there are multiple accountability requirements to be met and which often take precedence over a teaching and learning focus. Such schools or districts are often recipients of diverse funding streams tied to a set of discrete deliverables. Additionally, numerous challenging factors—federal, state, and district mandates; school reputation and rating; teacher and school leader turnover; societal perspectives of low-performing schools and/or students of color; schools in neighborhoods of concentrated poverty and public schools where students of color form the majority; and the multiple needs of students, staff, and the community—intersect to create a pervasive sense that full solutions are impossible, and one can only do what one can. A deliberate strategy and corresponding mobilization and alignment of all resources and talent is imperative to enable all within a district to stay focused on the possible: stellar student achievement.

## STEPS TO STRENGTHEN PROFESSIONAL LEARNING FOR ALL TEACHERS

To advance the practices of millennial teachers of color and their work with students of color, here are three recommendations and corresponding activities, based on the EquityEd framework, to strengthen professional learning for all teachers: (1) cultivate a districtwide equity mind-set, (2) lead the way by creating empowering cultures of learning, and (3) use culturally relevant texts as a springboard for culturally relevant and rigorous student learning.

### Recommendation 1: Cultivate a districtwide equity mind-set

An equity mind-set does not develop overnight. Mine began to form in my childhood through conversations with my parents about my black identity, through the books and cultural experiences shared with me, and through attending an elementary school with a philosophy of integration and social justice. My own equity mind-set became strengthened as my work as an educator and a doctoral student solidified my understanding of the vast inequalities that exist and the power of education to transform student learning and outcomes. These experiences framed my strong social, cultural, and political connections to people of color of all backgrounds. At the same time, it is my good fortune to also have white colleagues, friends and family members, and LBGTQ colleagues who positioned me to believe in equity and to work for it. My mind-set development has occurred over the course of my lifetime and has required a lot of reflection and work with others to use it for education improvement.

We cannot assume that millennial teachers have an equity mind-set or that millennial teachers of color have an inherent commitment to the education of students of color. Some teachers are not initially able to distinguish between equity and equality, often confusing equity with fairness, but they are eager and open to learning.[11] Educators need opportunities to learn about equity and then form their own understandings of the purpose of education and make their personal commitments. While some actions can and may need to be implemented quickly, fostering an equity mind-set takes time and focus. A one-day professional development workshop will not suffice. Just as we ask teachers to include modifications for English language learners and students with disabilities on every lesson plan, we need them to think about how every lesson and class routine can be designed to support the success of black and Latino/a students.[12] Several strategies can be implemented to cultivate an equity mind-set in teachers of all backgrounds and generations. Cultivating a districtwide equity mind-set will help to establish a culture that is a welcoming environment for millennial teachers of color.

## Strategy 1: Adopt a definition of equity

Using the EquityEd framework, districts and/or schools can establish or adopt definitions and goals for equity. These terms can be used to support productive dialogue and the goals can inform the district or school mission and school and professional development plans. Two examples: "To reach and teach all our students, staff will create rigorous, culturally relevant, and innovative teaching and learning strategies" and "to model our understanding of diversity, staff and students will be able to express their diverse experiences and corresponding perspectives and use them to serve our students."

In developing the definition of equity, district leadership should enlist the involvement of their teachers of color and ensure that the perspectives of their millennial teachers of color are included. The right definitions and goals can set the stage for millennial teachers of color to be inspired, purposeful, and supported.

## Strategy 2: Conduct focus groups

After the definitions and goals are established, districts can establish focus groups where all staff have the opportunity to talk about their culture with their colleagues; explore their beliefs about the connection between culture, race, socioeconomic status, gender, sexual orientation, and education; and discuss their understandings of the educational trajectories of the students in their school and the connection of all these variables to education for equity. Our experience suggests that all by themselves, these focus groups can jump-start the development of an equity mind-set based on the questions, perspectives, and experiences heard from colleagues. In one school we worked with, the focus group was the first time the staff had participated in any conversations about culture, race, or equity. These focus groups can at the very least promote a beginning awareness of equity issues and provide the opportunity for critical self-reflection.[13]

Consider these examples of focus group questions:

1. When you think of culture, what thoughts come to your mind?
2. How would you define your culture? What aspects of your social and cultural identities are most important to you?
3. How does culture in general and your culture specifically play a role in your work in your school?
4. How would you describe the cultures of the students in your school?
5. How might students' cultures affect their ability to succeed academically?
6. How might cultural differences and/or similarities between staff and students enhance or impede the school's educational objectives and student learning?
7. What unique role can teachers of color play in the improved achievement of students of color?
8. How do you and/or your team define equity? What pressing equity issues are students and families in your school community facing?
9. What cultures are represented in the school community you serve? In what ways does the school staff match the family and student cultures? What are the cultural assets?
10. To what degree are student learning experiences rigorous and culturally relevant? How do you know?
11. What action steps, informed by an equity mind-set, can be taken to strengthen the learning community to ensure that adults and students can access the skill, support, confidence, and resources to succeed?

*Strategy 3: Implement a series of equity workshops*

Districts can offer a series of workshops related to equity and education. These workshops should be open to all staff, and each workshop should include time for reflection on the implications of the workshop for one's practice and action planning. Ideally, the workshops should be offered during the workday to encourage participation. The content of the series can be customized based on the needs of the district, but the following outline can serve as a starting point.

Workshop 1: Exploring equity issues related to our students and their families

Workshop 2: Exploring the cultural assets of our students and their families

Workshop 3: Encountering deficit perspectives; how do I disrupt this mind-set?

Workshop 4: The research on teachers of color; what can we all learn?

Workshop 5: Our district equity mind-set; what does it mean in practice?

### Strategy 4: Allow affinity groups to form

Affinity groups offer benefits for teachers of color. They are well documented in the literature as a necessary strategy to support students and teachers of color. Affinity groups can be used to encourage teachers of color to form connections, support each other's development, share experiences, and develop ideas about how to use their experiences and perspectives as teachers of color to improve student achievement. District leaders must assert the importance of these groups, be able to stand up to any pushback about these groups being separatist or racist, and provide time for staff to meet within the school day or offer compensation for meetings held after the school day.

### Strategy 5: Form an equity scholars' teacher leadership group and school leader equity group

Leadership is needed to shepherd a district and its school to a place where all educators and staff hold extraordinarily high expectations for student achievement, where individual staff members feel empowered to speak up and interrupt a deficit perspective, and where staff can work together to close any achievement gap and provide stellar learning to all students. Principals need opportunities to think together, collaborate on how to lead with an equity mind-set, form empowering cultures of learning, and integrate culturally relevant curricula. Invariably, in any district, there will be teachers and school leaders who currently possess a passion to learn more about equity and to lead the way in their school communities. Districts can secure an internal or external facilitator to implement a teacher leader and a school leader group to explore equity deeply and develop district and school equity practices and transformative teaching and learning practices. Millennial teachers of color appreciate the opportunity to share dilemmas, learn together, and create action plans with other like-minded teachers. In one professional learning setting, their conversations surfaced specific school-based issues they wanted to address, such as the structure of professional development, the approach to family engagement activities, and the practice of tracking students by test scores. The EquityEd framework can be used to examine various school practices through the lens of equity and provide young teachers the opportunity and support to reflect on their perceptions and devise next steps to address inequities.

### Recommendation 2: Lead the way by creating empowering cultures of learning

Educators, then, need school and district leaders who act from a belief that teachers can also learn at high levels. To provide empowering cultures of learning for students, teachers need to work, learn, and grow in empowering cultures of adult learning. Often schools with large numbers of students of color and/or students of poverty are subject to significant accountability regulations. Educators regularly experience pressure to implement rigid curriculum and professional development approaches that limit the breadth and depth of what our students can learn, as well as the extent to which teachers can integrate their own experience, knowledge, and creativity into the classroom.

Millennial teachers of color need a supportive and empowering environment so they can learn, work, and grow as well as identify, plan, and implement improvements. All professional learning, including coaching, workshops, classes, and/or collaborative planning opportunities, needs to be offered within the context of supportive learning, and should model that approach as well as teach it. As teachers develop their equity mind-set and believe that students can learn at high levels, they need support to develop the skills to ensure student progress that closes the gaps and reinforces learning.

The cultivation of an equity mind-set and rigorous, engaging, culturally relevant teaching and learning doesn't necessarily make the work easier, but will make teachers' efforts more effective. Closing the opportunity gap requires thoughtful and strategic work over time. School leaders, teachers, community-based organizations, and parents need support to offset the barrage of new curricula, new assessments, and new standards with an unswerving equity mind-set and practice, yet they have not had the benefit of consistent, high-quality, supportive professional learning. School leaders and millennial teachers need support and inspiration to develop successful teaching and learning experiences that ensure student learning. For millennial teachers to foster confident, inspired learners who achieve at high levels, they need consistent empowering and interactive professional learning that explicitly models what they need to create for students. It is imperative that district and school leaders thoughtfully plan, organize, and lead empowering cultures of adult and student learning. When teachers report the cause of burnout, the feeling that their work is not making a difference outweighs the amount of work.

There are multiple entry points for school and district leaders who intend to develop empowering cultures of learning for all their learners, both adults and children, but support and accountability need to exist in balance.

*Entry Point 1: Set the stage for empowered adult learning*

At an opening staff conference, district and school leaders should share with teachers their own examples of learning how to teach and learning how to lead. They should provide examples of successful learning and practice as well as examples of failure. In describing their failures or missteps, they should delineate for staff their own learning associated with those failures. District and school leaders should explain to staff that it is okay to fail as long as they use failure as feedback to grow and improve their teaching practice. District and school leaders should communicate that the district will provide multiple opportunities for staff learning. Leaders should communicate that they will not penalize staff for not being knowledgeable on a topic, but they will hold staff accountable for learning and then sharing that learning. District and school leaders should also communicate the district vision for equity and their expectation that teachers will work together to develop a repertoire of excellent teaching and learning practices within the context of an equity mind-set to serve all students well.

*Entry Point 2: Schedule initial and ongoing planning meetings with all teachers, including millennial teachers of color*

District or school leaders should schedule initial planning meetings with each teacher. The purpose of these meetings can include (1) to develop an understanding of the insights, goals, and experiences that the teacher is hoping to use in his/her practice; (2) to develop an understanding of the teaching strengths and learning needs to inform a customized professional development plan; (3) to discuss ideas about how to improve the learning and school experiences of students of color; and (4) to develop a plan of action to help the teacher meet her/his goals. District and school leaders can use the information gathered in these meetings to leverage resources to provide professional development as well as scheduling support to allow millennial teachers of color to engage in targeted work to facilitate the learning and success of students of color and/or other populations of students.

*Entry Point 3: Provide opportunities for millennial teachers of color to share professional learning with their colleagues and learn from other teachers of color*

In a safe-to-fail culture, the teachers leading professional development don't need to be the most accomplished or the most confident, but they should be the teachers who are passionate about developing their practice and improving student results. Indeed, inviting millennial teachers of color to share their perspectives and their efforts to meet the learning needs of their students through an equity lens can shift the conversation and begin to change school culture. Using the EquityEd framework or a school's own definition of equitable teaching practice as a starting place, millennial teachers of color can lead their colleagues in a process of self-assessment and action planning. Tanya Friedman describes how this might work: "Teachers I have worked with described some of the most effective professional development as ongoing, collaborative study groups where participants chose topics to pursue, designed a course of study, had equal voice, and created quick feedback loops of learning, implementing, and reflecting. These kinds of collaborative inquiry groups become even more powerful when the participants or facilitators frame the learning around issues of equity.[14]

*Entry Point 4: Solicit ongoing feedback and ideas from millennial teachers of color on the quality of the professional learning and their experiences as teachers of color*

For multiple reasons, millennial teachers of color may be hesitant to share honest feedback on the professional learning they're receiving and on their experiences of a school culture. Because of this, it's incumbent on school leaders to actively solicit feedback in a variety of ways. One essential way is to schedule periodic one-to-one or small-group meetings with millennial teachers of color where the agenda is entirely focused on listening to them describe what things support their development as an effective teacher, what isn't working well for them, and what ideas they have. School leaders might use the EquityEd framework to structure the conversation. It's important that these meetings do not have a dual purpose of giving feedback on the teacher's practice or participation. Additionally, regular written feedback from millennial teachers of color can provide critical data for school leaders on the effectiveness of professional learning offerings and on how teachers of color experience the school climate.

## Recommendation 3: Use culturally relevant text and guiding questions as a springboard for culturally relevant pedagogy

Despite the efforts of some teacher education programs, some millennial teachers of color, like some of their white colleagues, feel unprepared to integrate culturally relevant approaches into their instruction. Through discussions with millennial teachers of color, through the survey, and through coaching support, I heard that many are concerned that they don't have the necessary skills to do this work, and some feel as though they are expected to do it without support. They realize that their own K–12 schooling, college, and teacher preparation did not afford them opportunities to learn about their own culture, the culture of others, or culturally responsive teaching.

Culturally relevant texts—those that reflect the life experience and cultural history of students in engaging and empowering ways—are an easy and essential way to jump-start school transformation. They also set the stage for school- or districtwide culturally relevant practices. Many of the curricula used in districts have a dearth of culturally relevant texts, and even when they are part of the curriculum, there is often little if anything to support their use in culturally relevant ways. Districts can take the following steps to integrate culturally relevant text within the existing curriculum and to provide millennial teachers of color with special opportunities to use such text to motivate and engage students of color.

*Step 1: Communicate an explicit commitment to the use of culturally relevant text*

District and school leaders need to make an explicit commitment to culturally relevant texts and encourage, not discourage, teachers to find such texts and other resources that fit into their programs. In some cases, this means that district and school leaders need to expand their definition of what fidelity to a curriculum can mean and consider substituting culturally relevant texts as enhancing a curriculum rather than not following it. Discussions with millennial teachers of color reveal high levels of student disengagement with the texts that are part of mandated curriculum, yet in many of their schools replacing a text is not allowed.

*Step 2: Provide professional development on how to use culturally relevant texts in meaningful ways*

We have had overwhelmingly positive responses from millennial teachers of color when we introduced them to culturally relevant texts and showed them how to develop questions that would help students make high-level connections with the texts. The teachers deeply appreciated the opportunity to use texts that celebrated their students' communities and identities, and prompted discussions that touched on cultural and racial identity with their young students.

For some millennial teachers of color, the books and questions helped them think about their own racial and cultural identities, and how they enact these identities in their classrooms. Some realized that they had never been explicit with their students about their own backgrounds and identities, and understood that is an essential step in supporting students to build their own positive cultural and racial identities. Without exception, teachers observed a higher level of engagement in their students, noting especially students' ability to make connection across various texts. Several teachers also mentioned the personal empowerment they felt using culturally relevant texts and reflected on how their own increased inspiration and connection to their cultural and racial identity contributed to a more positive classroom environment around literacy.

*Step 3: Ask rigorous, culturally relevant questions to support student and teacher engagement with the text and to integrate the text into existing curricula*

Importantly, millennial teachers of color were most excited about the way that culturally relevant texts and questions sparked higher-order thinking in their students, and how that engagement and connection with the texts paved the way for academic conversations. The following are examples of questions that can guide the use of the texts.

- How does this text relate to my life, the learning objective, the course?
- How does this book help me understand my culture, my language, my family, my community?
- What do I already know about my cultural identity?
- What do I know about the cultural identity of my classmates?
- How can I gain strength from my cultural identity?
- What more do I want to know?

- What would I like to learn more about and create?
- How does culture or cultural and racial identity impact what happens in this text?

*Step 4: Provide opportunities for millennial teachers of color to develop curriculum and/or student work products informed by the texts*

Culturally relevant texts can and should play a larger role in the curriculum than just as relatable materials for a literacy program. Culturally relevant texts should be integrated across the curriculum and can be the center of interdisciplinary units and a springboard for student projects. Millennial teachers of color whom we worked with used culturally relevant text that explored and celebrated a character's cultural and racial identity as a starting place for students' investigations of their own cultural and racial identities. Other teachers used stories about a character's relationship to their students' community to spark a study of that community. Teachers need dedicated time and coaching to develop or expand curriculum.

However, in our work with millennial teachers of color, this kind of curriculum planning supported their development as practitioners of culturally relevant pedagogy more than any other professional learning experience. Planning culturally relevant curriculum and designing student work products helped them to synthesize and integrate definitions of culturally relevant pedagogy with their own teaching practice and their best learning experiences. It is important that culturally relevant texts are not just an add-on to the main curriculum, but that teachers have the chance to build curriculum around their content and themes.

## CONCLUSION

Our country possesses the resources to effectively educate all students, close the achievement gap, and offer additional learning opportunities to ensure that students of color receive an education that prepares them for college and careers. While the value of teachers of color is clear and supported by research, we have not leveraged the experiences of veteran teachers of color to inform district practice and we are not actively cultivating, listening to, and using the experiences of the current generation's millennial teachers of color. If millennial teachers of color have been successfully recruited by school districts, districts would be well served to support their talent and advance their practices throughout their district community.

Districts can:

- Articulate the district expectation for an equity mind-set and commitment to the development of practices and strategies that target students of color, address societal challenges, and provide social justice learning opportunities.
- Hire and support a significant number of millennial teachers of color so that no one is the only one. Communicate the intent to recruit, hire, cultivate, and advance the practices of millennial teachers of color to enable their ideas and practices to inform classroom, school, and district transformation.
- Use the EquityEd framework to cultivate a district equity mind-set for all teachers, educators, staff, and parents. This will serve to lessen the instances of teachers of color being isolated and increase the likelihood that the perspectives and practices of millennial teachers of color will be appreciated and acted upon.
- Communicate directly to millennial teachers of color the district's understanding of their importance and the district's interest in adapting practices and ways of doing business to engage this generation. Encourage millennial teachers of color to develop new, innovative, even radical solutions for student learning.
- Aggressively develop professional learning opportunities and programs to support the improved learning and outcomes of students of color and students of poverty. Provide opportunities for millennial teachers of color to lead some of this work and for all interested teachers and staff to do so collaboratively.

While this chapter has focused on steps that school districts can implement to support millennial teachers of color in their professional learning and practices, the EquityEd framework can be used by teacher education institutions, community-based organizations, nonprofits, and other entities committed to transforming the life trajectories of students of color and students of poverty through empowering educational practices.

*Acknowledgments*

*The author would like to thank Tanya Friedman for her support with this chapter and the United Way of New York City for funding some of the work represented in this chapter.*

# 8

# Removing Barriers to the Recruitment and Retention of Millennial Teachers of Color

Zollie Stevenson Jr.

Since 2011, $15 billion in federal funds have been provided to state education agencies (SEAs) and, through SEAs, to school districts for the preparation, recruitment, and retention of qualified teachers using Elementary and Secondary Act (ESEA) Title II funds. Title II funds are specifically provided to help states and school districts recruit and prepare new teachers and to support and compensate teachers already in the classroom.[1] For millennial teachers of color, the Title II funds have likely contributed to the increase in the percentage of teachers of color since the 1980s from 12 percent to 17 percent of the teaching population.[2]

Although the numbers of African American, Latino/a, Asian Pacific, and Native American teachers in public schools has increased, the retention of millennial teachers of color in the public school systems is often stymied by systemic factors inherent in the licensing, preparation, hiring processes, and working conditions in schools, as well as the lack of autonomy of teachers of color. Specifically, Andrew Rotherham of Education Sector said of Title II funds that "tangible results from these efforts are scant, and there is little evidence that these funds are driving the sort of changes needed to help schools recruit, train, place, induct, and compensate quality teachers or changes that are aligned with broader human capital reform efforts in education."[3]

This chapter focuses on factors that have been identified from the field and research as having an impact on the recruitment and retention of millennial teachers of color in the public schools. Among those factors are (1) how federal Title II funds are used in school districts to recruit and retain teachers of color, (2) hiring and placement practices that impact teachers of color in school districts, (3) school affect issues, (4) state legislative actions that impact school district recruitment and retention practices, (5) district recruitment and retention efforts, and (6) collaborative efforts between school districts and universities. Additionally, strategies to improve the recruitment and retention of millennial teacher of color will be outlined.

## USE OF FEDERAL TITLE II FUNDS TO SUPPORT PREPARATION, RECRUITMENT, INCENTIVES FOR, AND RETENTION OF TEACHERS

My experience as a school district, state education agency, federal, and higher education administrator suggests that there are several areas where states, districts, and institutions can leverage current efforts to create diverse teaching and learning communities. Based on my years of service as the federal Title I director at the US Department of Education, I know how districts, which receive 95 percent of the Title II funding, spend these funds: they use them primarily to fund teacher professional development, to reduce class sizes, and to provide salary incentives to teachers in high-need content areas. Thus, the district focus is more on providing professional development to make sure existing teachers receive the additional training opportunities necessary to be effective in their classrooms, rather than having a primary focus on retaining existing teachers, even though recruitment and retention of minority teachers is an acceptable use of Title II funds.[4]

There has been significant federal investment in the preparation, recruitment, and retention of teachers. ESEA Title II funds may be used to increase the presence of teachers of color in K–12 schools. Ninety-five percent of Title II funds that a state receives from the federal government must be provided to the school districts for specific Title II activities. Chait and Miller reported that in 2008–09, 39 percent of the federal Title II funds was used by school districts to pay for professional development of teachers, support staff, and principals and 38 percent was used to provide teacher incentives and to lower class size.[5]

For example, the Colorado Department of Education analyzed how its school districts were using Title II funds and found that nearly 65 percent of the monies were being spent on professional development, 15 percent on class size reduction, 6 percent on recruitment and retention, and 2 percent on preparing highly qualified teachers.[6] Of the federal funds spent on recruitment and retention in Colorado, 63 percent was spent on induction and support for new teachers, 20 percent on teacher mentoring, 9 percent on recruitment activities, and 6 percent on teacher advancement activities. Likewise, Alyson Klein reported that Delaware has used Title II funds primarily to provide professional development to help teachers personalize student learning, and designates only a small amount of the funds for the recruitment and hiring of teachers.[7] In fact, Terrenda White noted that thirty-one states have minority recruitment policies and ten states have state-supported recruitment programs.[8]

In contrast, from 2011 through 2016, federal Title II competitive grant funds for school leader recruitment and support ranged from a high of $29 million in 2011 to lows of $16 million in both 2015 and 2016.[9] Title II school leader funds are focused on professional learning, alternative preparation programs, and opportunities to support collaboration between principals and teachers, ideally focused for use in districts with a high population of poor and minority children.[10] In addition to the small amount of funds available to support leadership development, the fact that these grants were competitive and thus not accessible to every school district limited the viability of this pot of Title II funds as a conduit for improving school leaders. From my experience, most of the thirteen thousand-plus school districts in the United States do not have the grant-writing infrastructure in place to even compete for these funds. As reported by Ingersoll and May, teachers who perceived their school leaders as good leaders had lower turnover rates than did schools perceived as having poor leaders.[11] The federal contribution to school leadership recruitment and support needs to be rethought and more funds made available to provide good leadership to schools with the greatest need and highest teacher turnover.

After so many decades of focusing federal Title II funds on a broad view of teacher professional development and smaller class sizes, perhaps the time has come to shift district use of ESEA Title II funds to focus more on strategies that will provide color-blind selection and placement processes for teachers of color and provide training and supports that will engage teachers in their learning environments. In addition, if good leadership encourages minority teachers to continue to teach in high-need schools, then perhaps one of the strategies to strengthen leadership that promotes teacher retention is to provide federal formula grant funding to districts for use in supporting schools with the greatest needs, rather than providing competitive grant opportunities for a small amount of funding for which only schools with well-developed grant writing offices are able to compete.

## HIRING AND PLACEMENT OF MILLENNIAL TEACHERS OF COLOR

There is disproportionality in the selection and placement of millennial teachers of color in schools. This opinion is supported by the work of D'Amico and colleagues as well as Klein.[12] Documentation supports my belief that black and Hispanic teacher candidates are not hired in the same proportions as white teacher candidates, and when teachers of color are hired, they are often placed in the most challenging settings and circumstances.[13]

D'Amico et al. analyzed the extent to which race was associated with some principals' hiring decisions in a large district, including the rates at which black and white candidates applied for teaching positions and the rates at which they were hired, as well as the demographics of the school district.[14] They found that black candidates were less likely to receive a job offer. When black teachers were offered teaching positions, they were most often placed in struggling schools with large minority and/or poor populations.

Rebecca Klein has focused on the role of racial/ethnic discrimination in the hiring process many school districts use in selecting millennial teachers of color.[15] The hiring process for many school districts entails the submission of an application for employment to a centralized district human resources department. After being processed to determine that minimum requirements for employment have been met, the applications are sent to school principals or school committees. Interviews are set up and decisions are made regarding whom to hire.

Klein cites teacher employment data for an unnamed school district in 2012 in which black and white teacher applicants were equally qualified to teach, but white teachers received a disproportionate number of job offers.[16] In the example cited only 6 percent of the black teachers received offers, although 13 percent of the job applicants were black. Seventy percent of the applicants were white and of that percentage, 77 percent received job offers. Asian and Hispanic teachers were hired proportionate to their representation in the application pool. The disproportionality was unique to black teacher applicants.

Additionally, Klein's study showed that black principals and schools with high percentages of high-poverty families and minority students disproportionately hired black teachers. To the surprise of the school district, this hiring pattern had persisted over time; it was not a fluke incident that occurred in 2012.

While millennial teachers of color like the idea of teaching and view it to be a worthy profession, the reality of working in high-stress settings and providing the extra effort to teach students who have not received the needed educational supports at school or at home causes these teachers to burn out and to leave. In addition, issues related to the hiring process and the disproportionate placement of teachers of color in the most challenging schools with the fewest resources also impact the length of time that a millennial teacher of color will stay in a school.

## SCHOOL AFFECT: WORKING CONDITIONS AND THE ABSENCE OF TEACHER VOICE IN SCHOOL DECISION MAKING

It is my belief that issues such as the disproportionate placement of millennial teachers of color in resource-deprived, high-poverty, and high-minority school settings where the environment is more like a prison than a school significantly contribute to their desire to leave the field of teaching. National Center for Education Statistics (NCES) survey findings as cited by Aragon inform us that minority teachers leave their schools at higher rates than nonminority teachers.[17] Minority teachers of color self-reported that they are disproportionately assigned to schools with high-minority, poor student populations with limited resources.[18] Attrition rates for teachers of color can be attributed, according to White, to three policy-related sources: school and student characteristics, school working conditions, and accountability mandates and sanctions.[19] Ingersoll and May concurred that those organizational conditions, such as the level of teacher involvement in decision making and the individual classroom autonomy, were more significant factors in minority teacher turnover than were salary or professional development.[20]

The 2015–2016 *School Survey on Crime and Safety* provides a snapshot of crime, violence, discipline, and safety in US public schools.[21] Among its findings, the survey stated that the rate of incidents of violence per 1,000 students was 16:1,000 in high schools, 27:1,000 in middle schools, and 15:1,000 in elementary schools. Threats of violence by a student with a weapon occurred in about 9 percent of the schools surveyed compared to threats of violence without a weapon (39 percent). Twenty-five percent of the schools reported an incident of distribution, possession, or use of illegal drugs in the school by students. However, it should be noted that the data in this survey was self-reported, and it is possible that the true numbers might paint a more negative picture of the conditions teachers must deal with.

Boyd et al. studied the influence of school administrators on first-year teachers' decisions to stay on the job.[22] The authors considered multiple measures of school context and found that working conditions (work environment, safety, infrastructure, etc.) and administrative support were important in the retention of teachers. Correlations between school context measures such as teacher influence, administration, staff relations, students, facilities, and safety showed that the highest correlations were between administration and facilities and administration and students. The lowest correlations were between teacher influence and facilities and safety. In terms of relative risk factors, administration was statistically significant for first-year teachers who left the school district or transferred to another school in the district, and teacher influence was the risk factor that was most predictive of which teachers would leave the district. Their study noted that it was not the student composition of the schools but the quality of the school leadership, and their engagement with and support of faculty in the school, that influenced whether teachers stayed or left.

The climate and culture of schools that are racially/ethnically diverse can play a role in the comfort level of minority teachers of color who navigate all the hurdles to be employed as teachers. Teachers of color sometimes find themselves as victims or in positions that require them to engage in policies that they do not agree with—policies that impact them or their students.[23] French cited antiquated policies that conflicted with current thinking and the absence of resources as factors that teachers named as the basis for their dissatisfaction and ultimate departure from the teaching profession.

At a meeting of the Education Writer's Association (EWA), Bristol described the different types of racism that blacks experience in school settings.[24] He offered several examples during his EWA panel presentation, including an episode in which a black educator shared a fellow educator's description of black children in the school as acting like monkeys. He also told of a black educator who resigned from his high school post because he was fed up with students being frisked by the principal in search of cell phones. The regular frisking of students made the teacher feel as if he was in a prison rather than a school. Factors such as these cause new teachers to lose the optimism they had when they entered the profession.

Bristol's research showed that racial hostility was experienced by black educators in both high- and low-performing schools. He also noted that black educators stayed longer in the schools that were high performing. Bristol further noted that black male teachers were often assigned the role of disciplinarian in high-poverty schools, which was another disincentive to stay in a school. For millennial teachers of color, school placement and the school culture encountered after placement likely play a role in their satisfaction with teaching as a profession and the likelihood that they will continue to teach.

## STATE LEGISLATIVE ACTIONS THAT IMPACT SCHOOL DISTRICTS' RECRUITMENT AND RETENTION OF MINORITY MILLENNIAL TEACHERS

How are efforts to recruit and retain millennial teachers of color being addressed by state governments, which have the responsibility to develop and implement educational policy? White reports that thirty-one states have approved legislation focused on the recruitment of minority teachers.[25] The paths that states are using to support teacher recruitment include providing financial incentives, creating government mandates, supporting specific types of recruitment programs, establishing recruitment centers, and establishing alternative certification programs. These efforts have contributed to the success that has occurred nationally in recruiting teachers of color into classrooms.

Examples of four such efforts are found in Colorado, Connecticut, Oregon, and Minnesota.[26] Legislative actions to support the recruitment, preparation, development, and retention of minority teachers include Colorado's House Bill (HB) 1175, passed in 2014, and Connecticut's Senate Bill (S.B.) 1098 (2015), both of which promoted strategies and additional support resources to increase the recruitment and retention of effective minority teachers. In Oregon, S.B. 755 (2013) requires a 10 percent increase in the number of minority teachers and administrators working in school districts and education service agencies as well as the number of minority students enrolled in state teacher education programs.[27]

Both Colorado (2014) and Connecticut (2015) studied minority pass rates on teacher licensing exams and required that changes be made if barriers such as cultural bias or technical problems affecting validity and reliability were uncovered. If the tests were found to be technically sound, then the state education agency was directed to develop a strategy to help minority teacher candidates to be successful on the licensing exam. The Oregon

Teacher Standards and Practices Commission eliminated the rule requiring the passage of a basic skills test for teacher licensure in June of 2015.

In Connecticut (2015), a new requirement was established mandating that
its education department review and approve alternative certification programs in the state and establish a teacher pathway pilot program to recruit
students of color to pursue a career in teaching. The pathway program is
orchestrated through state universities but targets minority high school
students. Minnesota (2015) implemented a new policy that permits people
with college degrees but without teaching certification to enter the profession and receive training that would lead to state licensure.

The states discussed in this section have taken steps to recruit and/or
retain minority teachers of color. Of interest are their efforts to look at cultural and statistical bias in required licensing tests and the steps taken to
provide supportive experiences, alternative certification polices, and scholarships that help millennial students to complete their college degrees and
enter the profession. It should be noted that state legislatures make the
funding decisions to address infrastructure issues (i.e., to repair decaying
schools, rewire for Internet access, etc.) and resource needs of schools. State
legislatures have approved only modest funding increases for infrastructure
and resources beyond the annual budget provisions.

## RECRUITMENT EFFORTS LAUNCHED BY SCHOOL DISTRICTS

Many school districts across the United States have reported that retention
of black and Hispanic teachers is a problem, citing the decline in minorities nationally who are choosing to teach as a career.[28] School districts have
tried many routes and have partnered with others to recruit Hispanic and
black millennial teachers to serve in their districts. Galarza reports that the
Gainesville and Hall County school districts (both in Georgia) have entered
into a faculty exchange agreement with Guanajuato school district in central
Mexico. Teachers from each district spend time in the other school district
as part of an exchange that is structured to help the Georgia teachers relate
culturally to Hispanic students and to strengthen the pipeline of Hispanic
teachers that the Georgia districts are able to recruit.[29] The Guanajuato
school district benefits by having American teachers support its efforts to
teach English and relate to American culture. Gainesville's Hispanic population is 40 percent of the city's population. The surrounding Hall County

school district reported that 87 Hispanic teachers were on board in their district out of 1,825 teachers employed, less than 5 percent of the teaching population.

The cities of Buffalo and Rochester in New York are also working together to recruit teachers of color at historically black colleges and universities (HBCUs) in the southern United States and Puerto Rico.[30] Ten percent of Rochester's students are white, compared to 80 percent of the school district's teachers.

On the opinion page of the *Post Bulletin* newspaper in Rochester, Minnesota, an editorial speaks of the promise of licensing reforms to improve teacher recruitment, especially of minority teachers and teachers in areas such as special education, English as a second language, math, and science.[31] Ninety-six percent of the teachers in Minnesota are white. In Rochester, 37 percent of the families are nonwhite, but only 2.9 percent of the teachers are nonwhite. Rochester has paired with the Austin, Minnesota, school district to form a partnership with Winona State University to train paraprofessionals, most of whom are minorities, to become teachers.

Pairing together makes great sense in terms of sharing the costs and the benefits of recruiting minority teachers of color. Partnerships that allow cross-cultural interchange can be most beneficial in engaging students in their learning and improving their performance outcomes.

## COLLABORATIVE EFFORTS TO RECRUIT AND RETAIN TEACHERS OF COLOR

A university, a school district, and a teacher's union in Buffalo, New York, partnered with the State of New York to recruit high school students to pursue a career in education.[32] Graduates of the Urban Teacher Academy receive job selection preference in the Buffalo school district if they commit to teaching in the school district for five years. High school students learn about special education and urban education while still in high school. When they are education students in college, they will get their field experience in the school district. The program is focused on closing the gap in the teacher/student ratio disparities that exist in the Buffalo city schools. This is another example of a school district working with other partners to supply its own teachers and fill critical resource needs. The build-your-own-teacher-corps model is becoming more prominent as a way for school districts to create a cadre of minority teachers. Some districts are also providing training support that enables their school paraprofessionals to move into the teacher ranks after completing teacher education courses.[33]

In another collaborative effort, Wilmington University in Delaware is one of four recipients of a $500,000 SEED (Supporting Effective Educator Development) grant from the National Center for Teacher Residencies for a year-long teacher residency initiative being implemented by the university's College of Education.[34] The grant is used to provide support for student teachers and their mentors. The Wilmington University initiative is focused on developing new strategies to recruit more teachers of color and bilingual teachers, preparing teachers for content and program areas with critical needs, and increasing teacher retention with partnering school districts. The year-long residency program, developed in collaboration with several Delaware school districts, is particularly focused on high-needs schools. The interns are treated as coteachers during the one-year internship and learn all aspects of the school year. Graduates of the program have experienced a 100 percent hire rate.

Legislative acts and collaborative efforts are just some examples of strategies that can be used to facilitate the recruitment, preparation, and retention of millennial teachers of color. However, the heavy lifting in addressing the challenges of recruitment and retention lies within school district programs, policies, and practices and in what millennial teachers of color, once selected, experience daily inside the public school settings.

## MAKING A DIFFERENCE IN RECRUITMENT AND RETENTION OF MILLENNIAL TEACHERS OF COLOR

Successful recruiting efforts have been stifled by high turnover rates of minority teachers who teach in high-poverty, high-minority school settings.[35] Dealing with the education needs of children with school preparation deficits is challenging, but experience informs me that teaching and learning for high-poverty and minority-majority students often occurs in crumbling infrastructures with many resource needs. Add to this the fact that most teachers do not have much of a say in what and how they teach, a scenario that limits or outright eliminates the creativity inherent in teaching. The additional effort required to teach in such settings becomes very stressful and can result in burnout. Teachers with other options leave schools in those settings.

## Recruitment strategies

A recruitment and selection process needs to be developed that enables teachers of color to receive a fair shot at being placed in schools where white candidates have traditionally been placed. Teachers of color should not disproportionately be placed in the lowest-performing, resource-deprived schools in a district just because the children in those schools might come from low-income homes or look like them. Nothing should be automatic about where a teacher candidate is placed to teach—our schools need to engage with diverse cultures and perspectives. Staffing of schools should be orchestrated in such a way that all students are exposed to white, black, Hispanic, and other racial/ethnic groups in the teaching/learning process.

In response to a question raised in a request for information, Stephanie Aragon of the Education Commission of the States (ECS) cited data from the NCES *Schools and Staffing Survey* to identify three broad recruitment strategies that would help improve minority teacher recruitment: reporting and data, financial investments, and preparation pathways. ECS stated that recent research supports the public reporting of teacher candidate outcomes disaggregated by race, disaggregated public reporting on each district's teacher workforce, and the establishment of forums where minority teachers can share and reflect on their own journey into teaching as a way to generate new ideas for minority teacher recruitment.[36] Those efforts certainly serve to highlight data on millennial teachers of color, but only the latter effort, which encourages teachers of color to examine their teaching experiences, would have an immediate impact on the teachers themselves.

Other practices ECS identified as being productive, based on research studies, included financial investments such as investment in high-quality teacher education programs at institutions of higher learning with high percentages of minority students, generous scholarship support for minority teacher education students, improved compensation packages on par with other professions requiring similar degrees, use of spending flexibilities under the Every Student Succeeds Act to support a variety of learning opportunities for minority teachers, and reducing the cost of achieving teacher certification. There is certainly some benefit to be gained by reaching out to HBCUs and Hispanic-serving colleges and universities as sources of millennial teachers of color, particularly when those institutions can begin the process of preparing their future teachers to function in challenging teaching and learning environments. Early inoculation can help prepare teachers for difficult work settings.

Aragon offers some creative possibilities for recruiting and retaining minority teachers.[37] Developing your own programs and career ladders for educational aides is one such promising practice. A similar path is to grow your own programs to develop future teachers while students are still enrolled in high school—sometimes in middle school—and expose students to shadowing and tutorial opportunities as well as offer the opportunity to earn college credit while still in high school.[38] Other promising practices cited by Aragon include development of incentives and supports that can be used to recruit high school and college students to pursue teaching as a profession, development of school- or community-based teacher preparation programs, making alternative certification programs affordable for minority participants and limiting program requirements to necessary learning experiences, and developing teacher preparation programs designed to meet the unique needs of minority teachers.

The ECS response also addressed disparities in test scores on the exams that teachers must pass in most states to achieve certification.[39] A national analysis of over three hundred thousand Praxis test takers between November 2009 and November 2015 showed a 41.4 percent pass rate gap between African American and Caucasian test takers in mathematics and a 40.8 percent gap in reading. A review and modification of Praxis cut scores by states could increase the number of minority teachers achieving licensure. Perhaps moving from a standardized test to performance-based assessments or portfolio assessment should be considered either individually or as a multimeasure approach to teacher licensure.

## Retention strategies

There are several things that can be done to increase the retention of millennial teachers of color in the public schools. A first step is to shift the emphasis of how ESEA Title II funds are spent at the district level to provide teacher development/incentive programs to teachers of color early in their careers. While still in the decision process or training, those preparing to become teachers should be exposed to classroom settings with positive role models so that they can begin to develop the effective strategies for functioning in a variety of classroom settings.

The environments where teaching occurs need to be transformed from toxic cultures into nurturing ones that offer support for both students and teachers. The environmental stresses of working in a setting that seems more like a jail than a school negate teachers' desire to work in the field of education. Good school leadership encourages teacher retention.[40] Positive school leadership can repair a toxic school work environment. More formula funding should be provided to strengthen principal leadership development and preparation—and move away from discretionary funding. This would require shifting a larger percentage of Title II funds from professional development to the development and preparation of school leaders. A change of this type would also require federal, state, and school district officials to implement stronger parameters regarding the use and monitoring of Title II funds.

Retention strategies that teachers of color felt were supportive, as cited in the ECS response, included innovative teacher education programs that prepare teachers of color to work in urban or high-poverty, high-minority settings; improved working conditions, including teacher participation in school decision making; greater instructional autonomy for teachers; and professional development that is focused on the experiences that teachers of color face in the classroom and school environments.[41] All three areas suffered from the absence of confirmatory research demonstrating the impact of those strategies.

Some of the same factors mentioned in the ECS response were echoed in a root-cause analysis focused on minority high school students and conducted by Eastern Connecticut State University.[42] Of interest were the responses to the open-ended questions. Students were asked what factors would make teaching an attractive profession for them. The dominant student responses were that teacher salaries and compensation (including a nine-month work schedule) were important. Other factors mentioned were the opportunity to influence youth and children and the respect generally afforded teachers.

Being able to teach what one loves without restrictions was also mentioned, as was teaching alongside multiracial and multicultural peers. Perhaps, then, another strategy to retain teachers of color is to make them integral to the teaching and learning process in their schools. The millennials who chose to work as teachers did so because they wanted to make a difference in the lives of the children that they teach. Give them some flexibility to make a difference.

The second question of the Eastern Connecticut State University analysis focused on factors that make teaching less attractive. Long days and stress were mentioned as deterrents along with disrespectful students, student attitudes, and low pay.

## The need for state support

Most state legislatures have moved in the right direction in terms of establishing policies that support the development, recruitment, and retention of teachers of color in schools. However, those same legislatures need to also make sure that funding is available for the instructional resources needed to provide equitable opportunities to children. In most states, school infrastructure support is expected to be provided by school districts and local taxes, with some additional assistance from state agencies. States should provide funds to achieve greater equity in school facilities so that twenty-first-century learning, including being able to access strong Wi-Fi signals, can occur. It is important to focus on school infrastructure and instructional resources so that even schools in high-poverty communities have certain minimum resources and an equitable distribution of support personnel to deal with the additional challenges they encounter daily. Teachers, whether new or veteran, need support personnel who can address their needs as well as those of students.

More states need to adopt legislation that promotes the recruitment and retention of millennial teachers of color, including incentives such as college scholarships, support for graduate school enrollment in education areas, salary supplements for teachers in high-need instructional areas, establishment of support systems, and ongoing professional development and training after teachers enter the classroom. Millennial teachers of color want to be engaged and creative in how they teach the children under their watch, and engaged in decision making about the school climate, policies, and practices.

## Other reasons for attrition by teachers of color

I would be remiss if I did not acknowledge that there are factors other than recruitment and retention policies and practices, including the need for some autonomy in teaching and learning, that impact the tenure of millennial teachers of color. Top among the more personal factors is that there are more competitive opportunities for people of color in the workforce today than ever before. When I was growing up in my predominantly black community in the South, the black middle class was largely composed of mothers who were public school teachers and fathers who worked for the post office or some other government agency. At least one parent of color worked in a white-collar setting. With so many employment options that pay much more than teaching does, millennials are able to choose among many professions. Even if a millennial decides to become a teacher initially, options beyond the classroom may lure them away, often to higher-paying positions. Family-related decisions and personal reasons are another source of attrition. Bottom line, this generation has more employment options than did the generation of baby boomers who preceded them.

## A last thought

Finally, the colorization of our school's student population has been foretold. Our public school populations will become majority minority during the lifetime of most millennials. It is critical that classrooms have teachers of quality who reflect the spectrum of diversity that exists in our world. We need teachers of color so that all children—those of color as well as other children—will be able to see diverse teachers as models of commitment and achievement. Let's break down the barriers that cause millennials to leave our schools.

# 9

# The Double-Edged Sword of Education Policy Trends

Michael Hansen

M illennials, as the generation coming of age in the educator labor force today, will control the future of education policy and will be most affected by its consequences in the years to come. They will inherit the assets and liabilities of education practices from prior generations and act as temporary stewards with an opportunity to make their mark before passing America's public schools on to the next generation. Minorities, as a growing percentage of the school-age populace, will also be increasingly affected by these new education policies. Yet teachers of color are acutely underrepresented in the public teacher workforce, and without significant changes to teacher recruitment and retention practices may not keep pace with the growth of the student population.

Thus, education policies of the future present a double-edged sword for millennial teachers of color: opportunities for influence abound even as risks of continued disenfranchisement increase as well. As minority groups, particularly parents of minority students, grow as a voting bloc, they should be positioned to advocate for their interests in more substantial ways than in the past, and millennial teachers of color could benefit. However, the underrepresentation and historical marginalization of minority teachers will continue to create barriers in the teacher workforce that must be overcome to enable millennial teachers of color to effect change from within the system.

This chapter analyzes millennial minority teachers in a different way than the preceding chapters. I corroborate earlier chapters' narratives with quantitative data from nationally representative surveys of teachers and American households.[1] Additionally, I zoom out, presenting a policy-oriented view of the threats and opportunities for influence described by many of the teachers interviewed for this volume. Ultimately, I aim to identify fruitful policy areas where millennial teachers of color can seize the opportunity to, hopefully, increase both their number and their status in the profession.

## CHARACTERISTICS OF MILLENNIAL MINORITIES

The discussions in the previous chapters—especially chapter 2 (Outtz and Coleman) and chapter 3 (Herrera and Morales)—established a matrix of interrelated characteristics, beyond year of birth, that describe this millennial generation. Before moving on to the intersection of millennials with minorities in the teacher workforce specifically, I find it useful to lay out this matrix:

1. Millennials came of age with the Internet and thus are more engaged with technology in their own lives and in their careers.
2. Millennials are more concentrated in urban areas than other generations and therefore experience increased racial and socioeconomic diversity. With the aid of social media, they envision themselves much more as members of expansive or even global communities rather than being oriented primarily toward family or local communities.
3. Raised in an increasingly multiracial and multicultural society, millennials envision the world through social justice struggles and commonly view their jobs as forms of activism, a position articulated in chapters 5 (Catone and Tahbildar) and 8 (Stevenson). Social media platforms are commonly used to advocate for or mobilize in service of their objectives.
4. Millennials are better educated than previous generations, and therefore have both more employment opportunities and substantial college debt. Perhaps as a consequence of the greater number of opportunities, millennials also switch jobs more frequently, reflecting a change in the labor market in the last fifty years toward transferable skills over specialization.
5. Finally, due to a combination of factors such as higher costs of living in urban areas, lower salaries of social justice–oriented employment, and college debt, millennials face significant financial barriers in accumulating wealth.

Millennial minority teachers demonstrate these characteristics in slightly different ways when compared with the average millennial. First, teachers overall represent a better-educated, less wealthy, and more social-justice-minded subset of the general population. Those characteristics match the preceding description of millennials, making millennial teachers especially prone to express those traits. Additionally, racial and ethnic minority groups have long occupied spaces on the margins of American society, forming their own unique subcultures. Thus, it is reasonable to infer that individuals identifying as both minority and millennial could manifest these characteristics in distinct ways from white millennials.

Millennial teachers of color may demonstrate magnified characteristics on some dimensions in comparison to white millennials (e.g., concentration in urban areas, financial barriers). Data from the American Community Survey bears out these hypotheses—millennial minority teachers are more than 20 percentage points more likely than their white counterparts to teach in urban schools, are 11 percentage points less likely to own their home, and pay $140 more for their monthly rental payment. On other metrics, millennial minorities may just be catching up to or lag slightly behind white millennials due to historical racial inequalities across subgroups (for example, on educational attainment and use of technology, where reported differences across racial groups are slight on both measures).

In a nation with a history of discrimination, millennials of color grew up differently than white millennials and therefore engage with the teaching profession differently. Notably, data from the Schools and Staffing Survey (SASS) show that millennial minority teachers serve many more minority students than white millennials and are roughly twice as likely to teach in charter schools. Household characteristics could be a factor in choosing to become a teacher, and here too millennial minority teachers differ from white millennials: minorities are more than 10 percentage points more likely to be unmarried singles. Millennial minorities also differ in important ways from older teachers of color, with notably lower levels of union membership and a higher stated interest in transferring to other schools.

In this chapter, however, I move beyond descriptive data alone to consider the relationship between education policy trends and the status and representation of minority millennials in the teacher workforce. To do this, I will first call attention to trends in education policy that create both opportunities and obstacles for millennial minority teachers to grow in number and status. I will then analyze successful organizing frameworks that millennial minorities can employ to advocate for change and influence the progress of those trends.

But first, I want to add a note about language. Each racial and ethnic group in this country enters the classroom with a distinct history and culture that has informed its upbringing and philosophy. These identities will affect each group's interests on education policy, with black families likely more concerned about segregation and Hispanic families more concerned about English language learners. Though this book and this chapter group these identities for ease of discussion, I acknowledge the diverse constituencies represented by the terms *minority* or *of color*, and urge researchers and practitioners to consider all these distinct identities in analyzing policy.

## EDUCATION POLICY AS A TESTING GROUND

In education policy, especially in areas where the ground is still shifting, opportunities abound for millennial minority teachers to exert influence but also to lose stature. Millennial minority teachers are particularly vulnerable to policies governing teacher licensure to enter the classroom and teacher evaluation systems that influence how long they stay there. Additionally, school choice policies continue a decades-long trend of expansion, while the Every Student Succeeds Act shepherds a push toward state and local control, potentially empowering low-performing schools and their mostly minority teacher workforce.

### Teacher retention and recruitment policy

From 1987 to 2012, the teacher workforce became more diverse, with increases in both the number and the proportion of minority teachers.[2] The number of minority teachers almost doubled, rising at a rate actually higher than the growth rate of the minority student population.[3] That being said, in chapter 2 Outtz and Coleman presented worrisome signs that minorities, still underrepresented among public school teachers in general, may find even less representation among the rising generation of millennials as they enter the teacher workforce.

Looking beyond the demographic data, along every step of the talent pipeline to the classroom, minorities are less well represented.[4] Teacher candidates themselves primarily determine differences in representation along the earliest steps of this path into the classroom (completing college and choosing to become a teacher), but states can and do manage the entrance of candidates through licensure. Indeed, because the hiring of teachers generally happens at the local level, licensure is the primary mechanism through which states can control their pipeline and therefore should be a target for action to increase minority teacher representation.

In their essence, licensure policies attempt to balance quality with quantity. Based on state staffing requirements and student enrollment, schools need a minimum quantity of eligible teachers; licensure policies, meanwhile, must impose conditions to ensure a minimum level of quality. Tests typically factor prominently in licensure policies. Along with requirements for a college degree and participation in some type of training program, most states require teachers to achieve a certain score on a standardized teacher licensure exam (or certain scores on specific components of a licensure exam). Until very recently, these exams were usually the Praxis series, developed and administered by the Educational Testing Service, or state-specific tests like the California Basic Educational Skills Test.

Passage rates of these licensure exams have historically cut against minority teacher candidates, constituting a formidable barrier to many pursuing a teaching career.[5] If minority teachers were truly less effective than white teachers in the classroom, then differential pass rates could be justified on the basis of ensuring a minimum level of quality. However, evidence from North Carolina suggests Praxis passage rates by race do not correspond to different levels of classroom performance by race (at least between black and white teachers).[6] In fact, based on students' value-added improvements on standardized tests, there was no statistically significant difference in the distributions of teacher performance by race.

Instead, the study found statistically significant benefits to racial matching when black teachers taught black students. In other words, licensure scores effectively screened out more black teacher candidates than white candidates from the workforce, implicitly replacing moderately performing black candidates with weak white ones at the margin. Since white candidates with the weakest scores tended to teach in the most disadvantaged schools serving communities with many black students, these students missed the opportunity of being taught by black teachers who would have been expected to boost achievement from the racial match. Such a phenomenon may plausibly be occurring among other minority teachers and student populations as well, though this is speculation at this point.

In recent years, many states have discontinued the use of the Praxis series of exams in favor of a new teacher assessment called the Teacher Performance

Assessment (widely known as edTPA). EdTPA is designed to provide a more holistic assessment of prospective teachers' practice, through its inclusion of lesson plans and teaching videos to demonstrate efficacy in addition to the standard written assessments. Early evidence from Dan Goldhaber and coauthors suggests that those who pass the exam on the first attempt are, in fact, stronger teachers based on classroom performance in reading, though not in math.[7] Worryingly, though, the authors continue to find evidence of differential passage rates for minorities: Hispanic teachers were three times more likely to fail on the first attempt than non-Hispanic whites.[8]

Some states struggling with teacher vacancies have opted to loosen licensure requirements in recent years.[9] These policies have included the adoption of tiered license policies (where teachers progress to higher tiers over time) or reciprocity for teachers licensed in other states. States also increasingly employ alternative certification paths, with these routes accounting for roughly 20 percent of new entrants into the classroom as of 2013.[10] These alternative licensure paths disproportionately benefit high-minority schools where minority teachers typically serve, with a recent study showing that higher concentrations of economically disadvantaged students and students of color are significantly associated with the share of teachers entering the profession through alternative pathways.[11]

Though many of these routes still require passing a licensure exam, these types of policies disproportionately stand to benefit prospective millennial minority teachers. Teachers entering the workforce either later in their careers or through alternative licensure programs are markedly more diverse than those entering the profession directly from an undergraduate education program.[12] Data from SASS reveal that these trends are even more pronounced among millennial minorities, almost 28 percent of whom reported entering the profession through alternative pathways compared to 23 percent of older minorities and just 14 percent of white millennials. Those same SASS data also show that millennial teachers of color reported thinking about transferring schools more often than older minorities and white millennials, meaning that state licensure reciprocity could disproportionately help this group as well.

Similar to teacher licensure, teacher evaluations attempt to evaluate a teacher's classroom effectiveness based on a limited set of ratings and data points. Due to their somewhat subjective nature, however, they can be vulnerable to bias in assessing what constitutes quality. Under the Obama administration, the vast majority of states updated and strengthened the rigor of their teacher evaluation standards—an issue frequently advanced by Secretary of Education Arne Duncan.[13] Since Duncan's resignation in late 2015, some states have begun to pause or reverse elements of these systems, though most continue to implement these revamped evaluation systems, which include measures of student progress that still impose high stakes on teachers.[14]

Policy makers designed these evaluation structures to increase accountability for teachers, but minority teachers may be particularly threatened by the advancement of these policies. Though the text of such policies may theoretically be neutral on race, risk may emerge from how individual elements of these evaluation systems are assessed. I see three ways these evaluations may threaten millennial minority teachers (who, based on SASS data, are much more likely to serve in high-minority schools than white millennials) and, to a lesser degree, older teachers of color. The data also show that millennial minority teachers teach in urban schools with a greater frequency than these other two groups. Since minority students historically underperform on achievement exams and since local funding formulas historically have underinvested in these schools, today's landscape shows that minority teachers disproportionately serve in schools designated low- or underperforming on school accountability ratings.[15]

First and foremost, these new evaluation systems often include measures that attribute student progress to teachers. It is well known that measures of achievement alone are highly correlated with student background variables like race and family income; hence, measures of student progress that isolate instructional inputs from student backgrounds are strongly preferred. However, these measures may not succeed in removing all vestiges of background and may therefore still include a bias that penalizes the disproportionately minority teachers serving large numbers of disadvantaged students.[16] Though statistical models can remove these penalties through adequate controls and various assumptions about the quality of teaching across schools, states and districts commonly choose not to include such variables in statistical models to avoid holding disadvantaged students to different standards than their better-off peers.

Second, observational ratings of teachers' instruction may also introduce bias into evaluation systems since they are based on an evaluator's subjective assessment of teacher performance against a predefined evaluation rubric. For most teachers outside of tested grades and subjects, these measures typically receive the highest weight in the overall evaluation rating.

Though intended to be focused on the instruction itself and theoretically blind to student factors that may otherwise influence student test scores, these measures are still correlated with classroom compositional factors, including student race and prior student achievement.[17] A recent study of comparisons between low-stakes principal ratings of teachers (collected by researchers only) and high-stakes ratings collected just weeks later for the district's evaluation system supports this conclusion; researchers found the principals' low-stakes assessments of black teachers significantly overpredicted the scores these teachers received on the actual high-stakes ratings.[18]

My third concern with evaluation systems is less specific, but rather an overall skepticism about how well evaluation measures designed with the best intentions can actually overcome common traps of implicit bias inherent in almost all professional settings.[19] Other components of teacher evaluations, such as principals' measures of professionalism or peer review, could suffer from cultural or implicit biases between the raters and teachers, disadvantaging minority teachers.[20] Theoretically, states or districts could vet these measures to check for empirical evidence of such bias, due to either teacher or student characteristics. However, I expect that, because minority teachers' interests tend to be underrepresented in state or district policy discussions of evaluation system design, few systems will actually vet evaluation measures this way.

I do, however, see some reasons for optimism among minorities in more rigorous teacher evaluations. Reporting evaluation scores to teachers promotes beneficial turnover—inducing low-performing teachers to exit and high-performing teachers to stay.[21] Because high-minority schools tend to exhibit the highest rates of teacher turnover (and most often this turnover does not directly benefit students), providing evaluation scores could help stabilize and even improve the quality of the teacher workforce in these contexts.[22] Moreover, rigorous evaluations accompanied by mentor programs appear to be particularly effective ways to promote teacher development and could be especially beneficial in retaining minority teachers in the classroom.[23] If these evaluations are delivered with adequate classroom and professional development supports, principals may better retain millennial teachers of color.[24]

## Expansion of school choice policies

Enrollment in school choice programs—whether in the form of charter schools, vouchers, or education savings accounts—has been steadily expanding over the last two decades.[25] Nationwide, charter schools now serve more than 6 percent of public school students, and several urban areas boast charter sectors that serve more than 20 percent of students.

How do these policy trends affect the status of millennial minority teachers? Due to differences in workforce diversity across the different school sectors—either charter or private in comparison to traditional public schools—the continued expansion of school choice has an ambiguous effect on the representation of minority teachers in the teacher workforce.

Race acts as a prominent fault line in differentiating charter schools from traditional public schools. The decoupling of school management from a school's geographical location (often in minority communities) has been a common point of criticism against the expansion of charter schools. It is this uncomfortable mismatch between charter managers and staff and the student communities they serve that makes Howard Fuller, a well-known charter school supporter and thought leader, somewhat ambivalent about their future prospects: "The one thing that concerns me about the charter movement . . . is the fact that it's the only social movement that I'm aware of where the people most impacted don't lead it. And that remains a significant problem."[26] For example, the takeover of Locke High School in Los Angeles by charter network Green Dot led to the large-scale resignation of a mostly minority teaching force. While test scores and graduation rates improved, achievement remains low overall and the mostly black community was alienated.[27] Similar trends have continued across the country when charter schools replace traditional public schools and their workforce composed mostly of teachers of color, disconnecting communities of color from their allies.[28]

That being said, charter schools represent a potential opportunity to increase the representation of millennial teachers of color. According to SASS data, almost 10 percent of millennial minority teachers serve in charter schools, compared to approximately 5 percent of white millennials and a similar percentage of older minorities. Millennial minority teachers are choosing to work in charters but their ranks are still slim overall, and since charters operate predominantly in urban areas with high-minority populations, the diversity gaps between students and teachers in these schools remain large.

Private schools may also benefit as more expansive school choice policies become more widespread across states. The teacher workforce in private schools is actually slightly more diverse than that observed in public schools as a whole. Overall, 18 percent of teachers in public schools are minorities compared to 22 percent in private schools, and we can examine this split by generation to predict future trends (see table 9.1). Particularly in light of the underrepresentation of minority students in private schools, I find this slightly more diverse workforce curious. Since private schools are predominantly white spaces, their diversification benefits white students while diffusing the political power of teachers of color, who might otherwise be more concentrated in high-minority schools.

Because the diversity of the teacher workforce varies across the different school sectors, the demographic composition of the future teacher workforce may depend in part on whether expanded choice primarily means greater access to private schools (through the use of educational savings accounts, tax credits, or vouchers) or the establishment of more public charter schools. Expanding access to private schools may plausibly result in slightly more minority teachers, but only if those institutions can scale up while maintaining their diversity, a lofty proposition. Charter schools, shown to be attractive to young minority teachers based on SASS data, present opportunities to concentrate millennial minority teachers and therefore increase their political power.

## ESSA and low-performing schools

The No Child Left Behind Act, signed into law in 2002, formally instituted school accountability measures nationwide and established a narrow set of interventions to help schools that failed to meet the new standards. These prescribed interventions intentionally removed autonomy from targeted schools, and in some cases districts, in an effort to accelerate improvement efforts.

TABLE 9.1   Minority representation in the teacher workforce in public and private schools

|  | Baby boomers | Generation X | Millennials |
| --- | --- | --- | --- |
| Minority share in public schools | 16.1% | 19.0% | 17.9% |
| Minority share in private schools | 19.1% | 23.1% | 22.1% |

Source: Author's calculations using American Community Survey, 2015, five-year estimates.

Though well intentioned, these policies effectively undermined minority teachers' influence in these low-performing schools. As mentioned previously, minority teachers disproportionately work in schools that serve large populations of minority students—the same schools commonly identified as failing to make adequate progress on accountability ratings. By disempowering schools, these initiatives indirectly disempowered the schools' minority teachers. No Child Left Behind's recommendations for school turnaround included the wholesale replacement of 50 percent or more of the school's teachers (who are more likely to be minorities at these underperforming schools); replacement of the principal (also more likely to be a minority); conversion of a traditional public school to a privately operated public charter school (diminishing the local community's direct influence on the school's operations); state or mayoral takeover of the school (transferring authority from local actors to those with more power); and closing the school (effectively severing long-established community ties and withdrawing access to public services in already disadvantaged communities).

The Every Student Succeeds Act (ESSA), which replaced No Child Left Behind in 2015, marked a dramatic change in school turnaround policy. Rather than prescribing a narrow set of interventions to be applied to all struggling schools nationwide, ESSA allowed states to establish their own policies, providing an opportunity for more local actors to influence the form and direction of turnaround interventions. Since minority teachers disproportionately serve at these struggling schools, this policy shift could empower teachers of color—but could also be treacherous for minority teachers, in light of historical marginalization of minority teachers and students at the local level.

If teachers can overcome these barriers, I expect to see minority influence on a variety of school turnaround issues, with those situated in site-based practices likely offering the most opportunity for change. For example, minority teachers could influence practices as varied as parent and community engagement strategies, spending priorities in school facilities, or common professional development sessions among teachers. Millennial minorities in low-performing schools will likely wield less leverage over decisions that may have consequences across a broad pool of schools where their influence is less concentrated, such as changing the district curriculum, opening a new magnet program, or extending the school day or year.

## AGENCY AND ORGANIZING FOR MILLENNIAL TEACHERS OF COLOR

Given the ways in which education policies of the past have contributed to the underrepresentation of minorities in the teacher workforce, the education policies of the present and future discussed above can be extraordinarily consequential for the next generation. Today's system may not be as overtly racist, but differences in the status of minority teachers continue to surface, with ramifications for their numbers in the workforce.

The history of social movements—from the civil rights movement to the Vietnam antiwar protests—has shown that systems typically do not change without pressure from outside advocates. This pressure must come from white as well as minority teachers and administrators. School districts, state education agencies, and the federal government—along with other education stakeholders—must work to effectuate change for this population, as minority teachers have been doing for decades.

In the following sections I present successful frameworks of agency developed by the hardworking advocates of the past that should allow millennial minorities specifically to leverage their unique skill sets to advocate for this change in new ways. This discussion should not burden the already overworked and underpaid millennial minority teachers of today but rather present policy-relevant lessons for those who wish to make change in the future.

### Relational agency

In chapter 5, Catone and Tahbildar define "relational agency" as the notion of organizing for change through cooperation and partnership. They begin with an example of a single teacher whose school community, through mentorship and partnership with a local organization, created a welcoming space for him and made the school a better place overall. Similarly, minority teachers successfully partner with churches, civic associations, or other programs already empowering minority neighborhoods. Local teacher preparation programs, particularly those that place large numbers of their graduates in high-minority schools, could be a great source of external support from within the education industry.

To influence education policy created by elected school boards, ambitious minority teachers could ally with community members through parents' associations in addition to community groups. These elected groups often view parents partially as voters and therefore as a vital constituency. For example, parents in Camden, New Jersey, pressed the superintendent and the school board to improve transportation and bilingual programming, among other causes, through the formation of Parents for Great Camden Schools.[29]

One feature of parent engagement that should encourage minority teachers is that minority voices are much more common among the parent communities of schools with many teachers of color than they are in other places. Hence, rallying vocal external support to agitate for internal change could be an effective strategy. As suburban[30] and rural[31] areas increasingly diversify, teachers of color (particularly Hispanic teachers) will have greater freedom to employ this parent-centered strategy in urban schools.

## Creative agency

Creative agency, or building alternative spaces from which to draw power, can also prove a potent force for change in education policy. I believe these spaces are already being constructed across the country in impactful ways, most notably in low-performing schools where minority teachers are most concentrated, but the scope of influence is poised to expand (as described in the previous section).

The district itself—especially a human resources department interested in helping minority teachers to feel more empowered and included in their schools—may prove to be accommodating to requests for outreach and creation of space along the lines of those discussed in chapter 8. Finally, if other modes prove unsuccessful, teachers could turn to the power of social networks, both online and in person, to connect with other teachers in the broader community. Millennial teachers are particularly well suited to make these connections given their proclivity to use social media and their more frequent transfers across schools and positions. Social networks can be an especially valuable tool within charter schools (a particularly strong magnet for millennial teachers of color), which commonly lack both union and district-level organizational ties.

Creative agency allows teachers to build support for policies especially relevant to them rather than compromising to form the broader alliances of relational agency–based strategies. Perhaps through the use of this type of agency, millennial minorities could advance policies that would be personally beneficial to them. For example, research has shown that bonuses for teachers in hard-to-staff schools can be an effective way to attract and retain high-performing teachers in disadvantaged, high-minority schools.[32] Despite that research, relatively few districts have adopted such policies, perhaps because the beneficiaries would often be a small group of mostly minority teachers in high-minority schools. As minority teachers build a vocal constituency across schools, unions and district leadership will find it more difficult to overlook their interests.

### Resistive agency

Finally, millennial minority teachers can employ resistive agency—forcing change on an existing power structure, such as teachers' unions or state or federal legislatures. Though nationally 74 percent of teachers reported being union members in 2015, only 66 percent of millennial minority teachers reported being so, according to the SASS data. A study of union practices showed that the median voter model—in other words, the voter whose preferences matched the fiftieth percentile on the spectrum of opinions—most closely predicted the outcome of a union's decision, meaning bargaining positions are relatively less likely to reflect the interests of a minority group like teachers of color.[33] This disenfranchisement within the local union was echoed in one of the millennial perspectives in chapter 1.

Since teachers' unions occupy a powerful perch in the education landscape, minority teachers can work to co-opt their structures and push for their own policies through membership. Teachers can utilize the union's established relationships across campuses to identify and communicate with others of similar backgrounds and interests and advocate for new policies in district negotiations.

To shape education policy on a larger scale, minority teachers must lobby for changes in either state capitals or in Washington, DC. In these halls of power, millennial minority teachers can follow the successful playbook of established special interest organizations that have fought discriminatory policies in the past, like the NAACP or La Raza. These teachers can arrange meetings with their local congressmen and women or state legislators and apply pressure through large-scale campaigns in their community.

### Successful combinations of agency frameworks

To be clear, these forms of agency are not mutually exclusive, and the most successful forms of advocacy have historically combined them. For example, in 2017 the NAACP altered its official position on charter schools, calling for the elimination of for-profit charter school operators and the creation of "more high-quality schools, regardless of the school's structure."[34] This change—a real shift from a year prior in which the NAACP called for a moratorium on all charter schools—resulted from advocacy by parents and teachers, who collectively resisted powerful constituencies by holding listening sessions across the country.

As school districts increasingly become aware of these issues, they can become partners in rather than the target of resistive action. DeRay McKesson embodies this transition, as a Black Lives Matter activist and former candidate for Baltimore mayor who later joined the Baltimore City Schools as chief human capital officer. McKesson spoke on this after a year on the job: "It was an honor to come back to city schools and serve in this role. . . . I think of it as complementary and inclusive to the other organizing work I do with social justice."[35]

## CONCLUSION

In the coming decades, millennial teachers of color will both shape and be shaped by education policy. I see both threats and opportunities for this group from changes to teacher recruitment and retention practices, expanding school choice, and increased efforts to turn around low-performing schools. Incoming millennial teachers will accept these developments as the status quo, but, for today's young minority teachers, the effects remain to be seen, and have important consequences.

The status of minority teachers, particularly those of the rising millennial generation, will affect students, the teaching profession, minority communities, and the nation at large. Though their numbers are currently small and their immediate influence may be limited, millennial minority teachers can wield influence in the niche spaces in which they have a critical mass and form alliances. Through these strategies, millennial minority teachers can advocate for their interests and ultimately advance the cause of minority students as well.

*Acknowledgments*

*Thanks to Diana Quintero, Sarah Novicoff, and Caitlin Dermody for excellent research and writing assistance in preparing this manuscript.*

# Notes

## Introduction

1. Generations roughly defined: centennials, generation Z, iGeneration—born 1998 on, with no defined cutoff; millennials, generation Y—born 1981–1997; generation X—born 1965–1980; baby boomers—born 1946–1964; silent generation—born 1928–1945; greatest generation—born before 1928. Richard Fry, "Millennials Overtake Baby Boomers as America's Largest Generation," Pew Research Center, April 25, 2016, http://www.pewresearch.org/fact-tank/2016/04/25/millennials-overtake-baby-boomers/.

2. Annie E. Casey Foundation, *2016 KIDS COUNT: Data Book* (Baltimore, MD: Annie E. Casey Foundation, 2016), http://www.aecf.org/m/resourcedoc/aecf-the2016kidscountdatabook-2016.pdf; Joel McFarland et al., *The Condition of Education 2017*, NCES 2017-144 (Washington, DC: US Department of Education, National Center for Education Statistics, 2017), https://nces.ed.gov/pubs2017/2017144.pdf; Steve Suitts, *A New Majority Update: Low Income Students in the South and Nation* (Atlanta: Southern Education Foundation, 2013).

3. Hua-Yu Sebastian Cherng and Peter F. Halpin, "The Importance of Minority Teachers: Student Perceptions of Minority Versus White Teachers," *Educational Researcher* 45, no. 7 (2016): 407–20, doi:10.3102/0013189X16671718; Thomas S. Dee, "A Teacher Like Me: Does Race, Ethnicity, or Gender Matter?," *American Economic Review* 95, no. 2 (2005): 158–65; Dan Goldhaber, Roddy Theobald, and Christopher Tien, "The Theoretical and Empirical Arguments for Diversifying the Teacher Workforce: A Review of the Evidence" (working paper 2015-9, Center for Education Data & Research, University of Washington–Bothell, Seattle, 2015), http://m.cedr.us/papers/working/CEDR%20WP%202015-9.pdf; Mari Ann Roberts and Jacqueline Jordon Irvine, "African American Teachers' Caring Behaviors: The Difference Makes a Difference," in *The SAGE Handbook of African American Education*, ed. Linda C. Tillman (Thousand Oaks, CA: SAGE Publications, 2009), 141–52.

4. Mary E. Dilworth, *Motivation, Rewards, and Incentives*, Trends and Issues Paper No. 3 (Washington, DC: ERIC Clearinghouse on Teacher Education, 1991), https://eric.ed.gov/?id=ED330692.

5. Fry, "Millennials Overtake Baby Boomers."

6. Hannah Putman et al., *High Hopes and Harsh Realities: The Real Challenges to Building a Diverse Workforce* (Washington, DC: Brown Center on Education Policy, Brookings Institution, 2016), https://www.brookings.edu/wp-content/uploads/2016/08/browncenter_20160818_teacherdiversityreportpr_hansen.pdf; Mary E. Dilworth and Marcus J. Coleman, *Time for a Change: Diversity in Teaching Revisited* (Washington, DC: National Education Association, Center for Great Public Schools, May 2014), https://www.nea.org/assets/docs/Time_for_a_Change_Diversity_in_Teaching_Revisited_(web).pdf.

7. Mary E. Dilworth and Carlton A. Brown, "Consider the Difference: Teaching and Learning in Culturally Rich Schools," in *Handbook of Research on Teaching*, 4th ed., ed. Virginia Richardson (Washington, DC: American Educational Research Association, 2001), 643–67.

8. Ana Maria Villegas and Jacqueline Jordan Irvine, "Diversifying the Teaching Force: An Examination of Major Arguments," *Urban Review* 42, no. 3 (2010): 175–92, doi: 10.1007/s11256-010-0150-1; Mary E. Dilworth with Anthony L. Brown, "Teachers of Color: Quality and Effectiveness One Way or Another," in *Handbook of Research on Teacher Education: Enduring Questions in Changing Contexts*, 3rd ed., eds. Marilyn Cochran-Smith et al. (New York: Routledge, Taylor & Francis Group and Washington, DC: Association of Teacher Educators, 2008), 424–44; Mary E. Dilworth, "Historically Black Colleges and Universities in Teacher Education Reform," *Journal of Negro Education* 81, no. 2 (2012): 138–52; Lauren Musu-Gillette, *Status and Trends in the Education of Racial and Ethnic Groups 2016*, NCES 2016-007 (Washington, DC: US Department of Education, National Center for Education Statistics, 2016), https://nces.ed.gov/pubs2016/2016007.pdf.

9. Linda Darling-Hammond, Mary E. Dilworth, and Marcy Bullmaster, "Educators of Color" (background paper for the invitational conference "Recruiting, Preparing, and Retaining Persons of Color in the Teaching Profession," January 22–24, 1996; sponsored by the National Alliance of Black School Educators, Inc.; Phi Delta Kappa Educational Foundation; Recruiting New Teachers, Inc.; and US Department of Education, Office of Educational Research and Improvement), http://files.eric.ed.gov/fulltext/ED474898.pdf.

10. Mary E. Dilworth, *Reading Between the Lines: Teachers and Their Racial/Ethnic Cultures*, Teacher Education Monograph No. 11 (Washington, DC: ERIC/American Association of Colleges for Teacher Education, 1990), http://files.eric.ed.gov/fulltext/ED322148.pdf; Mary E. Dilworth, Ebo Otuya Jr., and Peggy Carr, *Academic Achievement of White, Black, and Hispanic Students in Teacher Education Programs* (Washington, DC: American Association of Colleges for Teacher Education, 1992); http://files.eric.ed.gov/fulltext/ED353259.pdf; Jason Irizarry, *Latinization of US Schools: Successful Teaching and Learning in Shifting Cultural Contexts* (Abingdon, UK: Routledge, 2011); Tonia Durden, Caitlin McMunn Dooley, and Diane Truscott, "Race Still Matters: Preparing Culturally Relevant Teachers," *Race Ethnicity and Education* 19, no. 5 (2016): 1003–24, doi:10.1080/13613324.2014.969226.

11. Rachel Endo, "How Asian American Female Teachers Experience Racial Microaggressions from Pre-service Preparation to their Professional Careers," *Urban Review* 47, no. 4 (2015): 601–25; Gretchen McAllister and Jacqueline Jordan Irvine, "The Role of Empathy in Teaching Culturally Diverse Students: A Qualitative Study of Teachers' Beliefs," *Journal of Teacher Education* 53, no. 5 (2002): 433–43; Lisa D. Delpit, *"Multiplication Is for White People": Raising Expectations for Other People's Children* (New York: New Press, 2012).

12. Thomas D. Snyder and Sally A. Dillow, *Digest of Education Statistics 2012*, NCES 2014-015 (Washington, DC: US Department of Education, National Center for Education Statistics, 2013), https://nces.ed.gov/pubs2014/2014015.pdf.

13. Dilworth and Coleman, "Time for a Change."

14. Christine E. Sleeter, La Vonne I. Neal, and Kevin K. Kumashiro, eds., *Diversifying the Teacher Workforce: Preparing and Retaining Highly Effective Teachers* (New York: Routledge, 2015); Christine E. Sleeter, "Preparing Teachers for Culturally Diverse Schools: Research and the Overwhelming Presence of Whiteness," *Journal of Teacher Education* 52, no. 2 (March/April 2001): 94–106; Nancy Zimpher and Elizabeth A. Ashburn, "Countering Parochialism in Teacher Candidates," *Diversity in Teacher Education* (1992): 40–62.

15. Keffrelyn D. Brown, "Teaching in Color: A Critical Race Theory in Education Analysis of the

Literature on Preservice Teachers of Color and Teacher Education in the US," *Race Ethnicity and Education* 17, no. 3 (2014): 326–45; Tambra O. Jackson and Rita Kohli, "Guest Editors' Introduction: The State of Teachers of Color," *Equity & Excellence in Education* 49, no. 1 (2016): 1–8, doi:10.1080/10665684.2015.1130477.

16. Paul Taylor, *The Next America: Boomers, Millennials and the Looming Generational Showdown* (New York: Public Affairs, 2014).

17. Conra D. Gist, "Voices of Aspiring Teachers of Color: Unraveling the Double Bind in Teacher Education," *Urban Education*, January 12, 2016, 8, doi: 10.1177/00420859156233398.

18. Carl A. Grant and Vonzell Agosto, "Teacher Capacity and Social Justice in Teacher Education," in *Handbook of Research on Teacher Education: Enduring Questions in Changing Contexts*, 3rd ed., eds. Marilyn Cochran-Smith et al. (New York: Routledge, Taylor & Francis Group and Washington, DC: Association of Teacher Educators, 2008), 178.

19. Tondra L. Loder-Jackson, "The Confluence of Race, Gender, and Generations in the Lives of African American Women," in *The SAGE Handbook of African American Education*, ed. Linda C. Tillman (Thousand Oaks, CA: SAGE Publications, 2009), 223–36.

20. Dilworth and Coleman, "Time for a Change."

21. http://www.instituteforteachersofcolor.org/leadership-team.html.

22. Rita Kohli and Marcos Pizarro, "Fighting to Educate Our Own: Teachers of Color, Relational Accountability, and the Struggle for Racial Justice," *Equity & Excellence in Education* 49, no. 1 (2016): 72–84, doi: 10.1080/10665684.2015.1121457.

23. Betty Achinstein and Rodney T. Ogawa, *Change(d) Agents: New Teachers of Color in Urban Schools* (New York: Teachers College Press, 2011).

24. Prudence L. Carter and Linda Darling-Hammond, "Teaching Diverse Learners," in *Handbook of Research on Teaching*, eds. Drew Gitomer and Courtney Bell (Washington, DC: American Educational Research Association, 2016), 623.

25. Marilyn Cochran-Smith, *Walking the Road: Race, Diversity, and Social Justice in Teacher Education* (New York: Teachers College Press, 2004).

26. Gist, "Voices of Aspiring Teachers."

27. Ibid., 19; Dilworth, "Historically Black Colleges."

28. Sonia Nieto, "Placing Equity Front and Center: Some Thoughts on Transforming Teacher Education for a New Century," *Journal of Teacher Education* 51, no. 3 (2000): 181.

29. Christian J. Faltis and Guadalupe Valdes, "Preparing Teachers for Teaching in and Advocating for Linguistically Diverse Classrooms: A Vade Mecum for Teacher Educators," in *Handbook of Research on Teaching*, eds. Drew Gitomer and Courtney Bell (Washington, DC: American Educational Research Association, 2016), 555.

30. Kent C. McGuire, "Commentary: Access and Differentiation," in *Handbook of Education Policy Research*, eds. Gary Sykes, Barbara Schneider, and David N. Plank (New York: Routledge, 2012).

31. Sonia Nieto, "Solidarity, Courage and Heart: What Teacher Educators Can Learn from a New Generation of Teachers," *Intercultural Education* 17, no. 5 (2006): 457–73.

32. Bruce Fuller, Luke Dauter, and Anisah Waite, "New Roles for Teachers in Diverse Schools," in *Handbook of Research on Teaching*, eds. Drew Gitomer and Courtney Bell (Washington, DC: American Educational Research Association, 2016), 952.

33. Elan C. Hope, Micere Keels, and Myles I. Durkee, "Participation in Black Lives Matter and Deferred Action for Childhood Arrivals: Modern Activism Among Black and Latino College Students," *Journal of Diversity in Higher Education* 9, no. 3 (2016): 203.

## Chapter 1

1. Graham Lock, "Wang Dang Doodlin: An Interview with Frederick J. Brown," *International Review of African American Art Plus* (2015), http://iraaa.museum.hamptonu.edu/page/Wang -Dang-Doodlin.
2. Ibid.
3. Gloria Ladson-Billings, *The Dreamkeepers: Successful Teachers of African American Children*, 2nd ed. (San Francisco: Jossey-Bass, 2009).
4. Django Paris and H. Samy Alim, *Culturally Sustaining Pedagogies: Teaching and Learning for Justice in a Changing World* (New York: Teachers College Press, 2017), 1.
5. Examples of such research are Chris Emdin, *For White Folks Who Teach in the Hood* (Boston: Beacon Press, 2017); Django Paris and Samy Alim, *Culturally Sustaining Pedagogies* (New York: Teachers College Press, 2017); and Marc Lamont Hill, *Beats, Rhymes, and Classroom Life: Hip-Hop Pedagogy and the Politics of Identity* (New York: Teachers College Press, 2009).
6. Ladson-Billings, *Dreamkeepers*, 100–102.
7. Lock, "Wang Dang Doodlin."

## Chapter 2

1. Sandra L. Colby and Jennifer M. Ortman, "The Baby Boom Cohort in the United States: 2012 to 2016," *Current Population Reports*, P25-1141. (Washington, DC: US Census Bureau, 2014).
2. Sally Seppanen and Wendy Gualtieri, *The Millennial Generation Research Review* (Washington, DC: US Chamber of Commerce Foundation, November 12, 2012), https://www .uschamberfoundation.org/reports/millennial-generation-research-review.
3. Ibid.
4. Pew Research Center, *Millennials: A Portrait of Generation Next. Confident. Connected. Open to Change* (Washington, DC: Pew Research Center, 2010), http://www.pewsocialtrends.org /files/2010/10/millennials-confident-connected-open-to-change.pdf.
5. According to the US Census Bureau, Hispanic origin is considered an ethnicity, not a race. Hispanics may be of any race.
6. Scott Berridge, "Millennials After the Great Recession," *Monthly Labor Review* (Washington, DC: US Department of Labor, Bureau of Labor Statistics, September 2014), https://www.bls .gov/opub/mlr/2014/beyond-bls/millennials-after-the-great-recession.htm.
7. Pew Research Center, *Millennials*.
8. Urban Institute, *Nine Charts About Wealth Inequality in America* (Washington, DC: Urban Institute, 2015), http://apps.urban.org/features/wealth-inequality-charts/.
9. Sophie Quinton, "The Disproportionate Burden of Student Loan Debt on Minorities," *The Atlantic* (May 5, 2015), https://www.theatlantic.com/education/archive/2015/05/the -disproportionate-burden-of-student-loan-debt-on-minorities/392456/.
10. Ibid.
11. Common Core of Data, *State Nonfiscal Survey of Public Elementary/Secondary Education, 1997–98 through 2011–12* (Washington, DC: US Department of Education, National Center for Education Statistics, 2015), https://nces.ed.gov/ccd/stnfis.asp.
12. US Department of Education, *The State of Racial Diversity in the Educator Workforce* (Washington, DC: US Department of Education; Office of Planning, Evaluation and Policy Development; Policy and Program Studies Service, 2016), http://www2.ed.gov/rschstat/eval /highered/racial-diversity/state-racial-diversity-workforce.pdf.
13. Richard Ingersoll, Lisa Merrill, and Daniel Stuckey, *Seven Trends: The Transformation of the Teaching Force*, CPRE Research Report #RR-80, updated April 2014 (Philadelphia: University

of Pennsylvania, Consortium for Policy Research in Education, 2014), http://www.cpre.org/sites/default/files/workingpapers/1506_7trendsapril2014.pdf.

14. Richard Ingersoll and Lisa Merrill, *A Quarter Century of Changes in the Elementary and Secondary Teaching Force: From 1987 to 2012*, NCES 2017-092, Statistical Analysis Report (Washington, DC: US Department of Education, National Center for Education Statistics, 2017), https://nces.ed.gov/pubs2017/2017092.pdf.

15. Ibid.

16. Ibid.

17. William J. Hussar and Tabitha M. Bailey, *Projections of Education Statistics to 2022*, NCES 2014-051 (Washington, DC: US Department of Education, National Center for Education Statistics, 2013), https://nces.ed.gov/pubs2014/2014051.pdf.

18. Ingersoll, Merrill, and Stuckey, *Seven Trends*, 15.

19. Ingersoll and Merrill, *Quarter Century*.

20. Ibid.

21. 21. Dr. Roy Jones started the program in South Carolina to recruit black males from disadvantaged schools, provide those black males academic and professional enrichment, and to return those black males back to the disadvantaged schools as well-prepared teachers. Since its inception, it has spread to into states such as Mississippi, Kentucky, Missouri, and Minnesota, http://hechingerreport.org/call-me-mister-initiative-succeeds-in-recruiting-developing-black-teachers/

22. Anna J. Egalite, Brian Kisida, and Marcus A. Winters, "Representation in the Classroom: The Effect of Own-Race Teachers on Student Achievement," *Economics of Education Review* 45 (2015): 44–52.

23. Thomas S. Dee, "Teachers, Race and Student Achievement in a Randomized Experiment," *Review of Economics and Statistics* 86, no. 1 (2004): 195–210.

24. Seth Gershenson et al., "The Long-Run Impacts of Same-Race Teachers" (IZA Discussion Paper No. 10630, Institute for the Study of Labor, Bonn, Germany, 2017).

25. Ivory A. Toldson, "Black Male Teachers: Becoming Extinct?" *The Root*, http://www.theroot.com/black-male-teachers-becoming-extinct-1790896120.

26. Ibid.

27. Nicholas W. Papageorge, Seth Gershenson, and Kyungmin Kang, "Teacher Expectations Matter" (IZA Discussion Paper No. 10165, Institute for the Study of Labor, Bonn, Germany, 2017).

28. Gershenson et al., "Long-Run Impacts."

## Chapter 3

1. Sharn Donnison, "Unpacking the Millennials: A Cautionary Tale for Teacher Education," *Australian Journal of Teacher Education* 32, no. 3 (2007): 1–13.

2. Colleen Flaherty, "Regaining Public Trust," *Inside Higher Education*, January 27, 2017, https://www.insidehighered.com/news/2017/01/27/academics-consider-how-rebuild-public-trust-higher-education.

3. "New Census Bureau Statistics Show How Young Adults Today Compare with Previous Generations in Neighborhoods Nationwide," US Census Bureau, December 4, 2014, http://www.census.gov/newsroom/press-releases/2014/cb14-219.html.

4. Jean M. Twenge, *Generation Me: Why Today's Young Americans Are More Confident, Assertive, Entitled—and More Miserable Than Ever Before* (New York: Simon & Schuster, 2014).

5. Sally Koslow and Caity Weaver, "The Terrible 22s: Are Today's Young Adults Really Helpless Narcissists?," *AARP The Magazine* (2016), http://www.aarp.org/home-family/friends-family/info-2016/millennials-boomers-reaching-adulthood.html; Twenge, *Generation Me.*

6. Chip Espinoza, Mick Ukleja, and Craig Rusch, *Managing the Millennials: Discover the Core Competencies for Managing Today's Workforce* (Hoboken, NJ: Wiley, 2010); Joel Stein, "Millennials: The Me Me Me Generation," *Time*, May 20, 2013, http://time.com/247/millennials-the-me-me-me-generation/.

7. David Borrelli, "There's a Reason Millennials Want a Culture of Collaboration at Work," *Huffington Post: The Blog*, December 12, 2014, www.huffingtonpost.ca/david-borrelli/millennials-at-work_b_6315026.html; Arthur Levine and Diane R. Dean, *Generation on a Tightrope: A Portrait of Today's College Student* (San Francisco: Jossey-Bass, 2012).

8. Donnison, "Unpacking the Millennials."

9. Ibid.; Levine and Dean, *Generation on a Tightrope.*

10. Mary E. Dilworth and Marcus J. Coleman, *Time for a Change: Diversity in Teaching Revisited* (Washington, DC: National Education Association, Center for Great Public Schools, May 2014), https://www.nea.org/assets/docs/Time_for_a_Change_Diversity_in_Teaching_Revisited_(web).pdf.

11. Flaherty, "Regaining Public Trust."

12. Richard Fry, "Millennials Overtake Baby Boomers as America's Largest Generation," Pew Research Center, April 25, 2016, http://www.pewresearch.org/fact-tank/2016/04/25/millennials-overtake-baby-boomers/; Pew Research Center, "Millennials in Adulthood: Detached from Institutions, Networked with Friends," *Social & Demographic Trends* (Washington, DC: Pew Research Center, March 7, 2014), http://www.pewsocialtrends.org/2014/03/07/millennials-in-adulthood/; Louis Soares, *Post-Traditional Learners and the Transformation of Postsecondary Education: A Manifesto for College Leaders* (Washington, DC: American Council on Education, January 2013), http://www.acenet.edu/news-room/Documents/Post-Traditional-Learners.pdf.

13. "New Census Bureau Statistics."

14. Twenge, *Generation Me.*

15. Linda Hogg, "Funds of Knowledge: An Investigation of Coherence Within the Literature," *Teaching and Teacher Education* 27, no. 3 (2011): 666–77; Dolores Delgado Bernal, "Critical Race Theory, Latino Critical Theory, and Critical Raced-Gendered Epistemologies: Recognizing Students of Color as Holders and Creators of Knowledge," *Qualitative Inquiry* 8, no. 1 (2002):105–26.

16. Tara Yosso et al., "Critical Race Theory, Racial Microaggressions, and Campus Racial Climate for Latina/o Undergraduates," *Harvard Educational Review* 79, no. 4 (2009): 659–91.

17. Jannell Robles, "Barriers to Success: A Narrative of One Latina Student's Struggles," *Harvard Educational Review* 79, no. 4 (2009): 745–55.

18. Betty Achinstein and Julia Aguirre, "Cultural Match or Culturally Suspect: How New Teachers of Color Negotiate Sociocultural Challenges in the Classroom," *Teachers College Record* 110, no. 8 (2008): 1505–540; Danielle Magaldi, Timothy Conway, and Leora Trub, "'I Am Here for a Reason': Minority Teachers Bridging Many Divides in Urban Education," *Race Ethnicity and Education* (first published November 13, 2016), doi: 10.1080/13613324.2016.12488221-13.

19. Kathleen DeMarrais, "Qualitative Interview Studies: Learning Through Experience," in *Foundations for Research Methods of Inquiry in Education and the Social Sciences*, eds. Kathleen DeMarrais and Stephen D. Lapan (New York: Routledge, 2004), 51–68.

20. Ibid.

21. Margot Eyring, "How Close Is Close Enough? Reflections on the Experience of Doing Phenomenology," in *Inside Stories: Qualitative Research Reflections*, ed. Kathleen Bennett DeMarrais (Mahwah, NJ: Lawrence Erlbaum Associates, 1998), 142.
22. Dorothy Holland et al., *Identity and Agency in Cultural Worlds* (Cambridge, MA: Harvard University Press, 1998); Jack Mezirow, *Transformative Dimensions of Adult Learning* (San Francisco: Jossey-Bass, 1991).
23. Charles W. Mills, *The Racial Contract* (Ithaca, NY: Cornell University Press, 1991); Rita Kohli, "Behind School Doors: The Impact of Hostile Racial Climates on Urban Teachers of Color," *Urban Education*, March 11, 2016, 1–27, doi:10.1177/0042085916636653; Anthony Miele, "Beyond Race-Evasive White Teacher Identity: Toward Second-Wave White Teacher Identity Studies" (paper presented at the Annual Meeting of the American Association of Colleges for Teacher Education, Orlando, FL, March 2013); Daniel G. Solorzano and Dolores Delgado Bernal, "Examining Transformational Resistance Through a Critical Race and Latcrit Theory Framework: Chicana and Chicano Students in an Urban Context," *Urban Education* 36, no. 3 (May 1, 2001): 308–42; Tara J. Yosso, *Critical Race Counterstories Along the Chicana/Chicano Educational Pipeline* (New York: Routledge, 2006).
24. Achinstein and Aguirre, "Cultural Match"; Magaldi, Conway, and Trub, "'I Am Here for a Reason.'"
25. Danica G. Hays and Catherine Y. Chang, "White Privilege, Oppression, and Racial Identity Development: Implications for Supervision," *Counselor Education and Supervision* 43, no. 2 (2003): 134–45; Socorro G. Herrera and Amanda R. Morales, "Colorblind Non-accommodative Denial: Implications for Teachers' Meaning Perspectives Towards Their Mexican American Students," in *Race, Culture, and Identity in Second Language Education*, eds. Ryuko Kubota and Angel Lin (New York: Taylor & Francis, 2009), 197–214.
26. Christopher Hayter, *Innovation America: A Compact for Postsecondary Education* (Washington, DC: National Governors Association, 2007), https://www.nga.org/cms/home/nga-center-for-best-practices/center-publications/page-ehsw-publications/col2-content/main-content-list/innovation-america-a-compact-for.default.html; Burnie Bond et al., *The State of Teacher Diversity in American Education* (Washington, DC: Albert Shanker Institute, 2015), http://www.shankerinstitute.org/resource/teacherdiversity.; Christine E. Sleeter, La Vonne I. Neal, and Kevin K. Kumashiro, eds., *Diversifying the Teacher Workforce: Preparing and Retaining Highly Effective Teachers* (New York: Routledge, 2015).
27. Richard Ingersoll and Henry May, *Recruitment, Retention and the Minority Teacher Shortage*, CPRE Research Report #RR-69 (Philadelphia: Consortium for Policy Research in Education, University of Pennsylvania, 2011), 62–65, http://www.cpre.org/sites/default/files/researchreport/1221_minorityteachershortagereportrr69septfinal.pdf; Bond et al., *State of Teacher Diversity*.
28. Jason Irizarry, "En La Lucha: The Struggles and Triumphs of Latino/a Preservice Teachers," *Teachers College Record* 113, no. 12 (2011): 2804–835; Michelle Jay, "Race-ing Through the School Day: African American Educators' Experiences with Race and Racism in Schools," *International Journal of Qualitative Studies in Education* 22, no. 6 (2009): 671–85.
29. Achinstein, and Aguirre, "Cultural Match"; Ana Maria Villegas, Kathryn Strom, and Tamara Lucas, "Closing the Racial/Ethnic Gap Between Students of Color and Their Teachers: An Elusive Goal," *Equity & Excellence in Education* 45, no. 2 (2012): 283–301.
30. Sleeter, Neal, and Kumashiro, *Diversifying the Teacher Workforce*.
31. Cited in Pamala M. Norwood, "Teaching as an Emancipatory Endeavor: Can Racial Uplift Be Taught?," *Negro Educational Review* 49 (1998): 119–27.
32. Betty Achinstein et al., "Retaining Teachers of Color: A Pressing Problem and a Potential

Strategy for 'Hard-to-Staff' Schools," *Review of Educational Research* 80, no. 1 (2010): 71–107; Sabrina Hope King, "Why Did We Choose Teaching Careers and What Will Enable Us to Stay? Recruitment and Retention Insights from One Cohort of the African-American Teaching Pool" (paper presented at the annual meeting of the American Educational Research Association, San Francisco, CA, April 2–4, 1992).

33. Magaldi, Conway, and Trub, "'I Am Here for a Reason,'" 2.

34. Thomas S. Dee, "Teachers, Race and Student Achievement in a Randomized Experiment," *Review of Economics and Statistics* 86, no. 1 (2004): 195–210; Gloria Ladson-Billings and William F. Tate IV, "Toward a Critical Theory of Education," *Teachers College Record* 97, no. 1 (1995): 47–68; Dick Startz, "Teacher Perceptions and Race," *Brown Center Chalkboard*, Brookings Institution, February 22, 2016, https://www.brookings.edu/blog/brown-center-chalkboard/2016/02/22/teacher-perceptions-and-race/.

35. James C. Jupp and Timothy J. Lensmire, "Second-Wave White Teacher Identity Studies: Toward Complexity and Reflexivity in the Racial Conscientization of White Teachers," *International Journal of Qualitative Studies in Education* 29, no. 8 (2016): 985–88.

36. Linda Darling-Hammond, Ruth Chung Wei, and Christine Marie Johnson, "Teacher Preparation and Teacher Learning: A Changing Policy Landscape," in *Handbook of Education Policy Research*, eds. Gary Sykes, Barbara Schneider, and David N. Plank (New York: Routledge, 2009), 613–36; Kenneth J. Fasching-Varner and Dodo-Seriki,"Moving Beyond Seeing with Our Eyes Wide Shut," *Democracy and Education* 19, no. 1 (2012): 1–6; Amanda Roriquez Morales and M. Gail Shroyer, "Personal Agency Inspired by Hardship: Bilingual Latinas as Liberatory Educators," *International Journal of Multicultural Education* 18, no. 3 (2016): 1–21; Farima Pour-Khorshid, "H.E.L.L.A.: Collective 'Testimonio' That Speak to the Healing, Empowerment, Love, Liberation, and Action Embodied by Social Justice Educators of Color," *Association of Mexican American Educators Journal* 10, no. 2 (2016): 16–32; Elia Vázquez-Montilla, Megan Just, and Robert Triscari, "Teachers' Dispositions and Beliefs about Cultural and Linguistic Diversity," *Universal Journal of Educational Research* 2 (2014): 577–87, doi:10.13189/ujer.2014.020806.

37. Herrera and Morales, "Colorblind Non-accommodative Denial."

38. Dorothy Holland et al., *Identity and Agency*, 40–41.

39. Mikhail M. Bakhtin, "Discourse in the Novel," in *The Dialogic Imagination*, ed. Michael Holoquist, trans. Michael Holoquist and Caryl Emerson (Austin: University of Texas Press, 1981), 259–422; Dorothy C. Holland and Jean Lave, *History in Person: Enduring Struggles, Contentious Practice, Intimate Identities* (Santa Fe, NM: School of American Research Press, 2001).

40. Mezirow, *Transformative Dimensions*.

41. Ibid., 11.

42. Mills, *Racial Contract*.

43. Elvira J. Abrica and Amanda R. Morales, "Conceptualizing Latino Experiences and Outcomes in Post-Secondary Institutions: Deficiencies, Assets, and a Post-Racial Contract" (paper presented at the Childhoods in Motion: Children, Youth, Migration, and Education Conference, Los Angeles, CA, March 3–5, 2017).

44. Paul C. Gorski, "Poverty and the Ideological Imperative: A Call to Unhook from Deficit and Grit Ideology and to Strive for Structural Ideology in Teacher Education," *Journal of Education for Teaching* 42, no. 4 (2016): 378–86, doi:10.1080/02607476.2016.1215546378-86.

45. Abrica and Morales, "Conceptualizing Latino Experiences."

46. Wilma S. Longstreet and Harold G. Shane, *Curriculum for a New Millennium: Instructor's*

*Manual* (Boston: Allyn and Bacon, 1993); Abrica and Morales, "Conceptualizing Latino Experiences"; Adrienne D. Dixson and Jeannine E. Dingus, "Tyranny of the Majority: Re-enfranchisement of African-American Teacher Educators Teaching for Democracy," *International Journal of Qualitative Studies in Education* 20, no. 6 (2007): 639–54; Jeremy D. Franklin, William A. Smith, and Man Hung, "Racial Battle Fatigue for Latina/o Students," *Journal of Hispanic Higher Education* 13, no. 4 (2014): 303–22; Solorzano and Delgado Bernal, "Examining Transformational Resistance"; Yosso et al., "Critical Race Theory."

47. Julie Bettie, *Women Without Class: Girls, Race, and Identity* (Berkeley: University of California Press, 2003).

48. Susan Moore Johnson, *The Workplace Matters: Teacher Quality, Retention and Effectiveness* (Washington, DC: National Education Association, 2006).

49. Jay, "Race-ing Through the School Day"; Kohli et al., "Critical Professional Development: Centering the Social Justice Needs of Teachers," *International Journal of Critical Pedagogy* 6, no. 2 (2015): 7–24; Magaldi, Conway, and Trub, "'I Am Here for a Reason'"; Tiffany M. Nyachae, "Complicated Contradictions amid Black Feminism and Millennial Black Women Teachers Creating Curriculum for Black Girls," *Gender and Education* 28, no. 6 (2016): 786–806; Pour-Khorshid, "H.E.L.L.A."

50. Nyachae, "Complicated Contradictions"; Achinstein and Aguirre, "Cultural Match."

51. Nyachae, "Complicated Contradictions," 788.

52. Denis Talaferro-Baszile, "Rage in the Interests of Black Self: Curriculum Theorizing as Dangerous Knowledge," *Journal of Curriculum Theorizing* 22, no. 1 (2006): 90; Nyachae, "Complicated Contradictions."

53. Achinstein and Aguirre, "Cultural Match."

54. Ibid.

55. Education Northwest, "Working with Indigenous Communities," *Evidence Blast*, April 2014, http://educationnorthwest.org/resources/working-indigenous-communities%E2%80%93evidence-blast; Marcelle M. Haddix, "Talkin' in the Company of My Sistas: The Counterlanguages and Deliberate Silences of Black Female Students in Teacher Education," *Linguistics and Education* 23, no. 2 (2012): 169–81; Pour-Khorshid, "H.E.L.L.A."

56. Melissa Holmes et al., "Contextualizing the Path to Academic Success: Culturally and Linguistically Diverse Students Gaining Voice and Agency in Higher Education," in *Linguistic Minority Students Go to College: Preparation, Access, and Persistence*, eds. Yasuko Kanno and Linda Harklau (New York: Routledge, 2012), 201–19.

57. Magaldi, Conway, and Trub, "'I Am Here for a Reason'"; Amanda Rodriguez Morales, "Documenting Professional Development of Latino/a Preservice Teachers" (paper presented at the annual meeting of the American Association of Colleges for Teacher Education, Las Vegas, NV, February 2016).

58. Bond et al., *State of Teacher Diversity*, 96.

59. Delgado Bernal, "Critical Race Theory"; Solorzano and Delgado Bernal, "Examining Transformational Resistance"; Yosso, *Critical Race Counterstories*.

60. Delgado Bernal, "Critical Race Theory"; Dolores Delgado Bernal, Rebeca Burciaga, and Judith Flores Carmona, eds., *Chicana/Latina Testimonios as Pedagogical, Methodological, and Activist Approaches to Social Justice* (New York: Routledge, 2015).

61. Maria C. Ledesma and Dolores Calderon, "Critical Race Theory in Education," *Qualitative Inquiry* 21, no. 3 (2015): 206–22; Daniel G. Solórzano and Tara J. Yosso, "Critical Race Methodology: Counter-Storytelling as an Analytical Framework for Education Research," *Qualitative Inquiry* 8, no. 1 (2002): 23–44.

62. Helene Starks and Susan Brown Trinidad, "Choose Your Method: A Comparison of Phenomenology, Discourse Analysis, and Grounded Theory," *Qualitative Health Research* 17, no. 10 (2007): 1372–380.

63. Sharon Vaughan, Jeanne Shay Schumm, and Jane Sinagub, *Focus Group Interviews in Education and Psychology* (Thousand Oaks, CA: SAGE Publications, 1996).

64. Maria E. Matute-Bianchi, "Situational Ethnicity and Patterns of School Performance Among Immigrant and Nonimmigrant Mexican-Descent Students," in *Minority Status, Oppositional Culture, and Schooling,* ed. John U. Ogbu (New York: Routledge, 1991), 205–47.

65. Amanda Rodriguez Morales, "Factors That Foster Latina, English, Language Learner, Non-traditional Student Resilience in Higher Education and Their Persistence in Teacher Education" (PhD diss., Kansas State University, 2011).

66. Jack Mezirow, *Fostering Critical Reflection in Adulthood: A Guide to Transformative and Emancipatory Learning* (San Francisco: Jossey-Bass, 1990), 42.

67. Socorro G. Herrera and Kevin G. Murry, *Mastering ESL/EFL Methods: Differentiated Instruction for Culturally and Linguistically Diverse (CLD) Students* (Boston: Pearson, 2016).

68. Xaé A. Reyes and Diana I. Ríos, "Dialoguing the Latina Experience in Higher Education," *Journal of Hispanic Higher Education* 4, no. 4 (2005): 377–91.

69. Irizarry, "En La Lucha"; Delgado Bernal, "Critical Race Theory."

70. Morales and Shroyer, "Personal Agency."

71. Janie T. Carnock and April Ege, "The 'Triple Segregation' of Latinos, ELLs: What Can We Do?," New America, November 17, 2015, https://www.newamerica.org/education-policy /edcentral/latinos-segregation/.

72. Mezirow, *Transformative Dimensions.*

73. Mills, *Racial Contract.*

74. Irizarry, "En La Lucha"; Nyachae, "Complicated Contradictions"; Pour-Khorshid, "H.E.L.L.A."

75. Lori Assaf, Ruben Garza, and Jennifer Battle, "Multicultural Teacher Education: Examining the Perceptions, Practices, and Coherence in One Teacher Preparation Program," *Teacher Education Quarterly* 37, no. 2 (2010): 115–35.

76. Angelina E. Castagno, "'I Don't Want to Hear That!': Legitimating Whiteness Through Silence in Schools," *Anthropology & Education Quarterly* 39, no. 3 (2008): 314–33; Victoria S. Haviland, "'Things Get Glossed Over': Rearticulating the Silencing Power of Whiteness in Education," *Journal of Teacher Education* 59, no. 1 (2008): 40–54; Miele, "Beyond Race-Evasive."

77. Gorski, "Poverty and the Ideological"; Sleeter, Neal, and Kumashiro, *Diversifying the Teacher Workforce.*

## Chapter 4

1. Eileen Patten and Richard Fry, "How Millennials Today Compare with Their Grandparents 50 Years Ago," *Pew Research*, March 19, 2015, http://www.pewresearch.org/fact-tank/2015/03/19 /how-millennials-compare-with-their-grandparents/.

2. George Guilder, "Women in the Work Force," *The Atlantic*, September 1986, https://www .theatlantic.com/magazine/archive/1986/09/women-in-the-work-force/304924/.

3. Vanessa Kirsch and Dana O'Donovan, "Millennials Are Reshaping the World of Social Impact," *Fast Company*, February 2, 2016, https://www.fastcompany.com/3060085 /millennials-are-reshaping-the-world-of-social-impact"; Susan Emeagwali, "Millennials: Leading the Charge for Change," *Techniques: Connecting Education and Careers* 86, no. 5 (2011): 22–26.

4. Mark Teoh and Celine Coggins, *Great Expectations: Teachers' Views on Elevating the Teacher Profession* (Boston: Teach Plus, October 2012).
5. Tamara Hiler and Lanae Erickson Hatalsky, "Teaching: The Next Generation," *The Third Way*, April 29, 2014, http://www.thirdway.org/report/teaching-the-next-generation.
6. José Luis Vilson, "The Need for More Teachers of Color," *The Professional Educator* (Summer 2015): 27–31.
7. Patten and Fry, "How Millennials Today"; Samantha Raphelson, "Amid the Stereotypes, Some Facts About Millennials," *National Public Radio*, November 18, 2014, http://www.npr.org/2014/11/18/354196302/amid-the-stereotypes-some-facts-about-millennials; Sally Seppanen and Wendy Gualtieri, *The Millennial Generation Research Review* (Washington, DC: US Chamber of Commerce Foundation, November 12, 2012), https://www.uschamberfoundation.org/reports/millennial-generation-research-review.
8. Interview with an assistant professor of early childhood education, May 2017.
9. James Vaznis, "Boston Teachers Union Poised to Elect 1st Person of Color as President," *Boston Globe*, May 18, 2017, https://www.bostonglobe.com/metro/2017/05/17/boston-teachers-union-poised-elect-person-color-president/h1Qi7Nm776KatQezNHHy3H/story.html.
10. Britney Stringfellow Otey, "Millennials, Technology and Professional Responsibility: Training a New Generation in Technological Professionalism," *Journal of the Legal Profession* 37, no. 199 (2013), https://papers.ssrn.com/sol3/papers.cfm?abstract_id=2420153.
11. "Young, Connected and Black: African-American Millennials Are Driving Social Change and Leading the Digital Divide," *Nielsen Insights*, July 17, 2016, http://www.nielsen.com/us/en/insights/reports/2016/young-connected-and-black.html.
12. Ibid., 14.
13. Hebah H. Farrag, "The Spirituality of Resilience," *On Being* (blog), February 25, 2016, https://onbeing.org/blog/hebah-farrag-the-spirituality-of-resilience/; https://onbeing.org/tag/patrisse-cullors
14. Claudio Sanchez, "Gifted But Still Learning English, Many Bright Students Get Overlooked," *National Public Radio*, April 11, 2016, http://www.npr.org/sections/ed/2016/04/11/467653193/gifted-but-still-learning-english-overlooked-underserved.
15. Otey, "Millennials, Technology and Professional Responsibility."
16. Jonathan Zur (president and CEO, Virginia Center for Inclusive Communities), in discussion with the author, January 2017.

## Chapter 5

1. Arne Duncan, "Remarks in Chicago Announcing the Nomination of Arne Duncan as Secretary of Education" (speech, Chicago, IL, December 16, 2008).
2. Keith C. Catone, *The Pedagogy of Teacher Activism: Portraits of Four Teachers for Justice* (New York: Peter Lang, 2017).
3. Gloria Anzaldúa, *Borderlands/La Frontera: The New Mestiza*, 4th ed. (San Francisco: Aunt Lute Books, 2012), 101.
4. Catone, *Pedagogy of Teacher Activism*.
5. James M. Jasper, *The Art of Moral Protest: Culture, Biography, and Creativity in Social Movements* (Chicago: University of Chicago Press, 1997).
6. Nathan Teske, *Political Activists in America: The Identity Construction Model of Political Participation* (Cambridge, UK: Cambridge University Press, 1997).
7. Anzaldúa, *Borderlands*, 100.
8. Catone, *Pedagogy of Teacher Activism*.
9. Paulo Freire, *Pedagogy of the Oppressed* (New York: Continuum, 1993), 66.

10. Anzaldúa, *Borderlands*, 60.
11. Ibid., 61.
12. Catone, *Pedagogy of Teacher Activism*.
13. Mark R. Warren, *Fire in the Heart: How White Activists Embrace Racial Justice* (New York: Oxford University Press, 2010).
14. Molly Andrews, *Lifetimes of Commitment: Aging, Politics, Psychology* (Cambridge, UK: Cambridge University Press, 1991).
15. Mary Beth Rogers, *Cold Anger: A Story of Faith and Power Politics* (Denton: University of North Texas Press, 1990).
16. Ibid., 10.
17. Ibid.
18. Catone, *Pedagogy of Teacher Activism*.
19. Ibid.
20. Ibid., 138.
21. Bernard Loomer, "Two Conceptions of Power," *Criterion* 15, no. 1 (1976): 11–29; Seth Kreisberg, *Transforming Power: Domination, Empowerment, and Education* (Albany, NY: SUNY Press, 1992).
22. Catone, *Pedagogy of Teacher Activism*, 138.
23. Ibid.
24. See the Movement for Black Lives (https://policy.m4bl.org/) and United We Dream (https://unitedwedream.org/).
25. Catone, *Pedagogy of Teacher Activism*.
26. Jeffrey M. R. Duncan-Andrade, "Note to Educators: Hope Required When Growing Roses in Concrete," *Harvard Educational Review* 79, no. 2 (2009): 181–94.
27. Ibid.
28. Ibid.
29. Ibid.

## Chapter 6

1. Betty Achinstein et al., "Retaining Teachers of Color: A Pressing Problem and a Potential Strategy for 'Hard-to-Staff' Schools," *Review of Educational Research* 80, no. 1 (2010): 71–107.
2. Keffrelyn D. Brown, "Teaching in Color: A Critical Race Theory in Education Analysis of the Literature on Preservice Teachers of Color and Teacher Education in the US," *Race Ethnicity and Education* 17, no. 3 (2014): 326–45; Tambra O. Jackson, "Perspectives and Insights from Preservice Teachers of Color on Developing Culturally Responsive Pedagogy at Predominantly White Institutions," *Action in Teacher Education* 37, no. 3 (2015): 223–37; Rita Kohli, "Critical Race Reflections: Valuing the Experiences of Teachers of Color in Teacher Education," *Race Ethnicity and Education* 12, no 2 (2009): 235–51.
3. Derrick A. Bell, *Faces at the Bottom of the Well: The Permanence of Racism* (New York: Basic Books, 1992); Gloria Ladson-Billings, "Toward a Theory of Culturally Relevant Pedagogy," *American Educational Research Journal* 32, no. 3 (1995): 465–91.
4. Thomas C. Holt, "Marking: Race, Race-Making and the Writing of History," *American Historical Review* 100, no. 1 (1995): 1–20; Michael Omi and Howard Winant, *Racial Formation in the U.S.*, 3rd ed. (New York: Routledge, 2015).
5. Sharn Donnison, "Unpacking the Millennials: A Cautionary Tale for Teacher Education," *Australian Journal of Teacher Education* 32, no. 3 (2007): 1–13.
6. Dominique Apollon, *Don't Call Them "Post-Racial": Millennial Attitudes on Race, Racism and Key Systems in Our Society* (New York: Applied Research Center, 2011); Jennifer C.

Mueller, "Tracing Family, Teaching Race: Critical Race Pedagogy in the Millennial Sociology Classroom," *Teaching Sociology* 41, no. 2 (2013): 172–87.

7. Ruth Milkman, "A New Political Generation: Millennials and the Post-2008 Wave of Protest," *American Sociological Review* 82, no. 1 (2017): 1–31.

8. Apollon, *Don't Call Them*; Antonio J. Castro, "Themes in the Research on Preservice Teachers' Views of Cultural Diversity: Implications for Researching Millennial Preservice Teachers," *Educational Researcher* 39, no. 3 (2010): 198–210; Mueller, "Tracing Family."

9. Eduardo Bonilla-Silva, *Racism Without Racists: Color-Blind Racism and the Persistence of Racial Inequality in the U.S.* (Lanham, MD: Rowman and Littlefield, 2006); Mueller, "Tracing Family."

10. Apollon, *Don't Call Them*.

11. Ibid.

12. Ibid; Kohli, "Critical Race Reflections."

13. Jason Irizarry, "En La Lucha: The Struggles and Triumphs of Latino/a Preservice Teachers," *Teachers College Record* 113, no. 12 (2011): 2804–35; Marc P. Johnston-Guerrero, "The Meanings of Race Matter: College Students Learning About Race in a Not-So-Postracial Era," *American Educational Research Journal* 53, no. 4 (2016): 819–49; Jennifer C. Mueller and Joe Feagin, "Pulling Back the 'Post-Racial' Curtain: Critical Pedagogical Lessons from Both Sides of the Desk," in *Teaching Race and Anti-Racism in Contemporary America: Adding Context to Colorblindness*, ed. Kristen Haltinner (Sydney, AU: Springer, 2014), 11–24; Janet K. Swim et al., "African American College Students' Experiences with Everyday Racism: Characteristics of and Responses to These Instances," *Journal of Black Psychology* 29, no. 1 (2003): 38–67.

14. Daniel G. Solórzano, Miguel Ceja, and Tara Yosso, "Critical Race Theory, Racial Microaggressions, and Campus Racial Climate: The Experiences of African American College Students," *Journal of Negro Education* 69, no. 1–2 (2000): 60–73; Derald W. Sue et al., "Racial Microaggressions in Everyday Life: Implications for Clinical Practice," *American Psychologist* 62, no. 4 (2007): 271.

15. Swim et al., "African American College Students' Experiences."

16. H. Richard Milner, *Start Where You Are, but Don't Stay There: Understanding Diversity, Opportunity Gaps, and Teaching in Today's Classrooms* (Cambridge, MA: Harvard Education Press, 2010).

17. Sonya V. Scott and Louie F. Rodriguez, "'A Fly in the Ointment': African American Male Preservice Teachers' Experiences with Stereotype Threat in Teacher Education," *Urban Education* 50, no. 6 (2015): 689–717.

18. Mary L. Gomez, Terri L. Rodriguez, and Vonzell Agosto, "Who Are Latino Prospective Teachers and What Do They Bring to U.S. Schools?," *Race Ethnicity and Education* 11, no. 3 (2008): 267–83; Edith Guyton, Ruth Saxton, and Martin Wesche, "Experiences of Diverse Students in Teacher Education," *Teaching and Teacher Education* 12, no. 6 (1996): 643–52; Cinthia Salinas and Antonio J. Castro, "Disrupting the Official Curriculum: Cultural Biography and the Curriculum Decision Making of Latino Preservice Teachers," *Theory and Research in Social Education* 38, no. 3 (2011): 428–63; Chris Wilkins and Rajinder Lall, "'You've Got to Be Tough and I'm Trying': Black and Minority Ethnic Student Teachers' Experiences of Initial Teacher Education," *Race Ethnicity and Education* 14, no 3 (2011): 365–86.

19. Brown, "Teaching in Color."

20. Ranita Cheruvu et al., "Race, Isolation, and Exclusion: What Early Childhood Teacher Educators Need to Know about the Experiences of Pre-Service Teachers of Color," *Urban Review* 47, no. 2 (2015): 237–65.

21. Kohli, "Critical Race Reflections."

22. Jackson, "Perspectives and Insights"; Ana Maria Villegas and Danné E. Davis, "Preparing Teachers of Color to Confront Racial/Ethnic Disparities in Educational Outcomes," in *Handbook of Research on Teacher Education: Enduring Questions in Changing Contexts*, 3rd ed., eds. Marilyn Cochran-Smith et al. (New York: Routledge, Taylor & Francis Group and Washington, DC: Association of Teacher Educators, 2008), 583–605.

23. Brown, "Teaching in Color"; Irizarry, "En La Lucha"; Alice Quiocho and Francisco Rios, "The Power of Their Presence: Minority Group Teachers and Schooling," *Review of Educational Research* 70, no. 4 (2000): 485–528.

24. Theodorea R. Berry, "Black on Black Education: Personally Engaged Pedagogy for/by African American Pre-Service Teachers," *Urban Review* 37, no.1 (2005): 31–48; Marcelle M. Haddix, "No Longer on the Margins: Researching the Hybrid Literature Identities of Black and Latina Preservice Teachers," *Research in the Teaching of English*, 45, no 2 (2010): 97–123; Marcelle M. Haddix, "Talkin' in the Company: The Counterlanguages and Deliberate Silences of Black Female Students in Teacher Education," *Linguistics and Education* 23, no. 2 (2012): 169–81; Shuaib J. Meacham, "Black Self-Love, Language, and the Teacher Education Dilemma: The Cultural Denial and Cultural Limbo of African American Preservice Teachers," *Urban Education* 34, no. 5 (2000): 571–96.

25. Sheryl C. Cozart, "Becoming Whole: A Letter to a Young, Miseducated Black Teacher," *Urban Review* 42, no. 1 (2010): 22–38.

26. Gloria Ladson-Billings and William F. Tate IV, "Toward a Critical Theory of Education," *Teachers College Record* 97, no. 1 (1995): 47–68; Daniel G.Solórzano, "Images and Words that Wound: Critical Race Theory, Racial Stereotyping and Teacher Education," *Teacher Education Quarterly* 24, no. 3 (1997): 5–19.

27. Bonilla-Silva, *Racism Without Racists*.

28. Kimberle W. Crenshaw et al., eds., *Critical Race Theory: The Key Writings That Formed the Movement* (New York: The New Press, 1995).

29. Philomena Essed, *Understanding Everyday Racism: An Interdisciplinary Theory* (Newbury Park, CA: SAGE Publications, 1991).

30. Bonilla-Silva, *Racism Without Racists*.

31. Omi and Winant, *Racial Formation in the U.S.*

32. Bonilla-Silva, *Racism Without Racist*; Omi and Winant, *Racial Formation in the U.S.*

33. Holt, "Marking."

34. Robert E. Stake, *The Art of Case Study Research* (Thousand Oaks, CA: SAGE Publications, 1995).

35. Louis Cohen, Lawrence Manion, and Keith Morrison, *Research Methods in Education*, 5th ed. (London: RoutledgeFalmer, 2000).

36. James P. Spradley, *The Ethnographic Interview* (New York: Holt, Rinehart and Winston, 1979).

37. A. Strauss and J. Corbin, *Basics of Qualitative Research*, 4th ed. (Thousand Oaks, CA: SAGE Publications, 1998); Matthew B. Miles and A. Michael Huberman, *Qualitative Data Analysis: An Expanded Sourcebook*, 2nd ed. (Thousand Oaks, CA: SAGE Publications, 1994).

38. Bonilla-Silva, *Race Without Racists*; Kimberle W. Crenshaw, "Color-Blind Dreams and Racial Nightmares: Reconfiguring Racism in the Post-Civil Rights Era," in *Birth of a Nation'Hood*, eds. Toni Morrison and Claudia Brodsky Lacour (New York: Pantheon Books, 1997), 97–168.

39. Apollon, *Don't Call Them*.

40. Ibid.

41. Ibid.

42. Kohli, "Critical Race Reflections."

43. Kathy Nakagawa and Angela E. Arzubiaga, "The Use of Social Media in Teaching Race," *Adult Learning* 25, no. 3 (2014): 103–10.

44. Luis Urrieta, "Identity Production in Figured Worlds: How Some Mexican Americans Become Chicana/o Activist Educators," *Urban Review* 39, no. 2 (2007): 117–44.

45. Ladson-Billings, "Toward a Theory of Culturally."

46. Brown, "Teaching in Color"; Cheruvu et al., "Race, Isolation, and Exclusion"; Gomez, Rodriguez, and Agosto, "Who Are Latino Prospective Teachers"; Guyton, Saxton, and Wesche, "Experiences of Diverse Students"; Kohli, "Critical Race Reflections"; Salinas and Castro, "Disrupting the Official Curriculum"; Wilkins and Lall, "'You've Got to Be Tough.'"

47. Apollon, *Don't Call Them.*

48. Chester Pierce et al., "An Experiment in Racism: TV Commercials," in *Television and Education*, ed. Chester Pierce (Beverly Hills, CA: SAGE. 1978), 62–88; Solórzano, Ceja, and Yosso, "Critical Race Theory"; Sue et al., "Racial Microaggressions."

49. Lani Guinier and Gerald Torres, *The Miner's Canary: Enlisting Race, Transforming Power, Creating Democracy* (Cambridge, MA: Harvard University Press, 2002).

50. Mueller, "Tracing Family."

51. Johnston-Guerrero, "Meanings of Race Matter."

52. Irizarry, "En La Lucha."

53. Achinstein et al., "Retaining Teachers of Color."

## Chapter 7

1. Alvis Adair, *Desegregation: The Illusion of Black Progress* (Lanham, MD: University Press of America, 1984); Patricia Albjerg Graham, "Black Teachers: A Drastically Scarce Resource," *Phi Delta Kappan* 68 no. 8 (1987): 598–605; Gloria Ladson-Billings, "Liberatory Consequences of Literacy: A Case of Culturally Relevant Instruction for African American Students," *Journal of Negro Education* 61, no. 3 (1992): 378–91; Joseph Stewart, Kenneth Meier, and Robert England, "In Quest of Role Models: Change in Black Teacher Representation in Urban School Districts, 1968–1986," *Journal of Negro Education* 58, no. 2 (1989): 140–52; Ashley Griffin and Hilary Tackie, *Through Our Eyes: Perspectives and Reflections from Black Teachers* (Washington, DC: Education Trust, November 2016), https://edtrust.org/wp-content/uploads/2014/09/ThroughOurEyes.pdf.

2. Keffrelyn D. Brown, "Teaching in Color: A Critical Race Theory in Education Analysis of the Literature on Preservice Teachers of Color and Teacher Education in the US," *Race Ethnicity and Education* 17, no. 3 (2014): 326–45; Rita Kohli, "Critical Race Reflections: Valuing the Experiences of Teachers of Color in Teacher Education," *Race Ethnicity and Education* 12, no. 2 (2009): 235–51; Rita Kohli and Daniel G. Solórzano, "Teachers, Please Learn Our Names!: Racial Microaggressions and the K–12 Classroom," *Race Ethnicity, and Education* 15, no. 4 (2012): 441–62; Chris Wilkins and Rajinder Lall, "'You've Got to Be Tough and I'm Trying': Black and Minority Ethnic Student Teachers' Experiences of Initial Teacher Education," *Race Ethnicity and Education* 14, no. 3 (2011): 365–86; Christine E. Sleeter and H. Richard Milner, "Researching Successful Efforts in Teacher Education to Diversify Teachers," in *Studying Diversity in Teacher Education*, eds. Arnetha Ball and Cynthia Tyson (Lanham, MD: Rowman and Littlefield, 2011), 81–104.

3. Anjale D. Welton, Sarah Diem, and Jennifer Jellison Holme, "Color Conscious, Cultural Blindness," *Education & Urban Society* 47, no. 6 (September 2015): 695–722; Sarah Diem et al., "Racial Diversity in the Suburbs: How Race-Neutral Responses to Demographic Change Perpetuate Inequity in Suburban School Districts," *Race Ethnicity and Education* 19, no. 4

(2016): 731–62, doi: 10.1080/13613324.2014.946485; David M. Herszenhorn, "Complaint Says Schools Are Lacking in Diversity," *New York Times*, April 21, 2000.

4. Tyrone. C. Howard, "Culturally Relevant Pedagogy: Ingredients for Critical Teacher Reflection," *Theory into Practice* 42, no. 3 (2003): 195–202.

5. Kari Kokka, "Urban Teacher Longevity: What Keeps Teachers of Color in One Under-Resourced Urban School?," *Teaching and Teacher Education* 59 (2016): 169–79; Geoffrey Borman and Maritza Dowling, "Teacher Attrition and Retention: A Meta-analytic and Narrative Review of the Research," *Review of Educational Research* 78, no. 3 (2008): 367–409; Richard Ingersoll, Lisa Merrill, and Daniel Stuckey, *Seven Trends: The Transformation of the Teaching Force*, CPRE Research Report #RR-80, updated April 2014 (Philadelphia: University of Pennsylvania, Consortium for Policy Research in Education, 2014), http://www.cpre.org /sites/default/files/workingpapers/1506_7trendsapril2014.pdf; Matthew Ronfeldt, Andrew Kwok, and Michelle Reininger, "Teachers' Preferences to Teach Underserved Students," *Urban Education* 51, no. 9 (November 2016): 995–1030.

6. Heidi Hallman, *Millennial Teachers: Learning to Teach in Uncertain Times* (New York: Routledge, 2017).

7. Seth Gershenson, "Who Believes in Me: The Effect of Student-Teacher Demographic Match on Teacher Expectations," *Economics of Education Review* 52 (2016): 209–24; Thomas S. Dee, "A Teacher Like Me: Does Race, Ethnicity, or Gender Matter?," *American Economic Review* 95, no. 2 (2005): 158–65.

8. ReadNYC is United Way of New York City's Campaign for Grade Level Reading. More information can be found at http://www.unitedwaynyc.org/what-we-do/ReadNYC.

9. Gloria Ladson-Billings, *The Dreamkeepers: Successful Teachers of African American Children*, 2nd ed. (San Francisco: Jossey-Bass, 2009).

10. Mary Stone Hanley and George W. Noblit, *Cultural Responsiveness, Racial Identity and Academic Success: A Review of the Literature* (Pittsburgh: Heinz Endowments, June 2009); Sabrina Hope King, "The Limited Presence of African-American Teachers," *Review of Educational Research* 63, no. 2 (2016): 115–49.

11. Tanya Friedman (leadership, literacy, and equity coach, ATAPE Group), discussion with the author, March 2017.

12. Ibid.

13. Howard, "Culturally Relevant Pedagogy."

14. Friedman, discussion.

## Chapter 8

1. US Department of Education, President's 2016 Budget, Budget Fact Sheet (Washington: US Department of Education, 2016), https://www2.ed.gov/about/overview/budget/budget16 /budget-factsheet.pdf.

2. Stephanie Aragon, "Response to Information Request" (Denver: Education Commission of the States, July 20, 2016), http://www.ecs.org/ec-content/uploads/July-2016_Teacher-Licensure _certification_recruitment_retention-with-table.pdf.

3. Andrew Rotherham, *Title 2.0: Revamping the Federal Role in Education Human Capital* (Washington, DC: Education Sector, November 2008).

4. US Department of Education, "Title II—Preparing, Training, and Recruiting High Quality Teachers and Principals" (Washington, DC: US Department of Education, Elementary & Secondary Education, July 20, 2017), https://www2.ed.gov/policy/elsec/leg/esea02/pg20.html.

5. Robin Chait and Raegen Miller, "Ineffective Uses of ESEA Title II Funds; Funding Doesn't

Improve Student Achievement" (Washington, DC: Center for American Progress, 2010), https://cdn.americanprogress.org/wp-content/uploads/issues/2009/08/pdf/titleII_brief.pdf.

6. Colorado Department of Education, "Colorado Title II, Part A Evaluation Summary: Trends in IIA-Funded Activities" (Denver: Colorado Department of Education, Office of Federal Program Administration, May 2011), https://www.cde.state.co.us/sites/default/files /documents/fedprograms/dl/tii_a_iiadisseminationreport.pdf.

7. Alyson Klein, "What Would Trump's Proposed Cut to Teacher Funding Mean for Schools?," *Education Week Politics K–12*, March 28, 2017, http://blogs.edweek.org/edweek/campaign -k-12/2017/03/trump_cut_teacher_funding_meaning_schools.html.

8. Terrenda White, *Recruiting and Retaining Educators of Color: A Review of Research, Policy, and Practice* (Washington DC: White House Initiative on Educational Excellence for African Americans/Stanford Center for Opportunity Policy in Education, Recruiting and Retaining Educators of Color, May 7, 2015).

9. US Department of Education, "Summary of Discretionary Funds, FY 2011–FY 2017 President's Budget" (Washington: U.S. Department of Education, February 26, 2016), https:// ed.gov/about/overview/budget/budget17/summary/appendix1.pdf.

10. US Department of Education, *Non-Regulatory Guidance for Title II, Part A: Building Systems of Support for Excellent Teaching and Leading* (Washington, DC: US Department of Education, September 27, 2016), https://www2.ed.gov/policy/elsec/leg/essa/essatitleiipartaguidance.pdf.

11. Richard Ingersoll and Henry May, *Recruitment, Retention and the Minority Teacher Shortage*, CPRE Research Report #RR-69 (Philadelphia: Consortium for Policy Research in Education, University of Pennsylvania, 2011), 62–65, http://www.cpre.org/sites/default/files /researchreport/1221_minorityteachershortagereportrr69septfinal.pdf.

12. Rebecca Klein, "Why Aren't There More Black Teachers? Racial Discrimination Still Plays a Role," *Huffington Post: Black Voices*, April 12, 2017, http://www.huffingtonpost.com/entry /teacher-racism-black-discrimination_us_58ebdcc2e4b0c89f912083dc.

13. Klein, "Why Aren't There"; Diana D'Amico et al., "Where Are All the Black Teachers? Discrimination in the Teacher Labor Market," *Harvard Educational Review* 87, no. 1 (Spring 2017): 26–49; Ingersoll and May, "Recruitment, Retention."

14. D'Amico et al., "Where Are All the Black Teachers?"

15. Klein, "Why Aren't There."

16. Ibid.

17. Aragon, "Response to Information Request."

18. Ingersoll and May, "Recruitment, Retention."

19. White, *Recruiting and Retaining.*

20. Ingersoll and May, "Recruitment, Retention."

21. Melissa Diliberti, Michael Jackson, and Jana Kemp, *Crime, Violence, Discipline, and Safety in U.S. Public Schools: Findings from the School Survey on Crime and Safety: 2015–16, First Look.* NCES 2017-122 (Washington, DC: US Department of Education, National Center for Education Statistics, July 2017).

22. Daniel Boyd et al., "The Influence of School Administrators on Teacher Retention Decisions," *American Educational Research Journal* 48, no. 2 (2011): 303–33, doi:10.3102/0002831210380788.

23. Asha French, "Educators Examine Minority Teacher Retention Crisis," *NEA Today*, June 1, 2017, http://newsone.com/3720661/seminar-focuses-on-solving-black-tea.

24. Travis Bristol, "To Be Alone or in a Group: An Exploration into How the School-based Experiences Differ for Black Male Teachers Across One Urban School District," *Urban Education*, March 14, 2017, doi: 10.1177/0042085917697200.

25. White, *Recruiting and Retaining.*

26. Aragon, "Response to Information Request."

27. Ibid.

28. Carlos Galarza, "Hall School Districts Struggling to Find Hispanic Teachers," *Gainesville Times* (Gainesville, GA), April 2, 2017, http://www.gainesvilletimes.com/12274/; French, "Educators Examine"; Mary Mann, "Diversity Job Fair Draws More Than 100 Candidates to South Orange–Maplewood Schools," *The Village Green of Maplewood and South Orange* (Maplewood, NJ), May 19, 2017, http://villagegreennj.com/schools-kids/diversity-job-fair -draws-100; Emmanuel Felton, "Buffalo and Rochester Work Together to Recruit Teachers of Color," *Education Week Blogs*, February 28, 2017, http://blogs.edweek.org/edweek /teacherbeat/2017/02/upstate_new_york.

29. Galarza, "Hall School Districts."

30. Felton, "Buffalo and Rochester Work Together."

31. "Our View: Licensing Reforms Promise to Improve Teacher Recruiting," *Post Bulletin* (Rochester, MN), May 15, 2017, http://www.postbulletin.com/opinion/our-view-licensing -reforms-promise-to-improve-teacher-recruiting/article_c2c91201-428e-5f37-b392- 83d9f7d1d1f0.html.

32. Tiffany Lankes, "Buffalo Looks to Own Students to Diversify Teaching Force," *Buffalo News* (Buffalo, NY), April 2, 2017, http://buffalonews.com/author/tlankes/.

33. Ibid.

34. Wilmington University, "Wilmington University Awarded $500,000 to Transform Teacher Training" (press release), *Globenewswire*, June 22, 2017, https://globenewswire.com/news -release/2017/06/22/1027773/0/en/.

35. Aragon, "Response to Information Request."

36. Ibid.

37. Ibid.

38. Lankes, "Buffalo Looks."

39. Aragon, "Response to Information Request."

40. Ingersoll and May, "Recruitment, Retention."

41. Ibid.

42. Jacob Easley II et al., *Minority Teacher Recruitment: A Root Cause Analysis in Connecticut* (Willimantic: Eastern Connecticut State University, School of Education and Professional Studies/Graduate Division, March 2017).

## Chapter 9

1. Unless otherwise noted, the descriptive statistics presented throughout the chapter are derived from the 2011–2012 Schools and Staffing Survey—a survey of teachers and principals about the schools in which they work—and the American Community Survey in 2015 (the five-year sample)—a nationally representative dataset of Americans, allowing us to compare teachers to the general population and investigate additional information about their households not gathered in the other survey.

2. Richard Ingersoll and Lisa Merrill, *A Quarter Century of Changes in the Elementary and Secondary Teaching Force: From 1987 to 2012*, NCES 2017-092, Statistical Analysis Report (Washington, DC: US Department of Education, National Center for Education Statistics, 2017), https://nces.ed.gov/pubs2017/2017092.pdf.

3. Richard Ingersoll and Henry May, *Recruitment, Retention and the Minority Teacher Shortage*, CPRE Research Report #RR-69 (Philadelphia: Consortium for Policy Research in Education,

University of Pennsylvania, 2011), 62–65, http://www.cpre.org/sites/default/files
/researchreport/1221_minorityteachershortagereportrr69septfinal.pdf.

4. Hannah Putman et al., *High Hopes and Harsh Realities: The Real Challenges to Building a Diverse Workforce* (Washington, DC: Brown Center on Education Policy, Brookings Institution, 2016), https://www.brookings.edu/wp-content/uploads/2016/08/browncenter _20160818_teacherdiversityreportpr_hansen.pdf; US Department of Education, *The State of Racial Diversity in the Educator Workforce* (Washington, DC: US Department of Education; Office of Planning, Evaluation and Policy Development; Policy and Program Studies Service, 2016), http://www2.ed.gov/rschstat/eval/highered/racial-diversity/state-racial-diversity -workforce.pdf.

5. Michael T. Nettles et al., *Performance and Passing Rate Differences of African American and White Prospective Teachers on Praxis™ Examinations*, ETS RR–11-08, A Joint Project of the National Education Association (NEA) and Educational Testing Service (ETS) (Princeton, NJ: ETS Research Report Series, 2011), https://www.ets.org/Media/Research/pdf/RR-11-08.pdf.

6. Dan Goldhaber and Michael Hansen, "Race, Gender, and Teacher Testing: How Informative a Tool Is Teacher Licensure Testing?," *American Educational Research Journal* 47, no. 1 (2010): 218–51, http://www.jstor.org/stable/40645423?seq=1#page_scan_tab_contents.

7. Dan Goldhaber, Trevor Gratz, and Roddy Theobold, "What's in a Teacher Test? Assessing the Relationship Between Teacher Test Scores and Student Secondary STEM Achievement" (working paper 2016-4, Center for Education Data & Research, University of Washington-Bothell, Seattle, 2016), http://www.cedr.us/papers/working/CEDR%20WP%202016-4.pdf.

8. Some states have also adopted tests from the National Education Series (NES) developed by Pearson. Since we currently lack data on differential pass rates by race, we have excluded NES tests from our discussion.

9. Stephanie Aragon, "Response to Information Request" (Denver: Education Commission of the States, July 20, 2016), http://www.ecs.org/ec-content/uploads/July-2016_Teacher-Licensure _certification_recruitment_retention-with-table.pdf.; Stephen Sawchuk, "ESSA Loosens Reins on Teacher Evaluations, Qualifications," *Education Week* 35, no. 15 (2016): 14–15, http://www .coramcivic.org/resources/ESSA+Loosens+Reins+on+Teacher+Evaluations$2C+Qualifications _010616.pdf.

10. Julie R. Woods, *Mitigating Teacher Shortages: Alternative Teacher Certification* (Denver: Education Commission of the States, 2016), http://www.ecs.org/ec-content/uploads/ Mitigating-Teacher-Shortages-Alternative-Certification.pdf.; Jenny DeMonte, *A Million New Teachers Are Coming: Will They Be Ready to Teach?* (Washington, DC: American Institutes for Research, Education Policy Center, 2015), http://www.air.org/sites/default/files/downloads /report/Million-New-Teachers-Brief-deMonte-May-2015.pdf.

11. Thomas S. Dee and Dan Goldhaber, *Understanding and Addressing Teacher Shortages in the United States* (Washington, DC: Brookings, Hamilton Project, 2017), http://www .hamiltonproject.org/assets/files/understanding_and_addressing_teacher_shortages _in_us_pp.pdf.

12. Putman et al., *High Hopes.*

13. Sandi Jacobs et al., *State Teacher Policy Yearbook: National Summary* (Washington, DC: National Council on Teacher Quality, 2015), http://www.nctq.org/dmsView/2015_State _Teacher_Policy_Yearbook_National_Summary_NCTQ_Report.

14. Kaitlin Pennington and Sara Mead, *For Good Measure? Teacher Evaluation Policy in the ESSA Era* (Washington, DC: Bellwether Education Partners, 2016), https://bellwethereducation.org /sites/default/files/Bellwether_ForGoodMeasure-GPLH_Final.pdf.

15. Farah Z. Ahmad and Ulrich Boser, *America's Leaky Pipeline for Teachers of Color* (Washington, DC: Center for American Progress, 2014).

16. Mark Ehlert et al., "Selecting Growth Measures for Use in School Evaluation Systems: Should Proportionality Matter?," *Educational Policy* 30, no. 3 (2016): 465–500, http://journals.sagepub .com/doi/abs/10.1177/0895904814557593.

17. Grover J. (Russ) Whitehurst, Matthew M. Chingos, and Katharine M. Lindquist, *Evaluating Teachers with Classroom Observations* (Washington, DC: Brookings Institution, Brown Center on Education Policy, 2014), https://www.brookings.edu/wp-content/uploads/2016/06 /Evaluating-Teachers-with-Classroom-Observations.pdf.

18. Jason A. Grissom and Susanna Loeb, "Assessing Principals' Assessments: Subjective Evaluations of Teacher Effectiveness in Low- and High-Stakes Environments," *Education Finance and Policy* 12, no. 3 (2017): 369–95, http://dx.doi.org/10.1162/EDFP_a_00210.

19. Seth Gershenson and Thomas S. Dee, "The Insidiousness of Unconscious Bias in Schools," Brookings Institution, Brown Center Chalkboard, March 20, 2014, https://www.brookings .edu/blog/brown-center-chalkboard/2017/03/20/the-insidiousness-of-unconscious-bias -in-schools/.

20. A recent study from New York University of 1,700 sixth- through ninth-grade teachers in cities around the country showed that students of all races expressed more positive perceptions of their teachers of color than of their white teachers. Hua-Yu Sebastian Cherng and Peter F. Halpin, "The Importance of Minority Teachers: Student Perceptions of Minority Versus White Teachers," *Educational Researcher* 45, no. 7 (2016): 407–20, doi:10.3102/0013189X16671718.

21. Thomas S. Dee and James Wyckoff, "Incentives, Selection, and Teacher Performance: Evidence from IMPACT," *Journal of Policy Analysis and Management* 34, no. 2 (2015): 267–97, http:// onlinelibrary.wiley.com/doi/10.1002/pam.21818/full.; Cory Koedel et al., "The Impact of Performance Ratings on Job Satisfaction for Public School Teachers," *American Educational Research Journal* 54, no. 2 (2017): 241–78, http://journals.sagepub.com/doi/abs/10.3102 /0002831216687531.

22. Eric Isenberg et al., *Do Low-Income Students Have Equal Access to Effective Teachers? Evidence from 26 Districts*, NCEE 2017-4007 (Washington, DC: US Department of Education, National Center for Education Evaluation and Regional Assistance, 2016), https://ies.ed.gov/ncee/pubs /20174008/pdf/20174007.pdf.

23. John P. Papay et al., "Learning Job Skills from Colleagues at Work: Evidence from a Field Experiment Using Teacher Performance Data" (NBER working paper No. 21986, National Bureau of Economic Research, 2016), http://www.nber.org/papers/w21986.pdf.

24. Minority teachers in general and novices (i.e., millennials) in particular are much more likely to stay in schools where they feel supported. This relationship is even more acute when teachers of color are underrepresented in the school's workforce. Steven Bednar and Dora Gicheva, "Workplace Support and Diversity in the Market for Public School Teachers" (working paper series no. 16-05, Department of Economics, University of North Carolina–Greensboro, 2016), http://bryan.uncg.edu/econ/files/2016/11/Teacher_Support_Aug2016.pdf.

25. Sara Mead, Ashley LiBetti Mitchel, and Andrew J. Rotherham, "The State of the Charter School Movement" (Washington, DC: Bellwether Education Partners, 2015), http://www .suny.edu/about/leadership/board-of-trustees/meetings/webcastdocs/G2_Bellwether%20 Charter%20Research%20Report.pdf.

26. Howard Fuller, *Past, Present and Future of Charter Schools* (Washington, DC: Brookings Institution, April 26, 2016), https://www.brookings.edu/events/ examining-charter-schools-in-america/.

27. Howard Blume, "Transformation of L.A. Unified's Locke High into a Charter School Is Green Dot's Biggest Test Yet," *LA Times*, September 18, 2008, http://www.latimes.com/local/la-me-locke18-2008sep18-story.html.

28. Mary E. Dilworth and Marcus J. Coleman, *Time for a Change: Diversity in Teaching Revisited* (Washington, DC: National Education Association, Center for Great Public Schools, May 2014), https://www.nea.org/assets/docs/Time_for_a_Change_Diversity_in_Teaching_Revisited_(web).pdf.

29. Phaedra Trethan, "Parents Offer Platform for Better Camden schools," *USA Today*, March 28, 2017, https://www.usatoday.com/story/news/2017/03/28/parents-offer-platform-better-camden-schools/99725344/.

30. Sean Gill, Jordan Posamentier, and Paul T. Hill, *Suburban Schools: The Unrecognized Frontier in Public Education* (Seattle: Center on Reinventing Public Education, 2016), http://www.crpe.org/sites/default/files/crpe.suburban_schools_5.2016.pdf.

31. US Department of Agriculture, *Rural Hispanics at a Glance*, Economic Information Bulletin No. 8. (Washington, DC: US Department of Agriculture, Economic Research Service, 2005), https://www.ers.usda.gov/webdocs/publications/44570/29566_eib8_002.pdf?v=41305.

32. Charles Clotfelter et al., "Teacher Bonuses and Teacher Retention in Low-Performing Schools: Evidence from the North Carolina $1,800 Teacher Bonus Program," *Public Finance Review* 36, no. 1 (2008): 63–87, http://journals.sagepub.com/doi/abs/10.1177/1091142106291662.

33. Bruce E. Kaufman and Jorge Martinez-Vazquez, "Monopoly, Efficient Contract, and Median Voter Models of Union Wage Determination: A Critical Comparison," *Journal of Labor Research* 11, no. 4 (1990): 401–23, doi: 10.1007/BF02685360.

34. NAACP, *Task Force on Quality Education; Hearing Report. Quality Education for All . . . One School at a Time* (Baltimore, MD: NAACP, July 2017), 6, http://www.naacp.org/wp-content/uploads/2017/07/Task_ForceReport_final2.pdf.

35. Luke Broadwater, "Activist DeRay Mckesson to Leave Baltimore School System," *Baltimore Sun*, July 17, 2017, http://www.baltimoresun.com/news/maryland/education/k-12/bs-md-ci-deray-to-leave-20170714-story.html.

# Acknowledgments

I owe a debt of gratitude to a host of millennial, generation X, baby boomer, and silent generation colleagues who agreed to contribute their intellectual energy and time to help me groom this work. Key among them is H. Richard Milner IV who, without hesitation, encouraged me to pursue this particularly complex theme in a book.

In addition to a remarkably bright and open-minded group of contributors, I truly appreciate the range of knowledge and insights that the editorial advisory board brought to this effort. Their clear and informed guidance was significant and helped me see this work from a variety of perspectives. Many thanks to these individuals for lending their expertise:

Joseph A. Aguerrebere, California State University System, Office of the Chancellor*

Donna M. Gollnick, TeachNow

Raymond C. Hart, Council of the Great City Schools

Hollis W. Hart, Citi*

Colleen O'Brien, Butler University, College of Education, Board of Visitors

I also thank Peggy L. Brookins, Adriane E. L. Dorrington, A. Lin Goodwin, Carl A. Grant, Lauren Jones Young, Ellen Holmes, Warren Simmons and Lisa M. Stooksberry for directing me to a very keen group of people who gave millennial voice to this volume.

---

*Retired*

I could not have asked for a better team of reviewers who, given their enormous body of work, offered very solid comments and recommendations for me and the authors to consider:

Clyde C. Aveilhe, City University of New York, Office of the Chancellor*

Rosetta A. Brooks, St. Mark's Dance Studio, Washington, DC

Daniel L. Clay, University of Iowa, College of Education

Yvonne D. Coates, American University, School of Education

Segun C. Eubanks, University of Maryland

Beverly Caffee Glenn, The George Washington University*

Robert W. Glenn, National Education Association, Research*

Vincent T. Groh, Millennium Challenge Corporation

Patrick C. Ledesma, National Board for Professional Teaching Standards

Cristal M. Piper, School Without Walls, Washington, DC

Elizabeth Moore Rhodes, Xavier University of Louisiana*

Stephanie G. Robinson, Education Trust*

Special thanks to Sarah Ishmael for serving as my generational translator and graduate assistant for the multitude of tasks necessary to complete this work. Sincere appreciation to Judy A. Beck, who with much patience and grace lent her knowledge of the field and her skills as a technical editor to make what was an assortment of thought pieces into a coherent whole.

Most importantly, I thank my very wise husband Clyde, who for decades has mentored and encouraged me through every conceivable professional dream.

# About the Editor

Mary E. Dilworth (EdD, Catholic University of America) currently serves as an independent consultant to nonprofit organizations and educational institutions. Dilworth's career has centered on issues of teacher quality and preparation, with a keen focus on racial/ethnic and linguistic diversity and equity issues. She led a host of education research, policy, and program initiatives as vice-president of the National Board for Professional Teaching Standards and senior vice-president of the American Association of Colleges for Teacher Education. In addition, she served as visiting professor and director of the Center for Urban Education at the University of the District of Columbia. Earlier in her career Dilworth was affiliated with Howard University in Washington, DC. She was a research fellow with the university's Institute for the Study of Educational Policy (ISEP) and subsequently the coordinator of education and training for Howard University Hospital. While at ISEP, Dilworth wrote the book *Teachers' Totter: A Report on Teacher Certification Issues*, widely recognized as heightening the national discourse on the disparate impact of licensing tests on underrepresented groups. She recently completed work as coprincipal investigator for a National Science Foundation project (NSF-DR12) designed to recruit, prepare, license, and employ secondary science teachers from underrepresented groups. She has authored and contributed to scores of scholarly books, articles, and policy and research reports, including the 2014 report *Time for a Change: Diversity in Teaching Revisited*, a chapter in the 2013 *International Guide to Student Achievement*, and an entry in the 2012 *Encyclopedia of Diversity in Education*. Dilworth serves on a range of appointed and elected national commissions and boards.

# About the Contributors

## Keffrelyn D. Brown

Keffrelyn D. Brown (PhD, University of Wisconsin–Madison) is associate professor of cultural studies in education in the Department of Curriculum and Instruction and affiliated faculty in the Department of African and African Diaspora Studies at the University of Texas–Austin. Her research focuses on the sociocultural knowledge of race, teaching and curriculum, critical multicultural teacher education, and the education of black people in the United States. She is the author of numerous articles, books, and book chapters. Her most recent book, *Beyond the "At-Risk" Label: Reorienting Educational Policy and Practice*, explores the troubling discourse and practice around the risk of categorizing students as "at-risk." Brown was awarded the American Educational Research Association (AERA) Division K Midcareer Award in 2017 and the AERA Division K Early Career Research Award in 2013.

## Keith C. Catone

Keith C. Catone (EdD, Harvard University) is the executive director of the Center for Youth and Community Leadership in Education (CYCLE) at Roger Williams University. Previously, he served as associate director for community organizing and engagement at the Annenberg Institute for School Reform and as adjunct assistant professor of education at Brown University. He was the project director for the Youth 4 Change Alliance in Providence, Rhode Island, and cofounded the New York Collective of Radical Educators, a citywide grassroots teacher activist group, while teaching high school social studies in the Bronx. Catone serves on the advisory board for the Education for Liberation Network and has authored numerous research and opinion pieces. His first book, *The Pedagogy of Teacher*

*Activism: Portraits of Four Teachers for Justice*, explores connections between pedagogical purpose, power, and possibility in the context of working with teachers, youth, families, and communities to change the world.

## Genesis A. Chavez

Genesis A. Chavez (BA, University of Maryland–College Park) is a sixth-year teacher in the Montgomery County Public Schools in Maryland. She is currently teaching first grade at JoAnn Leleck Elementary School at Broad Acres. Chavez is pursuing her master's degree in equity and excellence in education at McDaniel College. In 2016, she was featured as a "Young Activist" in *ActionLine Magazine* of the Maryland State Education Association for her advocacy work for students of color and in poverty; her article "Breakthroughs in Pedagogy: Equity Literacy" was published in the April 2016 issue. Chavez was recognized in 2011 by the University of Maryland–College Park as Mentee of the Year for her work with the La Familia/o Peer Mentoring Program.

## Marcus J. Coleman

Marcus J. Coleman (PhD, University of Georgia) is an assistant professor of communication and interdisciplinary studies at the University of Southern Mississippi. Prior to his current position, he served as a research fellow in the Civic Engagement and Governance Institute at the Joint Center for Political and Economic Studies and as the senior research analyst for the Washington, DC, Department of Behavioral Health.

Coleman's research is interdisciplinary and calls attention to the persistence of African American ideals of community engagement despite perpetual and intentional efforts to deny opportunity and access to engage community. While at the Joint Center he researched the impact of voter photo identification requirements on African Americans in battleground states and in 2012, he wrote the report, "African American Voter Access: Reduced Opportunity to Political Participation." To commemorate the sixtieth anniversary of *Brown v. Board of Education*, in 2014 he coauthored with Mary E. Dilworth *Time for a Change: Diversity in Teaching Revisited*. This piece highlights not only the dearth of minority teachers, but also the increased need for teachers, regardless of race/ethnicity, to be culturally competent.

## Lisa Delpit

Lisa Delpit (EdD, Harvard University) is the Felton G. Clark Distinguished Professor of Education at Southern University and A&M College. She has received numerous honors and awards for her research, writing, and contributions to the field of education, including Outstanding Contribution to Education from the Harvard Graduate School of Education and a MacArthur "Genius" Fellowship citing her work in cross-cultural communication. Delpit has written scores of seminal articles and books, including *The Skin That We Speak: Thoughts on Language and Culture in the Classroom* (2012), coedited with Joanne Kilgour Dowdy; *Other People's Children: Cultural Conflict in the Classroom* (1995); *Multiplication Is for White People: Raising Expectations for Other People's Children* (2012); and *The Silenced Dialogue: Power and Pedagogy in Educating Other People's Children* (1988).

## Hollee R. Freeman

Hollee Freeman (PhD, Boston College) is the executive director of the MathScience Innovation Center in Richmond, Virginia. She is a National Board certified teacher and has worked as an elementary teacher, district mathematics coach, national mathematics trainer, educational researcher, curriculum developer, and professor. In her capacity as field director for the Boston Teacher Residency for over ten years, Freeman was instrumental in developing content, policies, and practices for in-service teachers and their mentors. Having earned degrees in the areas of educational administration, special education, and psychology/elementary education, she has written numerous book chapters and articles focused on science, technology, education, and mathematics (STEM); educational reform; gender; and educational equity in the United States and abroad. Freeman volunteers her time locally and serves on several boards.

## Michael Hansen

Michael Hansen (PhD, University of Washington) is a senior fellow at the Brookings Institution and director of the Brown Center on Education Policy. A labor economist by training, he has conducted original research on a wide array of teacher policy and accountability issues, primarily using state longitudinal data systems. Findings from Hansen's research have received media coverage from prominent outlets including the *Washington Post*, the *Atlantic*, the *Wall Street Journal*, *Politico*, and *Education Week*. His work has also been published in peer-reviewed research journals, including *American Economic Review, Education Finance and Policy, Economica, Educational Evaluation and Policy Analysis,* and *American Educational Research Journal.* Hansen is also editor for the *Brown Center Chalkboard.*

## Socorro G. Herrera

Socorro G. Herrera (PhD, Texas Tech University) serves as a professor of elementary education at Kansas State University and directs the Center for Intercultural and Multilingual Advocacy in the College of Education. Herrera has written several books, including *Mastering ESL/EFL Methods: Differentiated Instruction for Culturally and Linguistically Diverse (CLD) Students* (3rd edition, 2015), *Accelerating Literacy for Diverse Learners: Strategies for the Common Core Classrooms, K–8* (2013), and *Assessment Accommodations for Classroom Teachers of Culturally and Linguistically Diverse Students* (2nd edition, 2013). She has also authored numerous articles in nationally known, peer-reviewed journals such as *Bilingual Research Journal, Journal of Hispanic Higher Education, Journal of Research in Education,* and *Journal of Latinos and Education.*

## Sarah Ishmael

Sarah Ishmael (MEd, University of Texas–Austin) is a doctoral student in the Department of Curriculum and Instruction at the University of Wisconsin–Madison. Her area of study is multicultural education and her master's work was in educational administration. Ishmael's research interests include critical qualitative research, critical pedagogy, and curriculum theory. She is the author of "Dysconscious Racism, Class Privilege, and TFA," a chapter in *Teach for America Counter-Narratives: Alumni Speak Up and Speak Out* (2015). Additionally, she coauthored "Teach for America's Preferential Treatment: School District Contracts, Hiring Decisions, and Employment Practices" in *Educational Evaluation and Policy Analysis,* a peer-reviewed journal. Ishmael has presented papers and participated in multiple symposia at American Educational Research Association (AERA) conferences. In 2017 she organized the AERA session, "There Could Never Really Be Justice on Stolen Land." She currently works with preservice teachers in secondary and elementary education and with local school districts to support projects that focus on equity and critical multicultural education. Previously, Ishmael taught elementary school and secondary special education in Baton Rouge, Louisiana.

## Sabrina Hope King

Sabrina Hope King (EdD, Teachers College, Columbia University) leads a consulting firm focused on professional and organizational development within the framework of equity and culturally relevant practice. Her firm builds upon her significant contribution to the field of urban education as a teacher, scholar, professor, and school and district leader. Prior roles include teacher at Spofford Juvenile Detention Facility and Asa Phillip Randolph High School in New York City; professor at the University of Illinois–Chicago, Hofstra University, and Bank Street College; assistant superintendent in Mount Vernon City Public Schools; and chief academic officer for curriculum and professional learning at the New York City Department of Education. She is dedicated to improving students' educational experiences by working with educators, policy makers, and community partners to improve the educational experiences of students who need and deserve the best.

## Adam T. Kuranishi

Adam Kuranishi (MA, Teachers College, Columbia University) is a social studies and special education teacher in New York City and a doctoral student in social studies at Teachers College, Columbia University. His research interests include inclusive pedagogy, democratic classrooms, and disability studies. In addition to his degree in secondary inclusive education, Kuranishi also holds a two-hundred-hour teacher certification in yoga and wellness. He has researched and written on mindfulness practices in the classroom. Prior to teaching, Kuranishi worked as an immigrant rights organizer in Illinois and Georgia and as a policy advisor for Congressman Michael Honda (D-CA17).

## Lindsay A. Miller

Lindsay A. Miller (MEd, University of Illinois–Chicago) currently teaches third grade in Chula Vista, California. After receiving her bachelor's degree in communication and international studies, Miller began working with a political consulting organization. Recognizing the need for better and more effective education for young people as citizens of the world, she headed to graduate school to earn a master's degree and her teaching certificate. Her first teaching position brought her to an elementary school in Chicago's southwest side where she taught bilingual third grade for several years. She also developed a love for mathematics and curriculum writing, and subsequently earned an endorsement in English as a second language. Miller is a member of the National Council of Teachers of Mathematics and served as her school's instructional leader in mathematics. In addition, she was appointed to districtwide task forces to develop Common Core–aligned curriculum and assessments. Now in southern California, she is applying her strengths as an educator and is learning many new skills. She serves a mostly immigrant and transient population and enjoys celebrating their culture as well as meeting their educational needs.

## Amanda R. Morales

Amanda R. Morales (PhD, Kansas State University) is an assistant professor at the University of Nebraska–Lincoln (UNL). Prior to her work at UNL, Morales was an assistant professor and diversity coordinator for the College of Education at Kansas State University (KSU), and program manager in KSU's Center for Intercultural Multilingual Advocacy. She is the author of numerous peer reviewed journal articles, book chapters, and grant proposals that address issues of equity and access for culturally and linguistically diverse students across the preK–16 education continuum. In addition to studying teachers of color in predominantly white institutions, Morales's current research explores the lived experiences of immigrant/migrant, multicultural, and first-generation college students. She won two national awards, from the American Education Research Association and the American Association of Colleges for Teacher Education, for her dissertation *Factors That Foster Latina, English Language Learner, Nontraditional Student Resilience in Higher Education and Their Persistence in Teacher Education.*

## Janice Hamilton Outtz

Janice Hamilton Outtz (MA, Howard University) recently left her position as senior program officer with the Annie E. Casey Foundation and now leads her own independent research consulting firm. Her work with the foundation centered on measurement and evaluation, with a focus on issues ranging from community engagement to children's social, emotional, and educational development. Hamilton Outtz has considerable experience in collecting and using data for decision making and assisting non-profit organizations with strategic planning and establishing partnerships. Earlier in her career she worked for the Greater Washington (DC) Research Center (now Greater Washington Research at Brookings). Her portfolio includes numerous research reports and articles on issues such as changing demographics, employment, education, families, racial and ethnic diversity, and welfare.

## Zollie Stevenson Jr.

Zollie Stevenson (PhD, University of North Carolina) is the chief academic officer and associate professor of psychology at Philander Smith College. Stevenson served as an associate professor of educational leadership and policy studies for the doctoral program at Howard and Bowie State Universities. He has held leadership positions in three urban school districts and the North Carolina Department of Public Instruction with responsibility for research and assessment and at the US Department of Education as director of student achievement and school accountability programs. He is coauthor of the chapter "The State of Federal and State Accountability Systems That Support P–12 and Postsecondary Transition Services for English Learners with Disabilities: Do They Exist and What Is the Need?" in *Transitioning Children with Disabilities: From Early Childhood Through Adulthood* (2017). In 2010 he was recognized for his outstanding career contribution to the field of assessment by the National Association of Test Directors. Stevenson is a vice-president of the American Educational Research Association.

## Dulari Tahbildar

Dulari Tahbildar (MCP, Massachusetts Institute of Technology) is the director of student support at 360 High School in Providence, Rhode Island. Previously, she served as executive director at Breakthrough Providence and has worked in a number of education and youth development organizations, such as the Brotherhood/Sister Sol, City Year national headquarters, Urban Institute, and Urban Assembly School for Applied Math and Science. Tahbildar is a recipient of the Providence Student Union's A+ Youth Ally Award and the *Providence Business News* 40 Under 40 award. She has served on the boards of Latino Policy Institute at Roger Williams University and Providence Children and Youth Cabinet, and on the national planning team for the Free Minds, Free People conference. Tahbildar's degree fields are public policy and urban studies and city planning.

## Angela M. Ward

Angela M. Ward (MEd, University of Texas–Austin) manages the Austin Independent School District's focus on cultural proficiency and inclusiveness and restorative practices. She has a special interest in the implications of the multiple relationships of education to culture, power, and society. Prior to leading this effort as a district administrator, she served as a campus administrator, teacher leader, and classroom teacher. As an expert on differentiation of curriculum, she led her district in writing its first curriculum documents. Ward also served four years on the Learning Forward Texas Board of Directors, an affiliate of the international organization whose purpose is engaging adult learners in the field of education in meaningful, effective professional learning. She is a doctoral student at the University of Texas–Austin in the Department of Curriculum and Instruction, with a focus on cultural studies in education.

# Index